GLENCOE
Mathematics
with Business Applications

www.busmath.glencoe.com

The Princeton Review

Glencoe: Your *Real* Business Choice

Student Activity Workbook

Fifth Edition

McGraw Hill Glencoe

New York, New York · Columbus, Ohio · Chicago, Illinois · Woodland Hills, California

Glencoe

The McGraw-Hill Companies

Copyright © 2004 by Glencoe/McGraw-Hill, a division of the McGraw-Hill Companies. All rights reserved. Except as permitted under the United States Copyright Act, no part of this publication may be reproduced or distributed in any form or by any means, or stored in a database or retrieval system, without prior written permission of the publisher, Glencoe/McGraw-Hill.

Printed in the United States of America.

Send all inquires to:
Glencoe/McGraw-Hill
21600 Oxnard Street, Suite 500
Woodland Hills, CA 91367

ISBN 0-07-831373-2 (Student Activity Workbook)
ISBN 0-07-831374-0 (Student Activity Workbook, TAE)

7 8 9 009 08 07

TABLE OF CONTENTS

CHAPTER 1 Gross Income
1-1	Hourly Pay	1
1-2	Overtime Pay	1
1-3	Weekly Time Card	2
1-4	Piecework	3
1-5	Salary	4
1-6	Commission	5
1-7	Graduated Commission	5
Spreadsheet Application: Gross Income		6

CHAPTER 2 Net Income
2-1	Federal Income Tax	7
2-2	State Income Tax	8
2-3	Graduated State Income Tax	8
2-4	Social Security and Medicare Taxes	9
2-5	Group Health Insurance	10
2-6	Statement of Earnings	11
Simulation: Applying for a Job		12
Career Path: Chiropractor		16

CHAPTER 3 Recordkeeping
3-1	Average Monthly Expenditures	17
3-2	Preparing a Budget Sheet	18
3-3	Using a Budget	19
Spreadsheet Application: Recordkeeping		20
Career Path: Long-Distance Truck Driver		22

CHAPTER 4 Checking Accounts
4-1	Deposits	23
4-2	Writing Checks	24
4-3	Check Registers	25
4-4	Bank Statements	26
4-5	Reconciling the Bank Statement	27
4-6	Online Banking	28
Spreadsheet Application: Online Banking Check Register		30
Simulation: Reconciling a N.O.W. Account		31

CHAPTER 5 Savings Accounts
5-1	Deposits	33
5-2	Withdrawals	33
5-3	Account Statements	34
5-4	Simple Interest	35
5-5	Compound Interest	36
5-6	Compound Interest Tables	37
5-7	Daily Compounding	37
5-8	Annuities	38
Spreadsheet Application: Compound Interest		39
Career Path: Welder		40

CHAPTER 6 Cash Purchases
6-1	Sales Tax	41
6-2	Total Purchase Price	41
6-3	Unit Pricing	42
6-4	Comparison Shopping	42
6-5	Coupons and Rebates	43
6-6	Markdown	44
6-7	Sale Price	44
Spreadsheet Application: Cash Purchases		45
Career Path: Sales Associate		46

CHAPTER 7 Charge Accounts and Credit Cards
7-1	Account Statements	47
7-2	Finance Charge: Unpaid-Balance Method	48
7-3	Finance Charge: Average-Daily-Balance Method (No New Purchases Included)	49
7-4	Finance Charge: Average Daily-Balance Method (New Purchases Included)	49
Simulation: Charge Accounts		50
Career Path: Mathematician		52

CHAPTER 8 Loans
8-1	Single-Payment Loans	53
8-2	Installment Loans	54
8-3	Simple Interest Installment Loans	54
8-4	Installment Loans—Allocation of Monthly Payment	55
8-5	Paying Off Simple Interest Installment Loan	55
8-6	Determining the APR	56
Spreadsheet Application: Loans		57
Career Path: Firefighter		58

CHAPTER 9 Vehicle Transportation
9-1	Purchasing a New Vehicle	59
9-2	Dealer's Cost	59
9-3	Purchasing a Used Vehicle	60
9-4	Vehicle Insurance	61
9-5	Operating and Maintaining a Vehicle	62
9-6	Leasing a Vehicle	63
9-7	Renting a Vehicle	64
Simulation: Vehicle Expenses		65

CHAPTER 10 Housing Costs
10-1	Mortgage Loans	69
10-2	Monthly Payment and Total Interest	69
10-3	Closing Costs	70
10-4	The Monthly Payment	71
10-5	Real Estate Taxes	72
10-6	Homeowners Insurance	73
10-7	Homeowners Insurance Premium	73
10-8	Other Housing Costs	74
Simulation: Energy Savings— Home Weatherization		75

CHAPTER 11 Insurance
11-1	Health Insurance Premiums	77
11-2	Health Insurance Benefits	78
11-3	Term Life Insurance	79
11-4	Other Types of Life Insurance	79
Career Path: Psychologist		80

CHAPTER 12 Investments
12-1	Certificates of Deposit	81
12-2	Effective Annual Yield	81
12-3	Stocks	82
12-4	Stock Dividends	82
12-5	Selling Stocks	83
12-6	Bonds	84
Simulation: Selecting a Stock		85
Career Path: Stockbroker		88

CHAPTER 13 Personnel
13-1	Hiring New Employees	89
13-2	Administering Wages and Salaries	90
13-3	Employee Benefits	91
13-4	Disability Insurance	92
13-5	Workers Compensation and Unemployment Insurance	93
13-6	Travel Expenses	94
13-7	Employee Training	95
Spreadsheet Application: Personnel		96

CHAPTER 14 Production
14-1	Manufacturing	97
14-2	Break-Even Analysis	98
14-3	Quality Control	99
14-4	Time Study—Number of Units	101
14-5	Time Study—Percent of Time	101
14-6	Packaging	102
Spreadsheet Application: Production		103
Simulation: Manufacturing		105
Career Path: Cartoonist		106

CHAPTER 15 Purchasing
15-1	Trade Discounts	107
15-2	Trade Discount— Complement Method	107
15-3	Trade-Discount Rate	108
15-4	Chain Discounts	109
15-5	Chain Discounts— Complement Method	109
15-6	Cash Discounts—Ordinary Dating	110
15-7	Cash Discounts—EOM Dating	110
Spreadsheet Application: Purchasing		111

CHAPTER 16 Sales
16-1	Markup	113
16-2	Markup Rate	113
16-3	Net Profit	114
16-4	Net-Profit Rate	114
16-5	Determining Selling Price— Markup Based on Selling Price	115
16-6	Markup Rate Based on Cost	116
16-7	Determine Selling Price— Markup Based on Cost	116
16-8	Markdown	117
Spreadsheet Application: Sales		118
Career Path: Teacher		120

CHAPTER 17 Marketing
17-1	Opinion Surveys	121
17-2	Sales Potential	122
17-3	Market Share	122
17-4	Sales Projections	123

17-5	Sales Projections—Factor Method	123
17-6	Newspaper Advertising Costs	124
17-7	Television Advertising Costs	124
17-8	Pricing	125
Spreadsheet Application: Sales Analysis		126
Simulation: Major Foods Corporation		127

CHAPTER 18   Warehousing and Distributing

18-1	Storage Space	129
18-2	Taking an Inventory	130
18-3	Valuing an Inventory	130
18-4	Carrying an Inventory	131
18-5	Door-to-Door Transportation Cost	132
18-6	Transportation by Truck	133
Spreadsheet Application: Warehousing and Distributing		134
Career Path: Veterinarian		136

CHAPTER 19   Services

19-1	Building Rental	137
19-2	Maintenance and Improvement	138
19-3	Equipment Rental	139
19-4	Utilities Costs—Telephone	140
19-5	Utilities Costs—Electricity	140
19-6	Professional Services	141
Spreadsheet Application: Services		142
Simulation: The Plaza Five		144

CHAPTER 20   Accounting

20-1	Payroll Register	145
20-2	Business Expenses	146
20-3	Apportioning Expenses	147
20-4	Depreciation—Straight-Line Method	148
20-5	Depreciation—Book Value	148
20-6	Modified Accelerated Cost Recovery System (MACRS)	149
Spreadsheet Application: Accounting		150
Simulation: Copyfax Center I		151

CHAPTER 21   Accounting Records

21-1	Assets, Liabilities, and Equity	153
21-2	Balance Sheet	154
21-3	Cost of Goods Sold	155
21-4	Income Statement	155
21-5	Vertical Analysis	156
21-6	Horizontal Analysis	157
Simulation: Copyfax Center II		158

CHAPTER 22   Financial Management

22-1	Corporate Income Taxes	161
22-2	Issuing Stocks and Bonds	162
22-3	Borrowing	163
22-4	Investments—Treasury Bills	164
22-5	Investments—Commercial Paper	164
22-6	Growth Expenses	165
Spreadsheet Application: Financial Management		166
Simulation: The Stock Market		167

CHAPTER 23   Corporate Planning

23-1	Inflation	171
23-2	Gross Domestic Product	172
23-3	Consumer Price Index	173
23-4	Budget	174
Spreadsheet Application: Corporate Planning		175

APPENDIX   177

Student _____ Date _____

Class _____ Instructor _____

SECTIONS 1-1, 1-2 Hourly Pay and Overtime Pay

Some jobs pay a fixed amount of money for each hour you work. The hourly rate is the amount of money you earn per hour. Straight-time pay is the total amount of money you earn for a pay period at the hourly rate. The overtime rate may be 1½ times your regular hourly rate.

Straight-Time Pay = Hourly Rate × Hours Worked

Overtime Pay = Overtime Rate × Overtime Hours Worked

Total Pay = Straight-Time Pay + Overtime Pay

1. Pilar Perez is a truck driver. She earns $17.65 per hour. She worked 40 hours last week. What was her straight-time pay? _____

2. Helen Kulman is a secretary. She earns $10.65 per hour. She worked 38 hours last week. What is her straight-time pay? _____

3. What is the straight-time pay for each of the following for a 40-hour week?

    a. locker room attendant _____ b. server _____

    c. pantry help _____ d. bus server _____

    > **PRIVATE CLUB SERVICE HELP**
    > Has opening for locker room attendant (men's) to $6.90 per hr., bus server to $6.80 per hr., servers to $7.73 per hr., Pantry help to $6.30 per hr. Send resume to P.O. Box 1073, Toledo, OH

4. As an electronics technician, Ellen Bero earns $14.92 per hour. She earns double time for work on Sundays. Last week she worked 38 regular hours plus 5 hours on Sunday. What was her total pay for this week? _____

5. Eli Katcher is hired as a landscaper. He works 7¾ hours each day, Monday through Friday. What would his total pay be for the week if he is paid at the:

    > **LANDSCAPING/WILL TRAIN**
    > $7-$9.90 PER HOUR
    > CAREER CONNECTIONS
    > Free resume 865-9786 small fee

    a. bottom of the pay scale? _____

    b. top of the pay scale? _____

6. Georgia Kassem installs fencing. She is paid $7.50 per hour for an 8-hour day and time and a half for overtime for any work over 8 hours per day. What is her pay for a week when she worked, 7, 12, 9, 10, and 10 hours? _____

7. Malik Boykin is paid $8.20 per hour and time and a half for any work over 40 hours per week. Find his total hours and gross pay for each week.

	M	T	W	Th	F	S
Week of 3/10	5.5	6	9	12	7	0
Week of 3/17	8	8.5	9	13	4.5	4

8. You are a computer technician for Data Control. You earn a regular hourly rate of $15.40. You earn time and a half for overtime work on Saturdays and double time on Sundays. This week you worked 38 hours from Monday through Friday, 8 hours on Saturday, and 5 hours on Sunday. What is your total pay for the week? _____

Student _____ Date _____

Class _____ Instructor _____

SECTION 1-3 Weekly Time Card

When you work for a business that pays on an hourly basis, you are usually required to keep a timecard. The timecard shows the time you reported for work and the time you departed each day.

Total Hours = Sum of Daily Hours

Compute the hours worked for each day on the timecards. Round each half of the day to the nearest quarter hour. What are the total hours for the week? What is the total pay for the week?

1. **TEMPORARY EMPLOYEE TIMECARD**
   NAME: Amanda Tacket
   DEPT: Accounting
   Note: No overtime rate.
   EMPLOYEE SIGNATURE

DATE	IN	OUT	IN	OUT	HOURS
9/13	7:00	11:00	11:30	4:45	
9/14	8:10	11:35	12:30	4:35	
9/15	8:10	12:00	12:40	4:10	
9/16	8:20	11:50	12:50	4:50	
9/17	7:05	11:09	11:50	3:30	

RATE PER HOUR: $8.50   TOTAL HOURS _____

2. **TEMPORARY EMPLOYEE TIMECARD**
   NAME: Akina Tanaka
   DEPT: Auto Parts
   Note: Overtime is 1½ on hours over 40.
   EMPLOYEE SIGNATURE

DATE	IN	OUT	IN	OUT	HOURS
4/5	8:00	12:00	1:00	5:00	
4/6	8:10	11:40	12:40	4:10	
4/7	8:00	12:05	12:55	5:20	
4/8	8:30	11:35	12:15	4:30	
4/9	7:50	11:55	12:40	5:00	
4/10	7:30	11:45			

RATE PER HOUR: $8.40   TOTAL HOURS _____

3. **TEMPORARY EMPLOYEE TIMECARD**
   NAME: Eugene Mueller
   DEPT: Sales
   Note: No overtime rate.
   EMPLOYEE SIGNATURE

DATE	IN	OUT	IN	OUT	HOURS
8/8	7:00	11:15	12:10	4:10	
8/9	6:50	11:00	11:50	4:00	
8/10	7:10	11:46	12:34	3:58	
8/11	7:10	11:10	12:00	4:35	
8/12	7:05	10:55	11:41	3:25	

RATE PER HOUR: $7.50   TOTAL HOURS _____

4. **TEMPORARY EMPLOYEE TIMECARD**
   NAME: Nina Surovy
   DEPT: Factory Shop
   Note: Overtime is 1½ on hours over 40 and all Saturday hours.
   EMPLOYEE SIGNATURE

DATE	IN	OUT	IN	OUT	HOURS
3/19	3:30	7:30	8:15	12:10	
3/20	3:25	7:40	8:30	11:25	
3/21	3:32	7:29	8:10	11:30	
3/22	3:23	7:25	8:05	12:00	
3/23	3:40	7:40			
3/24	12:15	6:15			

RATE PER HOUR: $13.28   TOTAL HOURS _____

Student _____ Date _____

Class _____ Instructor _____

SECTION 1-4 Piecework

Some jobs pay on a piecework basis. You are paid for each item of work that you produce.

Total Pay = Rate per Item × Number Produced

1. Alva Nunez is a punch press operator for Drummond Machine Company. She earns $0.95 for every molding she presses. What is her total pay for a week in which she presses 310 moldings? _____

2. Keiji Kuroki delivers newspapers for *The Toledo News*. He is paid $0.06 for every daily paper (Mon.–Fri.) he delivers and $0.50 for every Sunday paper. What is his pay for a week in which he delivers 574 daily papers and 165 Sunday papers? _____

3. Odell Gleaves delivers Danberry Real Estate calendars to town residents after school. He is paid $0.074 for each calendar he delivers. What is his total pay for a week in which he delivered the following number of calendars? _____

Mon.	Tues.	Wed.	Thurs.	Fri.
100	130	145	138	210

4. During the spring Nina Milling assembles bicycles at The Wheeler Dealer. She is paid $10.00 for each bicycle assembled during a regular work week, $14.00 for each bicycle assembled on a Saturday, and $16.00 for each bicycle assembled on a Sunday. What is her total pay for a week in which she assembled the following number of bicycles? _____

Mon.	Tues.	Wed.	Thurs.	Fri.	Sat.	Sun.
4	7	6	10	8	4	5

5. You are a packer for Acme Bottling Company. You fill cartons with bottles, seal the cartons, and stack them on pallets. Monday through Friday you are paid $0.41 for each carton you fill. On Saturday you are paid an additional $0.21 for each carton you fill. What is your total pay for a week in which you filled the following number of cartons? _____

Mon.	Tues.	Wed.	Thurs.	Fri.	Sat.
210	175	224	160	216	90

6. You work in the upholstery department of a furniture factory. You are trained to upholster couches, loveseats, and chairs. You receive $105 for each couch, $85 for each loveseat, and $65 for each chair. During the last 4 weeks you upholstered 5 couches, 6 loveseats, and 5 chairs.

    a. What is your total pay for the 4 weeks? _____

    b. If you worked 160 hours, what was your hourly rate? _____

Student Date

Class Instructor

SECTION 1-5 Salary

A salary is a fixed amount of money that you earn on a regular basis. Your salary may be paid weekly, biweekly, semimonthly, or monthly. Your annual salary is the total salary you earn during a year.

Salary per Pay Period = $\dfrac{\text{Annual Salary}}{\text{Number of Pay Periods per Year}}$

1. Devon Price is a clerk typist. His annual salary is $18,720. What is his biweekly salary?

2. Lorenzo Caballero was just hired as an engineer for Saxon Engineering. His starting salary is $57,600 annually. What is his semimonthly salary?

3. Ralph Konsky was hired as an administrative assistant for Hereford Cattle Company. His annual salary is $34,100. What is his weekly salary?

4. Mary O'Connel is earning a weekly salary of $521.60 as a payroll clerk. She has accepted a new assignment in the tax processing department. In her new position, she will be paid an annual salary of $30,534. How much more will she earn per week in her new position?

5. Joseph Cheyenne is earning an annual salary of $24,895. He has been offered the job in the ad. How much more would he earn per month if he is paid the minimum? The maximum?

   SYSTEMS PROGRAMMER
   $28-36,000. Fee paid. If you have a degree in Computer Science plus 2 or more years experience with QUARK, send your resume today. Executive Data Processing, P.O. Box 1746.

6. Catherine Lewiston is currently earning an annual salary of $15,080 at Zimmerman Heating Company. She has been offered a job at a steel company at an annual salary of $16,120. How much more would she earn per week at the steel company than at Zimmerman Heating?

7. Debra Arthur earns a weekly salary of $472 at All Sports. Next month she will be promoted from assistant buyer to head buyer. In her new position she will be paid $1,200 semimonthly. How much more per year will she earn as head buyer than as assistant buyer?

8. You are a first year police officer in Swanton, Ohio. You are earning a monthly salary of $2,200. Next year you will be given a raise to $29,890 annually. How much more per month will you earn your second year?

9. Consider the two ads for an accounting clerk. If you worked 40 hours per week for 50 weeks, how much would each company pay per hour?

   ACCOUNTING CLERK: $18,500 Fast paced CRT, type 60 wpm, benefits, 865-9281. 5640 Southwyck

   ACCOUNTING CLERK: $14,500/yr Salary "Great company" Full benefits! Interviewing now! Call Polly/Sue 243-2222.

Student _____ Date _____

Class _____ Instructor _____

SECTIONS 1-6, 1-7 Commission and Graduated Commission

A commission is an amount of money that you are paid for selling a product or service. Your commission rate may be a specified amount of money for each sale or it may be a percent of the total value of your sales. A graduated commission offers a different rate of commission for each of several levels of sales.

Commission = Commission Rate × Total Sales

Total Graduated Commission = Sum of Commissions for All Levels of Sales

1. Jermain Oberlin sells cleaning supplies. He received a straight commission of 12 percent of the selling price of each item sold. What commission will he receive for selling $2,591.67 worth of cleaning supplies? _____

2. Filipa Robarge sells cosmetics. Her commission is 30 percent of the selling price of every item she sells. What is her commission when she sells cosmetics totaling $717.53? _____

3. You sell storm windows and doors. You receive a straight commission of 8 percent of the selling price of each storm window and 12 percent of the selling price of each door. What total commission will you receive for selling storm windows worth $5,400 and doors worth $790? _____

4. Audrey Sanders sells sports equipment. She is paid a commission of 5.14 percent of her first $1,500 in sales during the week and 10 percent on all sales over $1,500. What is her commission in a week during which she sells $2,510 worth of sports equipment? _____

5. Jasper Carrott sells farm chemicals. He is paid a commission of 9 percent of his first $6,000 in sales during the month and 14 percent on all sales over $6,000. What is his commission in a month in which he has sales worth $16,120? _____

6. Miguel Valdez sells appliances. He is paid an 8 percent commission on the first $2,000 worth of sales, 10 percent on the next $2,500, and 15 percent on all sales over $4,500. What is his commission on $4,910 worth of sales? _____

7. Cho Sasaki demonstrates microwave ovens at the National Home Show. She is paid $7 each for the first 7 demonstrations and $11 for each demonstration over 7. What is her commission for a day in which she makes 12 demonstrations? _____

8. You are paid a commission plus $5.40 per hour with time and a half overtime for all hours over 8 per day. Your commission consists of 4 percent of the first $3,000 in sales and 5 percent on all sales over $3,000. Find your gross pay for a week in which you worked 9 hours on Monday, 8 hours on Tuesday, 11 hours on Wednesday, 9 hours on Thursday, 10 hours on Friday, and 8 hours on Saturday. Your total sales for the week were $4,115. _____

9. You are the sales manager for Solar Panel Company. You receive a commission based on the total sales of all the salespeople you manage. Your commission is 2 percent of the first $80,000 of sales, 4 percent of the next $80,000, and 5 percent of all sales over $160,000. What is your commission for a month in which your salespeople sold $242,100 in solar panels? _____

Student   Date

Class   Instructor

Spreadsheet Application: Gross Income

DIRECTIONS:

1. Insert your *Student Activity Workbook CD* into your computer and click on Chapter 1 Gross Income. The spread sheet will appear.
2. Key your name into cell B1. Key the date into cell G1.
3. Key the information below into the appropriate cells. The spreadsheet application will compute the data for you automatically.
4. Save your spreadsheet as Ch1XXX, where XXX are your initials.
5. Print out your spreadsheet.

Find the straight-time pay, the overtime pay, and the total pay for each employee. Overtime pays time and a half unless otherwise specified.

1. Employee: D. Wyse.
   Rate per hour: $9.60.
   Regular hours: 40.
   Overtime hours: 6.

2. Employee: K. Najera.
   Rate per hour: $12.50.
   Regular hours: 36.
   Overtime hours: 8.

3. Employee B. Bond.
   Rate per hour: $15.50.
   Regular hours: 25.
   Overtime hours: 4.

4. Employee: G. Maruyama.
   Rate per hour: $22.00.
   Regular hours: 40.
   Overtime hours: 12.

5. Employee: A. Roth.
   Rate per hour: $27.22.
   Regular hours: 26.
   Overtime hours: 0.

6. Employee: W. Pawlowicz.
   Rate per hour: $8.55.
   Regular hours: 36.
   Overtime hours: 9 at time and a half, 4 at double time.

7. Marc Pempertolie earns $9.50 per hour plus time and a half for overtime. Last week he worked his regular 40 hours plus 6 hours overtime.

8. Luisa Palma earns $6.95 per hour plus time and a half for overtime. Last week she worked her regular 40 hours plus 12 hours overtime.

9. Hilarie Mapes earns $16.50 per hour. Last week she worked her regular 36 hours plus 7.5 hours overtime at time and a half and 4 at double time.

10. Gardenia Cleaves earns $25.25 per hour plus time and a half for overtime. She worked her regular 42 hours plus 9.25 hours overtime.

11. Vernon Viera earns $8.63 per hour plus time and a half for overtime on weekends. Last week he worked 35 hours Monday through Friday, 8 hours on Saturday, and 8 hours on Sunday.

12. Sherri Cordesa earns $18.875 per hour plus double time for overtime on weekends. Last week she worked 28 hours Monday through Friday, 7.5 hours on Saturday, and 9.5 hours on Sunday.

13. Angela Perez earns $11.36 an hour plus time and a half for overtime over 8 hours a day. Last week she worked 10 hours on Monday, 10 hours on Tuesday, 8 hours on Wednesday, 12 hours on Thursday, and 9 hours on Friday.

14. Robert Lewis earns $12.42 an hour plus double time for overtime. Last week he worked his regular 40 hours plus 6.5 hours overtime.

15. Enyeto Abenaki earns $8.50 an hour plus time and a half for overtime over 8 hours and double time for weekends. Last week he worked 11 hours on Monday, 8 hours on Tuesday, 12 hours on Wednesday, 8 hours on Thursday, 9 hours on Friday, and 6.5 hours on Saturday.

16. Dwight Madsen earns $17.25 an hour plus time and a half for overtime over 36 hours and double time for weekends. Last week he worked 48 hours during the week and 7.25 hours on Saturday.

SECTION 2-1 Federal Income Tax

Employers are required by law to withhold a certain amount of your pay for federal income tax (FIT). The Internal Revenue Service provides employers with tables that show how much money to withhold. The amount withheld depends on your income, marital status, and withholding allowances. You may claim 1 allowance for yourself and 1 for your spouse if you are married. You may claim additional allowances for any others you support.

Use the tax tables on pages 178–181 to find the amount withheld.

1. Beverly Hibbs earns $325.00 a week. She is single and claims 2 allowances. What amount is withheld weekly for federal income tax?

2. Sing-Chi Fong earns $415.00 a week. He is married and claims 3 allowances. What amount is withheld weekly for federal income tax?

3. Rebecca David earns $427.50 per week as manager at Marlin Department Store. She is married and claimed 1 allowance last year. She hopes to receive a refund on her next tax return by claiming no allowances this year. How much more in withholdings will be deducted weekly if she claims no allowances?

4. Andrew Kendall's gross pay for the week is $398.80. He is married and claims 2 allowances. Starting next week he will receive $20 more per week. How much more per week will he pay in federal income tax?

5. Charnita Jones earns $304.80 per week as a sales assistant. Next week she will be promoted to assistant manager. She will then earn $332.50 per week. She is single and claims 1 allowance. How much more will she pay in federal income tax?

6. You are an apprentice plumber for Pointer Plumbing. You are earning an annual salary of $21,060. You are married and claim 3 allowances. What amount is withheld from your weekly pay for federal income tax?

7. You are single and claim 1 allowance. You presently earn $319 per week. Starting next week you will receive a 5 percent increase in pay and will earn $335.00. How much more will you have withheld from your weekly pay for federal income tax?

8. Nico Joven presently earns $348.40 per week. He claims himself and his mother as allowances. He is single. He is to get a new job classification which will result in a 15 percent increase in pay. He also plans to marry. After his marriage, he will claim his wife, himself, and his mother as allowances. How much less will be withheld weekly for federal income tax?

Student _____ Date _____

Class _____ Instructor _____

SECTIONS 2-2, 2-3 State Income Tax and Graduated State Income Tax

Most states require employers to withhold a certain amount of your pay for state income tax. In some states, the tax withheld is a percent of your taxable wages. Your taxable wages depend on personal exemptions allowed for supporting yourself and others in your family. Most states have a graduated income tax that involves a different tax rate for each of several levels of income.

Taxable Wages = Annual Gross Pay − Personal Exemptions

Annual Tax Withheld = Taxable Wages × Tax Rate

$$\text{Tax Withheld per Pay Period} = \frac{\text{Annual Tax Withheld}}{\text{Number of Pay Periods per Year}}$$

For Problems 1–4, use the personal exemptions below to find the amount withheld.

PERSONAL EXEMPTIONS: Single — $1,500; Married — $3,000;
Each Dependent — $700

1. Jack Pasler earns $30,940 annually as an accountant. He is married and supports 1 child. The state tax rate in his state is 4.5 percent of taxable income. What amount is withheld yearly for state income tax? _____

2. Aziza Johnson earns $34,850 annually as an engineer. She is single and supports her father. The state tax rate in her state is 3.0 percent of taxable income. What amount is withheld yearly for state income tax? _____

3. Nehru Patel earns $42,500 annually as a new staff attorney. He is single. The state tax rate in his state is 3.5 percent of taxable income. What amount is withheld from his monthly pay for state income tax? _____

4. Kalila Haddad earns $394.00 per week. She is married and claims 3 children as dependents. The state tax rate in Haddad's state is 2.0 percent of taxable income. What amount is withheld from Haddad's weekly pay for state income tax? _____

5. You are a computer operator for Data Base, Inc. The state has the following personal exemptions and graduated income tax.

Personal Exemptions	
Single	$1,500
Married	$3,000
Each Dependent	$ 700

STATE INCOME TAX	
Annual Gross Pay	Tax Rate
First $1,000	1.5%
Next $2,000	3.0%
Next $2,000	4.5%
Over $5,000	5.0%

You earn $28,600 a year. You are single and are paid on a weekly basis. What amount is withheld from your weekly paycheck for state income tax? _____

---

8 Mathematics with Business Applications ♦ Sections 2-2, 2-3   Copyright © Glencoe/McGraw-Hill

Student _____ Date _____

Class _____ Instructor _____

SECTION 2-4 Social Security and Medicare Taxes

The Federal Insurance Contributions Act (F.I.C.A.) requires employers to deduct 6.2 percent of the first $84,900 of your annual income for Social Security taxes and 1.45 percent of all your annual income for Medicare taxes. The employer must contribute an amount that equals your contribution.

Tax Withheld = Gross Pay × Tax Rate

Use the Social Security tax rate of 6.2 percent on the first $84,900 earned and Medicare tax rate of 1.45 percent on all earnings to solve the following problems.

1. Roland Purcell, a draughtsman, has a gross monthly income of $2,400. His earnings to date for this year are $24,000. How much is deducted this month for Social Security? How much for Medicare? _____ _____

2. Lazaro Lopez, a store manager, has a gross weekly income of $721.15. His earnings to date for this year total $25,240.25. How much is deducted from his paycheck this week for Social Security? How much for Medicare? _____ _____

3. Maria Whetstone, a boiler operator, has a gross weekly income of $502.16. Her earnings to date for this year are $20,086.40. How much is deducted from her paycheck this week for Social Security? How much for Medicare? _____ _____

4. Adam Zetts is an aerospace engineer. He earns $78,000 a year and is paid on a semimonthly basis. How much is deducted per pay period for Social Security? How much for Medicare? _____ _____

5. Renae Walters is paid a salary of $8,000 per month.

    a. How much is deducted in January for Social Security? For Medicare? _____ _____

    b. How much is deducted in December for Social Security? For Medicare? _____ _____

6. Cleveland Woods earns $126,000 per year. He is paid monthly.

    a. How much is deducted in August for Social Security? For Medicare? _____ _____

    b. How much is deducted in September for Social Security? For Medicare? _____ _____

    c. How much is deducted in October for Social Security? For Medicare? _____ _____

Student _____ Date _____

Class _____ Instructor _____

SECTION 2-5 Group Health Insurance

Many businesses offer group insurance plans to their employees. You can purchase group insurance for a lower cost than individual insurance. Businesses often pay part of the cost of the insurance. The remaining cost is deducted from your pay.

$$\text{Deduction per Pay Period} = \frac{\text{Total Amount Paid by Employee}}{\text{Number of Pay Periods per Year}}$$

1. Ruth Lockwood earns $2,917 a month as a supervisor for Acme Steel. Her group medical coverage costs $3,120 per year. The company pays 75 percent of the cost of group insurance. How much is deducted each month from her paycheck for medical insurance?

2. David Herbert earns $2,475 a month as a security guard for Baldwin Enterprises. His group medical insurance costs $3,300 a year. The company pays 80 percent of the cost of group insurance. How much is deducted each month from his paycheck for medical insurance?

3. Kasey Marsenburg is a financial consultant for ABC Finance. She earns $748.00 weekly. Her annual group medical coverage costs $4,780, of which ABC Finance pays 65 percent. How much is deducted weekly from her paycheck for medical coverage?

4. Ishiro Murakami earns $697.50 a week as a fireman for the city. The city pays 85 percent of the cost of any insurance coverage. His family medical insurance costs $5,100 a year. How much is deducted each week for medical insurance?

5. Shashi Ram earns $620 per week as a chef. He has group medical and dental insurance. Medical coverage costs $4,780 a year and dental coverage costs $86 a year. The restaurant pays 80 percent of the medical and 65 percent of the dental insurance. How much is deducted each week for both insurance coverages?

6. Judy Carol has medical, prescription drug, and term life insurance coverages through the company for which she works. Medical coverage costs $3,500 a year and the company pays 80 percent. Prescription drug coverage costs $480 a year and the company pays 60 percent. Term life insurance is paid entirely by the company. How much is deducted each week for the coverage?

7. You are a traveling sales representative for Lawn-Care. You have medical, dental, term life insurance, and travel insurance coverages through the company. Medical coverage costs $3,690 a year, dental coverage costs $194 a year, and travel insurance costs $92 a year. The company pays 80 percent of the medical, 70 percent of the dental, and 85 percent of the travel insurance. Term life insurance is entirely paid for by the company. How much is deducted each month from your paycheck for these coverages?

SECTION 2-6 Statement of Earnings

You may have additional deductions taken from your gross pay for union dues, contributions to community funds, savings plans, and so on. The earnings statement attached to your paycheck lists all your deductions, your gross pay, and your net pay for the pay period.

Net Pay = Gross Pay − Deductions

1. Find the net pay.

DEPT.	EMPLOYEE	CHECK #	WEEK ENDING	GROSS PAY	NET PAY
236	Pinto, J.	54316	11/5/—	$452.50	

TAX DEDUCTIONS				PERSONAL DEDUCTIONS		
FIT	SS	MED.	STATE	LOCAL	MEDICAL	UNION DUES	OTHER
$70.00	$28.06	$6.56	$11.27	—	$15.50	—	$24.20

Complete the earnings statements. The Social Security tax rate is 6.2 percent of the first $84,900 earned and the Medicare tax rate is 1.45 percent of all earnings.

2. Lucy Kreb is a bookkeeper. Her state personal exemptions are $84.60 a week. State tax rate is 3.5 percent of taxable income. Local tax is 1.5 percent of gross pay.

DEPT.	EMPLOYEE	CHECK #	WEEK ENDING	GROSS PAY	NET PAY
25	Kreb, L.	3074	3/7/—	$405.00	

TAX DEDUCTIONS				PERSONAL DEDUCTIONS		
FIT	SS	MED.	STATE	LOCAL	MEDICAL	UNION DUES	OTHER
$27.00					$9.15	$3.00	$3.50

3. Malicia Gregory is a telephone installer. Her state personal exemptions total $98.00 per week. The state tax rate is 3.0 percent of taxable income. Medical insurance costs $1,940 a year, of which the company pays 60 percent.

DEPT.	EMPLOYEE	CHECK #	WEEK ENDING	GROSS PAY	NET PAY
A	Gregory, M.	8002	6/10/—	$440.00	

TAX DEDUCTIONS				PERSONAL DEDUCTIONS		
FIT	SS	MED.	STATE	LOCAL	MEDICAL	UNION DUES	OTHER
$57.00				—		—	$28.00

4. Your annual salary is $28,460. Your state personal deductions total $88.00 for a weekly pay period. The state tax rate is 3.6 percent of taxable income. The city tax rate is 1.7 percent of gross pay. Medical and group life insurance are paid by the company. Social Security and Medicare are withheld. Union dues are $156 per year. FIT is $90 per pay period. What is your net pay for each weekly pay period?

Student _____ Date _____
Class _____ Instructor _____

Simulation: Applying for a Job

Suppose you have decided to get a summer job to earn extra money. To decide what kind of work you might like to do, you talk to friends, family, teachers, and others. There are many factors to consider. Here are some of them.

Compensation	Transportation	Interest
hourly pay	location	interesting work
benefits	public transportation	work related to career goals
overtime pay	need for car	
tips	cost	
commission		

Hours	Conditions	
regular hours	duties	
night work	indoor work	
weekend work	outdoor work	
holiday work	clean, quiet environment	
overtime work		

In comparing the wages of different jobs, consider costs too. For example, if you have to spend a lot of money for automobile expenses to drive to and from a job, you may end up with less money to spend than if you had a lower-paying job closer to home.

1. Look at the list of factors above. You may consider other factors important. List the ten factors that are most important to you, with the most important one first. (If you have never had a job, you may want to discuss the factors with someone who has.)

_____
_____
_____
_____

Fill in the table below and calculate the spendable income for each job.

	Hourly Rate	Hours per Week	Gross Pay	Deductions	Net Pay	Transportation	Spendable Income
2.	$6.30	20	$126.00	$24.24	$101.76	$ 5	
3.	7.15	15		18.24		0	
4.	8.25	40		69.13		15	
5.	8.35	36		83.77		36	

12 Simulation: Applying for a Job

Student _____ Date _____
Class _____ Instructor _____

Simulation: Applying for a Job
(CONTINUED)

FINDING A JOB

There are many ways to find a job. Relatives and friends may know of job openings. Schools, churches, and other organizations may be able to help. Some cities have programs that find jobs for young people. State employment services list job openings. Newspaper help-wanted ads may be a good source. Some young people do odd jobs, such as gardening and painting, for their neighbors. If you want to do a particular kind of work, start early when writing or calling possible employers. You may also want to place a "Position Wanted" ad in a local newspaper.

6. Find the gross weekly pay for each of the jobs listed in the ads. Lunch time is unpaid.

HELP WANTED
CAR WASHER $6.50/hr. Tues-Sat, 9-6, 1 hr. lunch. Apply in person to Happy Time Auto Wash, 2167 Elm St.
CASHIER and sandwich maker. 11-2 and 4-8, Mon.-Fri. $7.05/hr. Call 555-3597 for interview appointment.
CLERK TYPIST Must type at least 50 wpm and be willing to be trained as data input operator. 8-4:30, Mon.-Fri. $320/wk. Assured Products, 621 East St., 555-3418 ex. 43.
COOK'S ASSISTANT for summer camp. No experience necessary, will train. 7 hr./day, 7 days/wk. Meals, lodging, $280/wk. Green Mt. Camp, Woodstock, Vermont.
RECREATION AIDE for city parks. Supervise games, teach crafts. Tues-Sat, 10-6. $6.95/hr. Experience w/ children required. Park Dept, 555-5000 ex. 104.
KENNEL HELP No experience necessary, love of animals needed. Clean, feed, exercise, bathe animals. 7-3:30 with 1/2 hr. lunch, Mon.-Fri. $7.25/hr. Wagon Wheel Kennel, 555-4225 before noon.
SWIMMING POOL SERVICE Cleaning & servicing pools, will train. $7.50/hr., 8-5 with 1 hr. lunch, Mon.-Fri. E-Z Pool Service, 555-8216.

7. If you could have any of these jobs, which one would you choose? Why? Keep in mind the factors on the preceding page. If you have trouble choosing between two jobs, write down the reasons you like each one and compare them. This may help you narrow your choice to one job.

_____
_____
_____
_____

Copyright © Glencoe/McGraw-Hill   Simulation: Applying for a Job   13

Student _____ Date _____
Class _____ Instructor _____

Simulation: Applying for a Job
(CONTINUED)

JOB APPLICATION

When you apply for a job, you will be asked to fill out a job application form. You should be prepared to complete all items on the form. Be sure to receive permission to use the names of your personal character references.

Here is a sample of a job application form. Write down your answers as if you were filling out the form.

EMPLOYMENT APPLICATION

Name _____
Address _____
Home Phone _____
Social Security Number _____
Date of Birth _____
In case of emergency notify _____
              Address _____

EDUCATIONAL BACKGROUND

Name and Address of School	Dates Attended From	Dates Attended To	Date Graduated	Major Area of Study
Elementary School				
High School				
College				
Other				

EMPLOYMENT

Name and Address of Employer	Dates Employed From	Dates Employed To	Position	Reason for Leaving

REFERENCES

Name _____ Address _____ Phone _____
Name _____ Address _____ Phone _____
Name _____ Address _____ Phone _____

MISCELLANEOUS

Hobbies _____
Hours Available for Interview _____
Number of Days per Week You Wish to Work: Minimum _____ Maximum _____
Are You Willing to Work Evenings? _____ Weekends? _____

Student _____ Date _____

Class _____ Instructor _____

Simulation: Applying for a Job
(CONTINUED)

JOB INTERVIEWS

Usually an employer interviews many applicants for a job opening. It is important that you dress neatly, speak clearly, and are able to answer the interviewer's questions. Many people are nervous before and during an interview. It is helpful to know what type of questions an interviewer might ask. Here are some of the most common questions.

Write your answers to the questions below as if you were being interviewed for the job you choose on page 13. If there is time, you and someone in your class might take turns interviewing each other.

8. What kind of work are you most interested in? Why?
   _____

9. What are your future vocational or educational plans?
   _____

10. What do you know about our company? Why do you think you might like to work for us?
    _____

11. What jobs have you held? What did you learn from them?
    _____

12. What courses in school did you like best? What courses did you like least? Why?
    _____

13. What is your average grade in school? Do you think you have done the best academic work of which you are capable? If not, why not?
    _____

14. In what school activities have you participated? Which did you like most? Why? Have you been an officer in any activity?
    _____

15. How do you spend your spare time? What are your hobbies?
    _____

16. Do you prefer working with others or by yourself?
    _____

17. What is your major strength? What is your major weakness?
    _____

18. What have you done that shows initiative and willingness to work?
    _____

19. What qualifications do you have that make you feel you will be successful in your field?
    _____

An interview is an opportunity for you to ask questions about the job and the company. You may want to ask about pay, benefits, duties, tuition credit, opportunities for advancement, or other factors.

| Student | Date |
| Class | Instructor |

Career Path: Chiropractor

A chiropractor is a health professional who treats patients with particular focus on the physiological and mechanical aspects of the body. Also called a doctor of chiropractic, or DC, a chiropractor is concerned with the structural, spinal, skeletal, muscular, and neurological systems of the patient. Treatment by a chiropractor does not involve drugs or surgery, but rather physical adjustment of the body.

The word chiropractor comes from two Greek words that mean "hand" and "practice." The chiropractor treats the patient with the hands, through manipulation and adjustment of the spinal column, seeking to put it in proper alignment and restore proper muscle and nerve functions.

Chiropractors prepare for their profession at a chiropractic college. This typically involves four years of study, with two years of basic science and two years of specialized clinical work.

According to the American Chiropractic Association, chiropractors usually are self-employed. They establish their own offices, manage their own staffs, set their own working hours, and arrange their own appointments and schedules. Along with their health practice, chiropractors must also be independent businesspeople and managers. As such, they are responsible for their own finances, billing, payroll, taxes, and recordkeeping.

Check Your Understanding

Dr. Charles DeFilippo is a chiropractor with an office in Glenwood. He pays the following weekly salaries to his three employees:

Employee	Weekly Gross Pay
Assistant	$925.00
Receptionist	675.00
Janitor	575.00

Remember that the Social Security tax rate is 6.2 percent of the first $84,900 earned and the Medicare tax rate is 1.45 percent of all earnings.

1. His assistant's biweekly health insurance premium is $72.00. Dr. DeFilippo pays 80 percent of it and she pays 20 percent. How much is withheld from each of her biweekly paychecks?

2. Warren Bly, the janitor, lives 25 miles away in an adjoining state that has a 3 percent state tax rate. How much does Bly pay in state taxes every two weeks?

3. How much is withheld for Medicare each week for all three of Dr. DeFilippo's employees?

4. Dr. DeFilippo's receptionist is getting a 5 percent raise in June. How much will be withheld each two weeks for Social Security after the raise?

Student _____ Date _____

Class _____ Instructor _____

SECTION 3-1 Average Monthly Expenditures

You can manage your money better by keeping an accurate record of your expenditures. You will be able to evaluate your spending habits by keeping detailed records for a number of months.

$$\text{Average Monthly Expenditure} = \frac{\text{Sum of Monthly Expenditures}}{\text{Number of Months}}$$

Complete the table below.

| | Name | Monthly Expenditures ||||Average Monthly Expenditure |
		July	August	September	October	
1.	P. Barker	$ 934.20	$1,317.27	$1,112.15	$1,019.20	
2.	L. Lee	823.40	917.17	1,012.10	987.43	
3.	K. Rue	1,134.14	1,572.99	1,996.61	1,475.50	
4.	T. Geariger	1,192.75	1,946.62	1,439.84	1,503.22	

5. In the table above, who had the highest average expenditure? _____

6. In the table above, who had the lowest average expenditure? _____

7. The Carsons' expenditures for this month are: rent, $412; groceries, $378; utilities, $219.55; gasoline, $50.50; entertainment, $54.80; medical bills, $62.40; and miscellaneous, $95.47. How much did they spend? _____

8. The Jacobs' expenditures for the past 7 months were: January, $1,084.45; February, $886.40; March, $968.45; April, $1,142.60; May, $995.80; June, $1,379.86; and July, $1,042.88. What is their average monthly expenditure? _____

9. Fay Teng's expenditures for the past 3 months were: August, $1,735.50; September, $1,829.42; and October, $1,793.88. What is her average monthly expenditure? _____

10. Adebe Cook has a budget of $990 per month. His budget includes rent, utilities, transportation, clothing, groceries, and miscellaneous expenses. For the past 6 months his expenditures were: January, $927.50; February, $984.40; March, $1,032.32; April, $1,195.55; May, $874.24; and June, $943.37.

    a. What is his average monthly expenditure? _____

    b. How much over his budget is this? _____

11. You use the utility company's budget plan for paying your home heating bills. You pay $75 a month for 9 months. Your actual bills are: September, $28.95; October, $46.15; November, $68.46; December, $109.34; January, $115.26; February, $94.19; March $75.66; April, $51.97; and May, $49.16. Compute the average for the 9 months. _____

Student _____ Date _____

Class _____ Instructor _____

SECTION 3-2 Preparing a Budget Sheet

A budget sheet outlines your total monthly expenses. It includes your living expenses, fixed expenses, and all annual expenses.

$$\text{Total Monthly Expenses} = \text{Monthly Living Expenses} + \text{Monthly Fixed Expenses} + \text{Monthly Share of Annual Expenses}$$

Diane and Cory Legrand have a combined monthly net income of $1,800. Use their budget sheet to answer the following questions.

1. What is the total of their monthly living expenses?

2. What is the total of their monthly fixed expenses?

3. What is the total of their annual expenses?

4. What is the monthly share of their annual expenses?

5. What is the total of their monthly expenses?

6. Are the Legrands living within their monthly net income?

7. The Legrands receive pay raises that increase their net income by 5 percent. What is their new combined monthly net income?

A MONEY MANAGER FOR: The Legrands		MONTH: October	
Monthly Living Expenses		**Monthly Fixed Expenses**	
Food/Grocery Bill	$315.65	Mortgage Payment	$428.64
Household Expenses		Car Payment	192.45
Electricity	48.40	Regular Savings	20.00
Heating Fuel	65.00	Emergency Fund	40.00
Telephone	40.50	Total	
Water	28.20	**Annual Expenses**	
Misc.		Life Insurance	244.00
Transportation		Home Insurance	357.00
Gasoline/Oil	118.82	Car Insurance	306.60
Parking	32.00	Real Estate Taxes	1,847.40
Tolls	11.00	Car Registration	60.00
Commuting		Contributions	872.00
Misc.		Total	
Personal Spending		Monthly Share (÷12)	
Clothing	114.00		
Credit Payments			
Newspapers, Gifts	27.27	**Monthly Balance Sheet**	
Pocket Money	25.00	Net Income	
Entertainment		(Total Budget)	
Movies/Theater	32.00	Living Expenses:	
Dining Out	57.00	Fixed Expenses:	
Total		Total Monthly Expenses	
		Balance	

8. Can the Legrands meet their total monthly expenses with their new monthly income?

9. If you have the same budget and the same net income as the Legrands had before their received their pay increases, on what items would you try to reduce your spending in order to live within your monthly net income?

18 Mathematics with Business Applications ◆ Section 3-2   Copyright © Glencoe/McGraw-Hill

Student _____ Date _____

Class _____ Instructor _____

SECTION 3-3 Using a Budget

You can use a budget to plan your future spending. Using an expense summary, you can compare the amount spent with the amount you budgeted. It is wise to include an emergency fund for unpredictable expenses, such as medical bills and repair bills.

Percent of Budget = Amount Budgeted ÷ Total Budget

Use the budget sheet on the preceding page to answer Problems 1–6. Round each percent to the nearest tenth.

	Expenses	Amount Budgeted	Total Monthly Living Expenses	Percent of Budget	Percent for Average Family	Percent More or Less Than Average
	Clothing	$114.00	$914.84	12.5%	6.8%	5.7% more
1.	Transportation		914.84		20.3%	
2.	Groceries		914.84		27.5%	
3.	Entertainment		914.84		15.0%	
4.	Pocket Money		914.84		5.0%	

5. The Legrands increased their transportation expenses by $40 and decreased their groceries by $40. What percent of the budget for living expenses is the new transportation amount of $201.82? _____

6. In June the Legrands' heating bill is reduced from $65.00 to $10.50.

   a. How much do they save? _____

   b. By what percent are their household expenses reduced if their other expenses remain the same? _____

7. Your monthly net income is $980. You allocate 10 percent for clothing, 27 percent for transportation, 30 percent for groceries, 8 percent for entertainment, 5 percent for pocket money, and the remainder for savings. Your actual expenses for 2 months are shown. What is the dollar amount allocated for each expense? Find the difference between the actual amount spent and the amount budgeted.

Item	Monthly Budget	Actual for Sept.	Difference	Actual for Oct.	Difference	2 Months Combined
Clothing	_____	$ 75.00	_____	$136.27	_____	_____
Transportation	_____	250.00	_____	275.68	_____	_____
Groceries	_____	324.50	_____	275.61	_____	_____
Entertainment	_____	121.60	_____	65.32	_____	_____
Pocket Money	_____	35.00	_____	54.00	_____	_____
Savings	_____	200.00	_____	175.00	_____	_____
Totals	_____					

Are you spending over or under your budget? _____

Student _____ Date _____

Class _____ Instructor _____

Spreadsheet Application: Recordkeeping

DIRECTIONS:

1. Insert your *Student Activity Workbook CD* into your computer and click on Chapter 3 Recordkeeping. The spreadsheet will appear.
2. Key your name into cell B1. Key the date into cell G1.
3. Key the information below into the appropriate cells. The spreadsheet application will compute the data for you automatically.
4. Save your spreadsheet as Ch3XXX, where XXX are your initials.
5. Print out your spreadsheet.

Find the total monthly budgeted amount, total monthly expenditures, and difference between amounts budgeted and spent for each month. Then answer the questions that follow.

MONTHLY BUDGET SHEET FOR JAMES AND SHIRLEY KUJKOWSKI							
Budget Category	Amount Budgeted	April Actual Spent	Differ-ence	May Actual Spent	Differ-ence	June Actual Spent	Differ-ence	Three Months' Differ.
Groceries	$200.00	$195.00		$197.00		$206.00		
Utilities	220.00	235.00		225.00		210.00		
House Payment	715.00	715.00		715.00		715.00		
House Insurance	30.00	30.00		30.00		35.00		
Transportation	215.00	205.00		212.00		210.00		
Clothing	40.00	25.50		45.00		48.00		
Credit Card Payment	100.00	100.00		100.00		100.00		
Entertainment	40.00	56.70		43.25		30.00		
Dining Out	50.00	42.85		61.95		51.85		
Savings	200.00	200.00		180.00		200.00		
Miscellaneous	100.00	89.80		107.90		93.45		
TOTAL								

1. What is the Kujkowskis' total amount budgeted? _____
2. What are the total expenditures for April? _____
3. What are the total expenditures for May? _____
4. What are the total expenditures for June? _____
5. Were they over or under their budget for April? By how much? _____
6. Were they over or under their budget for May? By how much? _____
7. Were they over or under their budget for June? By how much? _____
8. Were they over or under their budget for the three months combined? By how much? _____

Spreadsheet Application: Recordkeeping
(CONTINUED)

9. For April, in which category did they differ most from their budgeted amount? By how much?
   _____

10. For May, in which category did they differ most from their budgeted amount? By how much?
    _____

11. For June, in which category did they differ most from their budgeted amount? By how much?
    _____

12. Over the entire three months, in which category did they differ most from their budgeted amount? By how much?
    _____

13. Why did the actual amount of their house payment not change?
    _____
    _____

14. Explain why the actual amount of their house insurance payment went up.
    _____
    _____

15. Do you have any advice for the Kujowskis? Why or why not?
    _____
    _____
    _____
    _____

Student _____ Date _____

Class _____ Instructor _____

Career Path: Long-Distance Truck Driver

Long-distance truck drivers must keep complete and accurate records of their day-to-day, even hour-to-hour activities. Like anyone else running a business, they must estimate their income and plan their expenses accordingly. Unlike some, they must also keep detailed records on specific items required by government regulations. The Interstate Commerce Commission requires every long-distance trucker to keep a manifest (a record of what is loaded on the truck, where it goes, and when and where it is delivered), time and mileage records, and expense records. Here are just some of the items truckers must estimate and record: tolls, fuel, tires, fines, meals, lodging, showers, miles driven, hours driven, hours spent loading and unloading, and repairs.

Some of these expenses, such as fuel, can vary over time. A tankful of diesel fuel might well cost 10 percent more in July than it did in February, while the trucker's pay for hauling the load remains the same.

Check Your Understanding

Use the table below to answer the questions.

	January	February	March	April	May	June
Miles driven	8,820	9,165	7,579	8,150	10,224	8,468
Fuel expenses	$9,261.00	$9,806.55	$8,185.32	$8,394.50	$11,348.64	$9,738.20
Tolls paid	$286.00	$313.00	$224.00	$241.00	$345.00	$302.00

1. Calculate the average price per gallon the trucker paid each month for fuel.

January	February	March	April	May	June

2. What is the average amount this trucker spent each month on diesel fuel?

_____

3. If the trucker were to estimate a total expense figure for tolls for the calendar year, which of these is the most likely number?

   A. $3,181.00   **B.** $3,811.00   **C.**   **D.** $3,692.00

4. In which 2-month period did the expenses for tolls drop by the greatest amount? Why do you suppose this is?

_____

_____

_____

Student _____ **Date** _____

Class _____ **Instructor** _____

SECTION 4-1 Deposits

A deposit is an amount of money that you put into a bank account. You use a deposit slip to record the amounts of currency, coins, and checks that you deposit. To open a checking account, you must make a deposit.

Total Deposit = (Currency + Coins + Checks) − Cash Received

Find the subtotal and the total deposit.

1.

Cash		DOLLARS	CENTS
	Currency		
	Coins		
Checks	LIST SEPARATELY		
	117–4	$594	44
	71–97	301	03
	SUBTOTAL		
	▸ LESS CASH RECEIVED	40	00
	TOTAL DEPOSIT		

2.

Cash		DOLLARS	CENTS
	Currency	$68	00
	Coins	42	95
Checks	LIST SEPARATELY		
	712–08	129	44
	SUBTOTAL		
	▸ LESS CASH RECEIVED		
	TOTAL DEPOSIT		

3. Margo Xavier makes a deposit at an ATM. She has a paycheck for $375.42 and a refund check for $24.95. She would like to receive $45.00 in cash and deposit the remaining amount. What is her total deposit? _____

4. Nabora Nagamatus deposited a check for $299.45 and a check for $229.52. He received $42.00 in cash. What was his total deposit? _____

5. Paul and Ann Sherwin deposited their paychecks at an ATM. Their checks were for $375.45 and $614.20. They also had a check from their insurance company for $187.60. They received $500.00 in cash. What was their total deposit? _____

6. Akiba Ellis deposits the following in her checking account: 6 five-dollar bills, 5 two-dollar bills, 12 one-dollar bills, 9 half dollars, 6 quarters, 42 dimes, 10 nickels, 15 pennies, and a check for $97.23. What is her total deposit? _____

For Problems 7 and 8, use the deposit slips below to show your total deposit.

7. Randy Houck deposited his paycheck for $385.15, a refund check from a mail order purchase for $125.95, and $37.20 in cash.

8. You have a check for $223.47 and a check for $24.75. You would like to deposit the checks and receive 2 ten-dollar bills, 3 one-dollar bills, 10 quarters, and 10 dimes.

7.

Cash		DOLLARS	CENTS
	Currency		
	Coins		
Checks	LIST SEPARATELY		
	refund		
	paycheck		
	SUBTOTAL		
	▸ LESS CASH RECEIVED		
	TOTAL DEPOSIT		

8.

Cash		DOLLARS	CENTS
	Currency		
	Coins		
Checks	LIST SEPARATELY		
	SUBTOTAL		
	▸ LESS CASH RECEIVED		
	TOTAL DEPOSIT		

SECTION 4-2 Writing Checks

After you have opened a checking account and made a deposit, you may write checks. A check directs the bank to deduct money from your checking account to make a payment. Your account must contain as much money as the amount of the check you are writing so as to avoid overdrawing your account.

Write each amount in words as it would appear on a check.

1. $10.91

2. $228.00

3. $57.81

4. $7.62

5. $4,030.00

6. $8,461.00

7. Complete check #317 using today's date. Make it payable to Hartman Dental Clinic for $86.97 for an office visit.

8. Complete check #128 using today's date. Make it payable to First National Bank for $84.02 for car payment #14.

9. Complete check #142 using today's date. Make it payable to Rural Farm Electric for $364.90 for your monthly bill. Sign your name.

SECTION 4-3 Check Registers

You use a check register to keep a record of the deposits you make and the checks that you write. The balance is the amount of money in your account. You add deposits to the balance. When you write a check, you subtract the amount of the check from the balance.

New Balance = Previous Balance − Check Amount

New Balance = Previous Balance + Deposit Amount

1. Gustava Valadez opened a new checking account by depositing her paycheck for $347.95. The check register shows her transactions since opening her account. What should her new balance be?

CHECK NO.	DATE	CHECKS ISSUED TO OR DESCRIPTION OF DEPOSIT	AMOUNT OF CHECK		AMOUNT OF DEPOSIT		BALANCE
		BALANCE BROUGHT FORWARD ▶					
101	1/7	E&H Auto Clinic	$102	14			
102	1/11	Heising Builders	67	70			

2. Your checkbook balance was $206.42 on March 3. The check register shows your transactions since. What should your new balance be?

CHECK NO.	DATE	CHECKS ISSUED TO OR DESCRIPTION OF DEPOSIT	AMOUNT OF CHECK		AMOUNT OF DEPOSIT		BALANCE
		BALANCE BROUGHT FORWARD ▶					
284	3/9	Osborne Pharmacy	$32	50			
	3/15	ATM Deposit			$120	49	
AT	3/20	General Telephone	19	80			
285	3/21	Continental Foods	68	82			

3. Your checkbook balance was $492.16 on September 3. Use the check register below to record the following transactions: On 9/5 check #442 for $102.06 payable to Lenny's Deli; on 9/6 check #443 for $228.00 payable to Merchant's Bank; on 9/10 a deposit of $350.00; on 9/12 check #444 for $35.79 payable to Home Pharmacy; on 9/15 check #445 for $42.22 payable to Trenton Shoe Store; on 9/15 automatic transfer for $72.60 payable to Home Gas Company.

CHECK NO.	DATE	CHECKS ISSUED TO OR DESCRIPTION OF DEPOSIT	AMOUNT OF CHECK	AMOUNT OF DEPOSIT	BALANCE
		BALANCE BROUGHT FORWARD ▶			

SECTION 4-4 Bank Statements

When you have a checking account, you receive a statement and canceled checks from the bank each month. Canceled checks are the checks that the bank has paid by deducting money from your account. Your statement lists all your checks that the bank has paid, any automatic transfers, any ATM or debit card transactions, and any deposits that the bank has recorded since your last statement. The statement may include a service charge for handling the account.

Present Balance = Previous Balance + Deposits Recorded − Withdrawals − Service Charge

Find the present balances in the table below.

	Previous Balance	Total Deposits	Withdrawals	Service Charge	Present Balance
1.	$ 42.30	$ 502.00	$ 80.60	$ 6.75	
2.	220.72	304.50	398.63	2.80	
3.	37.09	806.51	329.77	2.85	
4.	849.83	795.14	900.62	0	
5.	19.84	1,136.22	1,108.00	48.06	

6. A portion of Edna Betahkatoch's bank statement is shown. Her previous balance was $286.91. What is her present balance?

CHECKS AND OTHER CHARGES			DEPOSITS AND CREDIT		BALANCE
Date	Number	Amount	Date	Amount	
9/24	210	$ 39.95	9/10	$464.00	
9/27	211	110.27	9/18	ATM 148.90	
9/29	AT-Phone	97.58	9/30	45.21	
Service charge		2.25			

7. A portion of your bank statement is shown. Your previous balance was $228.73. What is your present balance?

CHECKS AND OTHER CHARGES			DEPOSITS AND CREDIT		BALANCE
Date	Number	Amount	Date	Amount	
10/13	AT-Sprint	$ 43.60	10/5	$146.90	
10/18	143	112.76	10/12	188.42	
10/27	144	10.64	10/19	ATM 135.65	
10/31	ATM	50.00			
Service charge		5.14			

SECTION 4-5 Reconciling the Bank Statement

When you receive your bank statement, you compare the cancelled checks, the bank statement, and your check register to be sure they agree. You may find some outstanding checks and deposits that appear in your register but did not reach the bank in time to be processed and listed on your statement. You reconcile the statement to make sure that it agrees with your check register.

$$\text{Adjusted Balance} = \text{Statement Balance} - \text{Outstanding Checks/Payments/Debits} + \text{Outstanding Deposits}$$

Find the new balances and adjusted balances in the table below.

	Check Register Balance	Service Charge	NEW BALANCE	Statement Balance	Outstanding Checks/Payments/Debits	Outstanding Deposits	ADJUSTED BALANCE
1.	$ 275.14	$ 4.81		$ 549.95	$ 529.63	$ 250.01	
2.	378.95	4.35		231.36	190.00	333.24	
3.	1,591.40	6.20		1,027.33	0	557.87	
4.	1,202.91	0		2,174.00	1,046.20	75.11	
5.	1,861.20	0		2,361.40	812.14	311.94	

Do the new and adjusted balances agree? _____

6. After comparing your bank statement, canceled checks, and checkbook register, complete the reconciliation statement shown below. What are the new and adjusted balances?

RECONCILIATION STATEMENT

Check Register Balance $ __285.14__

Service Charge − __8.10__

NEW BALANCE $ _____

Statement Balance $ __182.63__

Outstanding Checks

#202 $35.92

#203 $28.75

_____ −$ _____

$ _____

Outstanding Deposits

$129.08

$30.00 +$ _____

ADJUSTED BALANCE $ _____

**RECONCILIATION STATEMENT For Your Convenience

Do the balances agree? _____

Student   Date

Class   Instructor

SECTION 4-6 Online Banking

Online banking, or Internet banking, allows you to do your banking from your home or business by connecting to the Internet. You may access your account(s) round-the-clock, even on weekends. When you are online, you can transfer funds from checking to savings, savings to checking, make loan payments from checking to loan accounts, and make payments to third parties such as utility companies. You may be charged a fee for these services. The table below shows some online banking charges.

Service	Fee	ATM Transaction Charges:	Fee
Basic Monthly Charge	$ 6.95	Local Network	No Charge
Bill Payment—First 5 No Charge	0.50	Regional Network Surcharge	$1.00
Printed Statement	4.00	National Network Surcharge	2.00
Replace Lost Card	5.00	Out of Network Surcharge	3.00
Overdraft	25.00	Cash Advance—2.00% of Amt., $10.00 Max	

Total Fees = Basic Charge + Bill Payments + Statement + ATM Surcharge + Cash Advance Fee

1. Dale Elamuses uses online banking. He pays the basic monthly charge, 9 bills, and requests a printed statement. He also has ATM transactions that include 2 out of network transactions and a cash advance of $200.00. What are his total fees for the month?

2. Mark Antonio uses online banking. He pays the basic charge, pays 8 bills, has a lost card replaced. He also has ATM charges that included 2 national network and 2 out of network transactions, and a $33 cash advance. What are his total fees for the month?

When you bank online, you need to maintain a check register to keep a record of your finances. One feature of online banking is that you can download your current online transactions and put the information into a computer program such as an Excel Spreadsheet, Microsoft Money, or Quicken that contains a check register.

3. On March 15, Atsuko Nagamatus uses online banking to download the transactions on the next page so she can put them on her spreadsheet where she keeps a check register. Note that the transactions since her last logon are shown. Update the check register below the online banking account.

28   Mathematics with Business Applications ◆ Section 4-6   Copyright © Glencoe/McGraw-Hill

Date	Amount	Check Number	Description
03/05	$ 200.00		ATM Withdrawal
03/05	2.00		ATM National Network Fee
03/14	1,251.60	+	**Payee/Description:** AT DEPOSIT **Memo:** MEDIVAC PAYROLL 05555
03/14	0.50		**Memo:** BILL PAYMENT FEE
03/14	0.50		**Memo:** BILL PAYMENT FEE
03/14	1,541.29		CARD PYMT TO 004:555-565 Online Payment
03/14	100.00		ISAAC WALTON PYMT TO 009:W455 Online Payment
03/14	54.55	122	CHECK **Memo:** Winn Dixie
03/14	198.54		AT WITHDRAWAL **Memo:** RO 16 INSURANCE 031202
⦿	**DOWNLOAD**	⦿	**CUSTOMIZE**

Transaction Type or Check No.	Date	Check Register			
		Description of Transaction	Payment/ Debit (−)	Deposit/ Credit (+)	Balance
					$ 2,987.59
ATM	05-Mar	ATM withdrawal			
ATM	05-Mar	ATM fee			
AT	14-Mar	MEDIVAC Payroll			
Online	14-Mar	Bill Payment Fee			
Online	14-Mar	Bill Payment Fee			
Online	14-Mar	Card Pmt			
Online	14-Mar	Isaac Walton			
122	14-Mar	Winn Dixie			
AT	14-Mar	Insurance			

Student   Date

Class   Instructor

Spreadsheet Application: Online Banking Check Register

DIRECTIONS:

1. Insert your *Student Activity Workbook CD* into your computer and click on Chapter 4 Checking Accounts. The spreadsheet will appear.
2. Key your name into cell B1. Key the date into cell G1.
3. Key the information below into the appropriate cells. The spreadsheet application will compute the data for you automatically.
4. Save your spreadsheet as Ch4XXX, where XXX are your initials.
5. Print out your spreadsheet.

Input the transactions that have been downloaded from an online-banking account and enter the transactions on the check register spreadsheets in the following problems.

1. Alan Cook downloaded these transactions. Put them on his spreadsheet where he keeps a check register. His beginning balance is $2,415.32.

Date	Amount		Check Number	Description
03/05	$ 200.00			ATM Withdrawal
03/05	2.00			ATM National Network Fee
03/17	2,751.55	+		Payee/Description: AT DEPOSIT Memo: Dean Corp. Payroll PAYMENT 0555
03/17	0.50			Memo: BILL PAYMENT FEE
03/17	0.50			Memo: BILL PAYMENT FEE
03/18	1,521.82			CREDIT CARD PYMT TO 004:555-666 Online Payment
03/18	100.00			Waterford Commons PYMT TO 009:KW55 Online Payment
03/25	59.55		351	CHECK Memo: Foodland
03/25	230.15			AT WITHDRAWAL Memo: American INSURANCE 031202
⦿	DOWNLOAD		⦿	CUSTOMIZE

2. On June 12, P.J. Perez uses First Bank online banking to download these transactions so he can put them on his spreadsheet where he keeps a check register. His beginning balance is $436.66.

Date	Amount		Check Number	Description
06/01/20	$ 6.95			Online Banking Basic Charge
06/02/20	150.00			ATM Withdrawal
06/05/20	1,250.00	+		AT DEPOSIT Memo: Transfer From Savings Act. 06655
06/05/20	0.50			Memo: BILL PAYMENT FEE
06/05/20	0.50			Memo: BILL PAYMENT FEE
06/05/20	452.23			CREDIT CARD PYMT TO 008-555-555 Online Payment
06/05/20	55.00			Music Booster PYMT TO 002:W6325 Online Payment
06/12/20	85.55		320	CHECK Memo: Plumbing Repairs
06/14/20	745.32			AT WITHDRAWAL Memo: American INSURANCE 031202 Auditor #555

---

30   Spreadsheet Application: Online Banking Check Register   Copyright © Glencoe/McGraw-Hill

Student _____   Date _____

Class _____   Instructor _____

Simulation: Reconciling a N.O.W. Account

Your Negotiable Order of Withdrawal (N.O.W.) account is similar to a checking account except that it earns interest for you. Interest is the amount you earn for permitting the bank to use your money. A service charge of $5 is imposed if the balance in the account falls below $500 on any day of the cycle. You also make your mortgage payment to Peoples Savings through an automatic transfer arrangement. In addition, the interest on your certificate of deposit is automatically credited to your N.O.W. account. Using your N.O.W. account statement from the bank and your checkbook register, complete the reconciliation form on the next page.

N.O.W. ACCOUNT STATEMENT

Check Number	Amount +/−	Date	Description	Bank Reference Number	Date	Balance
ATM	$ 50.00−	12/03	Check Withdrawal: 24-hour	681765	12/01	$768.70
315	275.80−	12/07	Check	249247	12/03	718.70
	132.42+	12/07	CD Interest Credit	756358	12/07	575.32
316	99.22−	12/10	Check	249861	12/10	992.30
AT	516.20+	12/10	Deposit − Payroll	332196	12/11	892.30
ATM	100.00−	12/11	Cash Withdrawal: 24-hour	681983	12/15	579.37
317	312.93−	12/15	Check	249187	12/17	435.77
318*	143.60−	12/17	Check	249193	12/23	951.97
AT	516.20+	12/23	Deposit − Payroll	332552	12/28	390.78
322	96.19−	12/28	Check	249337	12/31	390.53
	465.00−	12/28	Peoples Savings Transaction	817130		
	4.75+	12/31	N.O.W. Account Interest	527168		

Items Enclosed	Balance Last Statement	Total Amount Charged	Total Amount Credited	Balance
5	$768.70	$1,547.74	$1,169.57	$390.53

* Indicates the next sequentially numbered check or checks may have (1) been voided by you, (2) not yet been presented to the bank, or (3) appeared on a previous statement.

PLEASE BE SURE TO DEDUCT ANY PER CHECK CHARGES OR SERVICE CHARGES THAT MAY APPLY TO YOUR ACCOUNT

CHECK OR TRANS. NO.	DATE	DESCRIPTION OF TRANSACTION	CHECK OR TRANSACTION AMT.	√T	(−) CHECK FEE	(+) AMOUNT OF DEPOSIT	BALANCE $768 70
	12/03	Cash Withdrawal	$50 00	✓			718 70
315	12/07	Car Payment	275 80	✓			442 90
316	12/10	King Food Locker	99 22	✓			343 68
	12/10	Deposit Paycheck		✓		$516 20	859 88
	12/11	Cash Withdrawal	100 00	✓			759 88
317	12/14	Ace Appliances	312 93	✓			446 95
318	12/17	Electric Co.	143 60	✓			303 35
	12/23	Deposit Paycheck		✓		516 20	819 55
319	12/25	King Drugstore	17 93				801 62
~~320~~		VOID					
321	12/27	Suburban News	15 80	✓			785 82
322	12/28	King Food Locker	96 19	✓			689 63

Student _____ Date _____

Class _____ Instructor _____

Simulation: Reconciling a N.O.W. Account
(CONTINUED)

BALANCING MADE EASY

To adjust your checkbook register balance for reconciliation with your N.O.W. Account Statement, enter your checkbook balance here. _____

1. Add to your checkbook balance all deposits, interest, and other credits posted on this statement that you have not already recorded.   1. _____ (+)

2. Subtract all automatic and other charges such as automatic savings posted on this statement that you have not already recorded.   2. _____ (−)

3. Subtract from your checkbook balance any service charges.   3. _____ (−)

4. The steps above will give you your adjusted balance. Enter this adjusted balance here.   4. [_____]

Reconcile your N.O.W. Account Statement with your adjusted balance in your checkbook register.

1. Write the amount shown on the N.O.W. Account Statement under "Balance this Statement."   1. _____

2. Add any deposits you have made that the Bank has not shown.

   2. Date _____ Amount
   $ _____
   _____
   _____
   _____

   SubTotal $ _____ (−)

3. Subtract outstanding checks not shown.

   3. Check # _____ Amount
   $ _____
   _____
   _____
   _____
   _____
   _____
   _____
   _____
   _____

   SubTotal $ _____ (−)

4. Now you should have the same figure as your adjusted checkbook register.   4. [_____]

32   Simulation: Reconciling a N.O.W. Account

Student	Date
Class	Instructor

SECTIONS 5-1, 5-2 Deposits and Withdrawals

To open a savings account, you must make a deposit. Every deposit you make is added to the balance of your account. Every withdrawal you make is subtracted from the balance of your account. Your bank may provide deposit and withdrawal slips for you to fill out for each transaction.

Total Deposit = (Currency + Coins + Checks) − Cash Received

1. Your account number is 718512. You wish to deposit $34 in currency, $6.25 in coins, and a check for $228.91. Complete the savings deposit slip.

2. Your account number is 421746. You wish to deposit 120 dimes, 25 quarters, and checks for $184.63 and $196.17. You wish to receive $50 in cash. Complete the savings deposit slip.

3. Your account number is 0651831. You wish to withdraw $332.16. Complete the savings withdrawal slip.

4. Your account number is 9841730. You wish to withdraw one hundred twenty-three dollars and sixty-four cents. Complete the savings withdrawal slip.

Student _____ Date _____

Class _____ Instructor _____

SECTION 5-3 Account Statements

Your bank may provide you with a savings account passbook. When you make a deposit or withdrawal, a bank teller records in your passbook the transaction, any interest earned, and the new balance. Your bank may mail a monthly or quarterly account statement showing all deposits, withdrawals, and interest credited to your account since the last statement date.

New Balance = Previous Balance + Interest + Deposits − Withdrawals

Fill in the table below with the new balances.

	Previous Balance	Interest	Deposit	Withdrawals	New Balance
1.	$ 504.23	$ 1.87	$ 98.25	$ 150.00	
2.	597.70	1.80	—	—	
3.	882.85	1.94	—	20.00	
4.	8,412.56	28.04	—	8,000.00	
5.	3,294.00	10.98	75.00	217.49	
6.	2,218.47	5.55	612.89	750.00	

7. Find the balance for each date on this savings account passbook.

Passbook Account Number 07-623456				
Date	Deposit	Withdrawal	Interest	Balance
1/04				$ 285.85
3/15	$ 25.00			_____
4/03			$ 2.86	_____
4/14		$175.00		_____
6/20	814.50			_____
7/03			9.53	_____
7/20	814.50			_____
9/23		125.00		_____
10/03			16.52	_____

8. You receive this savings account statement. What is the balance in your account on June 30?

Passbook Account Number 07-623456				
Date	Deposit	Withdrawal	Interest	Balance
4/08		$ 315.28		$ 152.07
5/25	$ 261.30			
6/10	201.20			
6/30			$ 1.54	

Previous Statement		This Statement	
Date	Balance	Date	Balance
3/31	$467.35	6/30	

34 Mathematics with Business Applications ◆ Section 5-3   Copyright © Glencoe/McGraw-Hill

SECTION 5-4 Simple Interest

When you deposit money in a savings account, you are permitting the bank to use the money. The amount you earn for permitting the bank to use your money is called interest. The principal is the amount of money earning interest. The annual interest rate is the percent of the principal that you earn as interest based on one year. Simple interest is the interest paid on the original principal.

Interest = Principal × Rate × Time

---

1. Alice Tsongas deposited $600 in a new savings account at Bradinton Savings and Loan Association. No other deposits or withdrawals were made. After 3 months the interest was computed at an annual interest rate of 3½ percent. How much simple interest did her money earn?

2. Henry Bonnacio deposited $1,000 in a new savings account at First National Bank. He made no other deposits or withdrawals. After 6 months the interest was computed at an annual rate of 6½ percent. How much simple interest did his money earn?

3. On June 1, Elena Moore deposited $610 in a savings account at Metro Savings and Loan Association. At the end of November her interest was computed at an annual interest rate of 4.5 percent. How much simple interest did her money earn?

4. On March 31, you opened a savings account at Main Street Savings Bank with a deposit of $817.25. At the end of October the interest was computed at an annual rate of 5¾ percent and added to the balance in your account.

   a. How much simple interest did your money earn?

   b. What was your new balance?

5. On February 1, the balance in your account is $516.81. On July 1, you deposit $310.90. Your bank pays 6¼ percent interest.

   a. How much interest have you earned on July 1?

   b. What is your balance, including your deposit, on July 1?

   c. How much interest have you earned on November 1?

   d. What is your balance on November 1?

Some banks calculate the interest on a daily basis. The daily interest is added to the account at the end of the month.

6. On May 1, Cleveland Livingston opened a savings account that paid 3.5 percent exact interest at Fulton Savings Bank with a deposit of $5,000. Ten days later he deposited $2,000. Fourteen days later he deposited $8,000. No other deposits or withdrawals were made. Six days later the bank calculated the daily interest.

   a. How much simple interest did his money earn?

   b. How much was in the account at the end of the 30 days?

Student _____ Date _____

Class _____ Instructor _____

SECTION 5-5 Compound Interest

Interest that you earn in a savings account during an interest period is added to your account. The new balance is used to calculate the interest for the next interest period. Compound interest is interest earned not only on the original principal but also on the interest earned during previous interest periods.

Amount = Principal + Interest

Compound Interest = Amount − Original Principal

1. Michael Arthur deposited $2,900 in a new regular savings account that earns 5.5 percent interest compounded semiannually. He made no other deposits or withdrawals.

   a. What was the amount in the account at the end of 1 year? _____

   b. What is the compound interest? _____

2. Trella Alcala deposited $1,950 in a new credit union savings account on the first of the quarter. The principal earns 4.25 percent interest compounded quarterly. She made no other deposits or withdrawals.

   a. What was the amount in her account at the end of 6 months? _____

   b. What is the compound interest? _____

3. Joseph Black Bear Renfer deposited $2,400 in a new savings account on March 1. The savings account earns 6.0 percent interest compounded monthly.

   a. How much was in the account on June 1? _____

   b. What is the compound interest? _____

4. Jeanne Crawford had $9,675.95 deposited in an account paying 6¼ percent interest compounded semiannually.

   a. How much would she have in her account 2 years later? _____

   b. What is the compound interest? _____

5. You deposit $2,500 in a special savings account. The account earns interest at a rate of 3.25 percent compounded monthly.

   a. What amount will be in your account at the end of 5 months if no deposits or withdrawals are made? _____

   b. What is the compound interest? _____

SECTIONS 5-6, 5-7 — Compound Interest Tables and Daily Compounding

To compound interest quickly, you can use a compound interest table, which shows the amount of $1.00 for many interest rates and interest periods. To use the table, you must know the total number of interest periods and the interest rate per period. The more frequently interest is compounded, the more interest you will earn.

Amount = Original Principal × Amount of $1.00

Compound Interest = Amount − Original Principal

Use the compound interest tables below to solve the problems. Round answers to the nearest cent.

Amount of $1.00

Total Interest Periods	1.250%	1.375%	1.500%
1	1.01250	1.01375	1.01500
2	1.02516	1.02769	1.03023
3	1.03797	1.04182	1.04568
4	1.05095	1.05614	1.06136
5	1.06408	1.07067	1.07728
6	1.07738	1.08539	1.09344
7	1.09085	1.10031	1.10984
8	1.10449	1.11544	1.12649

Amount of $1.00 at 5.5% Compounded Daily, 365-Day Year

Day	Amount	Day	Amount	Day	Amount
21	1.00316	30	1.00452	80	1.01212
22	1.00331	40	1.00604	90	1.01364
23	1.00347	50	1.00755	100	1.01517
24	1.00362	60	1.00907	120	1.01823
25	1.00377	70	1.01059	140	1.02131

1. Valley Savings and Trust pays 5 percent interest compounded quarterly on regular savings accounts. Leland Davis deposited $2,000 in a regular savings account and left it there for 1½ years. He made no other deposits or withdrawals during the period. How much interest did his money earn? _____

2. Charles Johnson deposited $4,400 in a savings account earning 6 percent interest compounded quarterly. If he makes no other deposits or withdrawals, how much will his money earn in 2 years? _____

3. On January 4, Janelle Ruskinoff deposited $2,192.06 in a savings account that pays 5.5 percent interest compounded daily. How much will her money earn in 24 days? _____

4. Tak Murakami has a savings account at City Savings Bank. The account earns 5.5 percent interest compounded daily. On February 2, the amount in his account was $580. How much will be in the account in 40 days? _____

5. On October 1, Manda Loya deposited $1,120 in a savings account that pays 5.5 percent interest compounded daily. On October 22, how much interest had been earned on the principal in her account? _____

6. You have a savings account at Federal Savings. The account earns 5.5 percent interest compounded daily. On March 6, you had $1,645.72 in your account. How much would be in the account on July 4? _____

Student _____ Date _____

Class _____ Instructor _____

SECTION 5-8 Annuities

When an equal amount of money is deposited into an account at equal periods of time, this is called an annuity. An ordinary annuity occurs when equal deposits are made at the end of each interest period. The future value is the amount of money in the annuity account at the end of a specific period of time. To find the future value of an ordinary annuity, find the value of one dollar from the table and multiply by the amount of the regular deposit. To use the table you need to know the rate per period and the total number of periods.

Future Value = Amount of Deposit × Future Value of $1.00

Use the table to solve the problems.

1. Rodolfo Balderas deposits $400 in an ordinary annuity at the end of each quarter in an account earning 6 percent interest compounded quarterly. What is the future value of the account in 2 years?

   _____

2. Djana Pollard deposits $1,000 in an ordinary annuity at the end of each quarter in an account earning 4 percent interest compounded quarterly. What is the future value of the account in 1½ years?

   _____

Future Value of an Ordinary Annuity for $1.00 per Period

Period "n"	Rate Per Period			
	0.50%	1.00%	1.50%	2.00%
1	$1.00000	$1.00000	$1.00000	$1.00000
2	2.00500	2.01000	2.01500	2.02000
3	3.01502	3.03010	3.04522	3.06040
4	4.03010	4.06040	4.09090	4.12161
5	5.05025	5.10101	5.15227	5.20404
6	6.07550	6.15202	6.22955	6.30812
7	7.10588	7.21354	7.32299	7.43428
8	8.14141	8.28567	8.43284	8.58297

3. Peggy Mays deposits $100 in an ordinary annuity at the end of each month in an account earning 6 percent interest compounded monthly. What is the future value of the account in 6 months? _____

4. Dai Nakamura deposits $500 in an Individual Retirement Account in the form of an ordinary annuity at the end of each quarter. The account earns 8 percent interest compounded quarterly. What is the future value of the account in 2 years? _____

An annuity due occurs when equal deposits are made at the beginning of each interest period. In an annuity due the money starts earning interest immediately since it is deposited at the beginning of the interest period.

Future Value of an Annuity Due = Future Value of an Ordinary Annuity × (1.00 + the Rate per Period)

5. Leah Troeller deposits $400 in an Individual Retirement Account in the form of an annuity due at the beginning of each quarter. The account earns 8 percent interest compounded quarterly. What is the future value of the account in 2 years? _____

Student _____ Date _____

Class _____ Instructor _____

Spreadsheet Application: Compound Interest

DIRECTIONS:

1. Insert your *Student Activity Workbook CD* into your computer and click on Chapter 5 Savings Accounts. The spreadsheet will appear.
2. Key your name into cell B1. Key the date into cell G1.
3. Key the information below into the appropriate cells. The spreadsheet application will compute the data for you automatically.
4. Save your spreadsheet as Ch5XXX, where XXX are your initials.
5. Print out your spreadsheet.

Find the amount and the interest for each individual below.

1. Mike Oyer.
   Principal: $1,000.
   Interest rate: 6 percent.
   Periods per year: 4.
   Total time: 2 years.

2. Akiko Nakata.
   Principal: $10,000.
   Interest rate: 6.5 percent.
   Periods per year: 12.
   Total time: 1 year.

3. Helen Hallett.
   Principal: $5,000.
   Interest rate: 7.5 percent.
   Periods per year: 4.
   Total time: 0.5 years.

4. Tywanda Delaney.
   Principal: $6,540.
   Interest rate: 8 percent.
   Periods per year: 2.
   Total time: 4 years.

5. Jean Deilman.
   Principal: $568.65.
   Interest rate: 5.5 percent.
   Periods per year: 365.
   Total time: 2 years.

6. Angelo Diaz.
   Principal: $6,987.25.
   Interest rate: 9.5 percent.
   Periods per year: 365.
   Total time: 0.25 years.

7. Elmer O'Neal deposited $40,000 in a savings plan paying 9.85 percent interest compounded monthly for 5 years.

8. Cheryle Contikos opened a $40,000 savings account at 9.85 percent interest compounded quarterly for 5 years.

9. Juan Carrero deposited $2,000 in a passbook savings account paying 5.5 percent interest compounded quarterly for 2 years.

10. Elva and Paul Schrerez deposited $5,000 in a 5-year certificate of deposit paying 7½ percent interest compounded daily (365).

11. Laticia Olrich deposited $1,308.25 in a passbook savings account earning 5.5 percent interest compounded quarterly for 1 year.

12. Maria and Randall Zapata deposited $50,000 in a 20-year certificate of deposit paying 6.5 percent interest compounded monthly.

Student _____ Date _____

Class _____ Instructor _____

Career Path: Welder

A welder's job is to join two pieces of metal together, using ancient or modern tools to apply heat, pressure, or both. Welding is used in manufacturing furniture, automobiles, and just about anything else made of metal. Welders work joining metal to metal in buildings.

The basic process of putting two pieces of metal together has been around for centuries. Blacksmiths and sculptors, for instance, can both be welders. A blacksmith uses heat from a forge and pressure from a hammer to join two pieces of steel in a tool. A sculptor might do the same in joining the pieces of a work of art.

The most commonly used processes today include gas welding, arc welding, and resistance welding. Gas welding applies heat from a gas flame to the edges of the pieces being joined at the same time as it applies it to a welding rod, a filler that is melted to the joint being formed. Arc welding uses electricity to create an electric arc that is hot enough to melt the metal being joined. Resistance welding uses a combination of electricity and pressure, and the heat needed to melt them together is generated from electrical resistance in the metals at the point at which they meet. More modern welding methods include using electron beams and lasers. This kind of welding is used in automobile and aerospace manufacturing.

Welding requires a number of mathematical skills. Welders must be able to calculate measurements and compute the combined weight of pieces being joined. Welding also requires a working knowledge of geometry.

Check Your Understanding

Salvador Ibarra belongs to Local 980 of the Welders Union, which has its own credit union. He transferred $1,400 from his checking account into his credit union savings account and left it there for a year. The account earns 5 percent interest and is compounded quarterly. To answer the questions, show your calculations. Remember to use the following formulas:

Principal × Rate × Time = Interest

Interest + Principal = Total

1. How much was in his savings account at the end of the first quarter?
   _____

2. How much was in his savings account at the end of the second quarter?
   _____

3. How much was in his savings account at the end of the third quarter?
   _____

4. How much was in his savings account at the end of the fourth quarter?
   _____

Student	Date
Class	Instructor

SECTIONS 6-1, 6-2 Sales Tax and Total Purchase Price

Many state, county, and city governments charge a sales tax on certain items or services that you buy. The sales tax rate is usually expressed as a percent. Most stores give you a sales receipt as proof of purchase. The receipt shows the selling price of each item or service you purchased, the total selling price, the sales tax (if any), and the total purchase price.

Sales Tax = Sales Tax Rate × Total Selling Price

Total Purchase Price = Total Selling Price + Sales Tax

1. A store in Madison, Wisconsin, advertised an HDTV for $1,224.95.

   a. What is the sales tax if the combined state and city rate is 6 percent? _____

   b. What is the total purchase price? _____

2. Ramon Escalante purchases a digital camera for $399.99 in Omaha, Nebraska, where the sales tax rate is 5.75 percent.

   a. What is the sales tax? _____

   b. What is the total purchase price? _____

3. Tikia Garrow purchased fishing gear from a store in Toledo, Ohio, where the tax rate is 6.25 percent. She purchased a spinning combo rod and reel for $59.99, 4 spinner baits at $5.49 each, 3 lures for $3.89 each, and a landing net for $24.99. What is the total purchase price, including sales tax? _____

4. Ling Garn purchased 4 tires at $129.99 each, 2 sheepskin car seat covers at $79.89 each, a battery for $89.88, a muffler for $87.50, and 2 shock absorbers for $49.95 each. The sales tax rate is 4.75 percent. What is the total purchase price, including sales tax? _____

5. You purchase a $205.00 camera, a case for $23.89, a wide-angle lens for $127.88, and a zoom lens for $189.89. The sales tax rate is 6.0 percent.

   a. What is the total price of your purchases before sales tax? _____

   b. What is the sales tax on your purchases? _____

   c. What is the total purchase price? _____

Complete the following sales receipts.

6.
Foil	$2.88
Tissue	1.83
Aspirin	3.59
Cat food	6.51
Bleach	.97
Pantyhose	3.89
Towels	1.89
Soap	1.59
SUBTOT	_____
TX 6%	_____
TOT PUR PR	_____

7.
Paint	$18.90
Paint	18.90
Paint	18.90
Brush	7.89
Brush	3.29
Roller	9.49
Thinner	4.39
Dropcloth	2.29
SUBTOT	_____
TX 5.5%	_____
TOT PUR PR	_____

8.
Blouse	$39.98
Shirt	24.00
Skirt	54.98
Shoes	39.98
Slacks	49.95
Tie	16.50
Socks	6.00
Belt	17.00
SUBTOT	_____
TX 8%	_____
TOT PUR PR	_____

Student _____ Date _____

Class _____ Instructor _____

SECTIONS 6-3, 6-4 Unit Pricing and Comparison Shopping

Many grocery stores give unit pricing information for the products they sell. You can use this information to determine which size of a product is the better buy based solely on the price. The unit price of an item is its cost per unit of measure or count.

Unit Price = $\dfrac{\text{Price per Item}}{\text{Measure Count}}$

1. Willis Rusch recently purchased a 5-pound box of treats for his dog. The total purchase price was $4.87. What was the price per pound? _____

2. Leslie Thompson purchased a 64-oz bottle of juice for $2.07. What is the price per ounce? _____

3. Thirza Bernel wants to purchase some detergent. A 100-oz bottle costs $2.97 and a 200-oz bottle costs $5.78.

    a. What is the unit price of each per ounce?

    _____   _____

    b. Which is the better buy? _____

4. Boris Kruse wants to purchase some sport drink. A 64-ounce bottle costs $2.07, a 32-oz bottle costs $1.17, and an 8 pack of 20-oz bottles costs $5.47.

    a. What is the unit price of each per ounce?

    _____   _____   _____

    b. Which size is the best buy? _____

5. Yoon Weng wants to purchase some potato chips. A 1¾-oz bag costs $0.50, a 6-oz bag costs $1.00, and a 12-oz bag costs $1.88.

    a. What is the unit price of each per ounce?

    _____   _____   _____

    b. Which size is the best buy? _____

6. You are shopping for soda in the Food Town Supermarket. Soda is priced as: three "12-pack, 12-oz cans" for $9.00 or three "6-pack, 24-oz plastic bottles" for $9.00. What size is the best buy? _____

7. A store has a special price on "1/5 Cut Color Hanging Folders" 25 to a box. The regular price is $7.49 per box. The special price is "Buy 2, Get 1 Free."

    a. What is the unit price per folder of 1 box? _____

    b. What is the unit price on the special offer? _____

    c. Which is the better buy? _____

8. You are purchasing cotton swabs that come in 2 different sized containers. One box contains 300 swabs for $2.99 and the other box is specially marked at 30 percent more swabs for the same price. How much will you save per swab by buying the larger box? _____

Student _____ Date _____

Class _____ Instructor _____

SECTION 6-5 Coupons and Rebates

Manufacturers, stores, and service businesses offer customers discounts through coupons and rebates. Manufacturers' or store coupons are redeemed at the time of purchase. Manufacturers' rebates are obtained by mailing in a rebate coupon along with the sales slip and the U.P.C. (Universal Product Code) label from the product.

Final Price = Total Selling Price − Total Savings

1. Jesse Aranud purchased a half gallon of ice cream for $4.69. He had a store coupon for $1.00. What is the final price of the ice cream? _____

2. Bertha DeVys had the oil changed in her company car. She had a $3.00 off coupon from the Grease Monkey oil change service. The regular price of an oil change is $29.99. What is the final price? _____

3. Lamont Gatling purchased a phone answering system for his home office. The list price was $99.86. He also purchased a 12-foot handset cord for $8.95 and 50 feet of telephone wire for 45¢ per foot. He received a $5.00 rebate on the phone system and had a store coupon for $1.00 off each accessory. If he paid a 6 percent sales tax on the final price, how much did he pay? _____

4. A Thanksgiving Day promotion included a $1.00 mail-in rebate for the purchase of a turkey weighing at least 20 lbs. Esther Rothert purchased a 22-lb turkey for $1.79 a pound. What did it cost her after the rebate if an envelope costs 15¢ and a stamp costs 39¢? _____

5. A Fourth of July promotion included a $5.00 mail-in rebate for the purchase of a picnic cooler and a store coupon for 50¢ off the price of a case of 24 cans of soda. For the company picnic, Carl Rhiel purchased a 48-quart cooler for $32.99 and a case of soda for $6.99. What did it cost him after the rebate if an envelope costs 15¢ and a stamp costs 39¢? _____

6. A laptop computer sells for $2,149.99 and has a mail-in rebate for $200. What is the cost after the rebate if an envelope costs 15¢ and a stamp costs 39¢? _____

7. If you purchase business software for $69.95 and anti-virus software for $49.95, you get a $20 mail-in rebate for the business software and a $30 mail-in rebate for the anti-virus software.

   a. If each envelope costs 20¢ and each stamp costs 39¢, what is the total cost after the rebates? _____

   b. How much is the actual rebate after your expenses? _____

Student _____ Date _____

Class _____ Instructor _____

SECTIONS 6-6, 6-7 Markdown and Sale Price

Stores often sell products at sale prices that are lower than their regular selling prices. The markdown or discount is the amount of money that you save by purchasing a product at the sale price. The markdown rate or discount rate of an item is its markdown expressed as a percentage of its regular selling price.

Markdown = Regular Selling Price − Sale Price

Markdown = Markdown Rate × Regular Selling Price

Sale Price = Regular Selling Price − Markdown

For Problems 1 and 2, determine the markdown.

1. **Button front tank.** Ribbed cotton in blue, olive, or yellow. S-M-L. Orig. $29, **sale $20.30**

2. **Tattersall blouse.** Roll sleeves, patch pockets. Cotton: sizes 4–14. Reg. $48, **sale $36**

For Problems 3 and 4, determine the markdown and the sale price.

3. **Petite Coordinates** 25% Off REG. 40.00 Blazers, skirts & pants in navy, black or tan. Sizes 6–16.

4. **Spring Jackets** UP TO 30% Off Wide range of basic and fashion colors in nylon or poplin jackets. S, M, L, XL. REG. 59.99

5. A book store has paperback books marked down 25 percent. What is the total sale price of four books that regularly sell for $8.95, $9.55, $6.85, and $12.95?

6. During a September Sale, Camper Supply has marked down all items 30 percent. Judy Vaughn purchases a deluxe portable grill that regularly sells for $79.99 and a set of barbecue tools that regularly sells for $19.98. What is the total sale price?

7. Gechina Galvez shopped at a department store during the end-of-summer sale. All luggage was marked down 35 percent. She purchased a suitcase that regularly sells for $74.95, a garment bag that regularly sells for $80.00, and a tote bag that regularly sells for $39.99. What is the total sale price?

8. During the winter clearance sale, The Cyclery has marked down all bicycles 20 percent and all accessories 25 percent. You purchase a 26-inch 10-speed bike that regularly sells for $399.95, a chain and lock that regularly sell for $16.99, a tire gauge and pump that regularly sell for $24.49, and a deluxe generator and light package that regularly sells for $79.95. What is the total sale price for your purchases?

Student _____ Date _____

Class _____ Instructor _____

Spreadsheet Application: Cash Purchases

DIRECTIONS:

1. Insert your *Student Activity Workbook CD* into your computer and click on Chapter 6 Cash Purchases. The spreadsheet will appear.
2. Key your name into cell B1. Key the date into cell G1.
3. Key the information below into the appropriate cells. The spreadsheet application will compute the data for you automatically.
4. Save your spreadsheet as Ch6XXX, where XXX are your initials.
5. Print out your spreadsheet.

Find the sale price and total purchase price for each item.

1. Item: Office chair.
   Selling price: $129.95.
   Percent markdown: 50 percent.
   Sales tax rate: 6.5 percent.

2. Item: Electric hedge trimmer.
   Selling price: $34.77.
   Percent markdown: 15 percent.
   Sales tax rate: 4 percent.

3. Item: Dishwasher.
   Selling price: $599.99.
   Percent markdown: 5 percent.
   Sales tax rate: 7.55 percent.

4. Item: Car battery.
   Selling price: $79.99.
   Percent markdown: 15 percent.
   Sales tax rate: 7.25 percent.

5. Item: Leather wallet.
   Selling price: $39.99.
   Percent markdown: 25 percent.
   Sales tax rate: 6.50 percent.

6. Item: Jeans.
   Selling price: $24.99.
   Percent markdown: 15 percent.
   Sales tax rate: 7 percent.

7. Mary Zimmerman purchased a personal computer that was marked down 20 percent. The regular price is $599.99 and the sales tax rate is 8.5 percent.

8. Cleo Voss purchased a laptop computer that was marked down 30 percent. The regular price is $2,945 and the sales tax rate is 6.5 percent.

9. A lawn mower regularly sells for $339.99. It is currently marked down 15 percent. The sales tax rate is 6 percent.

10. A DVD player regularly sells for $999.99. It is currently marked down 20 percent. The sales tax rate is 6.25 percent.

11. An auto dealer advertised 10 percent off the list price of all vans. A van has a list price of $34,990. The sales tax rate is 8 percent.

12. A clothing store advertised 45 percent off all winter clothing. Herman Diez picked out several items with a total selling price of $435.42. The sales tax rate is 5.25 percent.

13. A tool set regularly sells for $589.99. It is marked down 20 percent. The sales tax rate is 4.875 percent.

14. Your total order of office products was $519.99. All orders over $500 are subject to a 10 percent discount. The sales tax rate is 5.75 percent.

15. A clothing dealer advertised 25 percent off the list price of all spring fashions in its online catalog. Your order totaled $439.87. There is no sales tax for online orders.

16. An online health foods dealer advertised 10 percent off the list price of herbs. Sue Trundell selected items that totaled $122.43. There is no sales tax for online orders.

Student _____ Date _____

Class _____ Instructor _____

Career Path: Sales Associate

If you've ever gone to a store and bought something, you've dealt with a sales associate. A sales associate helps you find a shirt in a department store, sells you tickets over the phone for a concert, comes to your house to spray your lawn for weeds, or helps you configure your new computer system at the electronics store.

Sales associates are the front line of retail. They are the people the customers do business with directly, the face of the store, the point at which the money comes in and the products go out. When you work as a sales associate, as far as the customer is concerned, you are the company. The customers not only get from you the things they came to buy; they also get information, hospitality, and an overall feeling for what the organization is like. A sales associate must communicate with all kinds of people, know all about what the company sells, and know where to find the answers to questions.

Sales associates working in stores run the cash register, of course, and must be familiar with such calculations as sales tax and percentage discounts. Electronic cash registers do these for you, but you should always be able to double-check yourself in case there is a question. A customer who disagrees about the amount of change given will be talking to the sales associate, not to the cash register.

Check Your Understanding

Lisa Munoz works the floor at BigBoxCo. The table below lists this week's advertised prices. Show your calculations to answer the questions that follow.

Item	Regular Price
Blanko CD-Rs, 100-pack	$ 26.99
Burnware CD-Rs, spindle of 25	8.95
Gektronix 2002 desktop computer (This week only: 5% off plus $75 mail-in rebate)	1,499.00
Yak@Ya cell phone (with 2-year contract at $29.95/month)	49.99
BlabStream Wireless cell phone (with 2-year contract at $19.95/month plus $50 activation fee)	69.99

1. Which pack of CD-Rs is a better deal?

   _____

2. How much is the markdown on the Gektronix 2002 computer? How much will it cost including the 6 percent sales tax and after the mail-in rebate?

   _____

3. Would you get a better deal from Yak@Ya or from BlabStream?

   _____

Student _____ Date _____

Class _____ Instructor _____

SECTION 7-1 Account Statements

When you have a credit card or charge account, you receive a monthly statement. The statement lists all transactions that were processed by the closing date for that month. If your previous bill was not paid in full by the closing date, a finance charge is added. The finance charge is interest that is charged for delaying payment.

$$\text{New Balance} = \text{Previous Balance} + \text{Finance Charge} + \text{New Purchases} - (\text{Payments} + \text{Credits})$$

1. What is the new balance for the credit statement shown?

Billing Date	Previous Balance	Finance Charge	Payments & Credits	New Purchases	New Balance
10/01/--	$139.50	$2.32	$45.00	$29.98	

2. What is the new balance for the credit statement shown?

Billing Date	Previous Balance	Finance Charge	Payments & Credits	New Purchases	New Balance
12/11/--	$185.74	$2.71	$70.94	$49.80	

3. You received this monthly statement from Bank Card. What is your new balance?

Billing Date	Previous Balance	Finance Charge	Payments & Credits	New Purchases	New Balance
09/22/--	$374.06	$6.55	$10.00	$144.99	

4. Complete the account statement. Previous balance of $716.45; payments of $150 and $75; new purchases of $29.98, $129.90, and $10.46; finance charge of $12.54.

Billing Date	Previous Balance	Finance Charge	Payments & Credits	New Purchases	New Balance
02/01/--					

5. Complete the account statement. Previous balance of $78.80; payment of $78.80; new purchases of $24.60 and $54.98; no finance charge.

Billing Date	Previous Balance	Finance Charge	Payments & Credits	New Purchases	New Balance
04/01/--					

6. Complete the account statement. Previous balance of $410.91; payments of $150 and $150; return credit of $21.90; new purchases of $71.80, $21.90, $116.60, $10.49, $51.80, and $6.75; finance charge of $7.19.

Billing Date	Previous Balance	Finance Charge	Payments & Credits	New Purchases	New Balance
06/01/--					

Student _____ Date _____

Class _____ Instructor _____

SECTION 7-2 Finance Charge—Unpaid-Balance Method

Some companies use the unpaid-balance method of computing finance charges. This is when they compute the finance charge based on that portion of the previous balance that you have not paid.

Unpaid Balance = Previous Balance − (Payments + Credits)

Finance Charge = Periodic Rate × Unpaid Balance

New Balance = Previous Balance + Finance Charge + New Purchases − (Payments + Credits)

Complete the account statements below using the unpaid-balance method.

1. Rosie Lane has a charge account at the Cosmopolitan Department Store where the periodic rate is 1.58 percent. A portion of her account statement is shown.

Billing Date	Previous Balance	Finance Charge	Payments & Credits	New Purchases	New Balance
05/20/--	$194.06		$61.50	$29.80	

2. You have a charge account with a periodic rate of 2.08 percent. Your monthly statement shows purchases totaling $416.49 and a payment of $750.

Billing Date	Previous Balance	Finance Charge	Payments & Credits	New Purchases	New Balance
02/01/--	$981.35				

3. The periodic rate is 2.0 percent; previous balance is $291.84; payment of $200; new purchases of $17.40, $17.70, and $46.04.

Billing Date	Previous Balance	Finance Charge	Payments & Credits	New Purchases	New Balance
07/01/--					

Student		Date	
Class		Instructor	

SECTIONS 7-3, 7-4
Finance Charge— Average-Daily-Balance Method

Many companies calculate the finance charge using the average-daily-balance method. The average daily balance is the average of the account balance at the end of each day of the billing period. New purchases posted during the billing period may or may not be included when figuring the balance at the end of the day. The finance charge is calculated by multiplying the periodic rate by the average daily balance.

Average Daily Balance = $\dfrac{\text{Sum of Daily Balances}}{\text{Number of Months}}$

Finance Charge = Periodic Rate × Average Daily Balance

New Balance = Unpaid Balance + Finance Charge + New Purchases

---

1. Fill in the table below.

Billing Periods	Payment	End-of-day Balance	Number of Days	Sum of Balances
09/01–9/10		$410.20	10	$4,102.00
09/11	$150.00	260.20	1	260.20
09/12–9/30		260.20	19	
		TOTALS		

What is the average daily balance without new purchases? _____

2. Compute the average daily balance, finance charge, and new balance as of July 1 using the average-daily-balance method where no new purchases are included. The periodic rate is 1.4 percent.

Date	Transaction	Amount
June 1	Balance	$800.00
June 11	Payment	200.00
June 25	Purchase	150.00

3. A portion of your account statement for November from Charge-All Credit Company is shown. The finance charge is computed using the average-daily-balance method where new purchases are included. Find the average daily balance, the finance charge, and the new balance.

REFERENCE	POSTING DATE	TRANSACTION DATE	DESCRIPTION	PURCHASES & ADVANCES	PAYMENTS & CREDITS
001781	3/12		PAYMENT		$45.00
007619	3/21	3/17	Corner Drug Co.	$31.75	

BILLING PERIOD	PREVIOUS BALANCE	PERIODIC RATE	AVERAGE DAILY BALANCE	FINANCE CHARGE
3/05–4/04	$161.43	2.0%		

PAYMENTS & CREDITS	PURCHASES & ADVANCES	NEW BALANCE	MINIMUM PAYMENT	PAYMENT DUE
$45.00	$31.75		$20.00	3/24

Student _____ Date _____

Class _____ Instructor _____

Simulation: Charge Accounts

You receive your monthly statement from the bank that issued your bank credit card. A portion of the credit card statement is shown.

REFERENCE	POSTING DATE	TRANSACTION DATE	DESCRIPTION	PURCHASES & ADVANCES	PAYMENTS & CREDITS
142116	7/07	7/01	Village Sports	$98.20	
132157	7/17	7/12	Adams Ins.	292.80	
270-32	7/22		PAYMENT		$100.00
122384	7/24	7/24	Ace Tire	84.80	

BILLING PERIOD	PREVIOUS BALANCE	PERIODIC RATE	FINANCE CHARGE
7/01–7/31	$186.80	1.5%	

1. If your credit card company used the unpaid-balance method of computing the finance charge, it would compute the charge on the portion of the previous balance that you have not paid. Complete the statement below to determine the unpaid balance, the finance charge, and the new balance.

Billing Period 7/01–7/30					
PREVIOUS REFERENCE	PAYMENTS & CREDITS	UNPAID BALANCE	FINANCE CHARGE	NEW PURCHASES	NEW BALANCE
$186.80	$100.00				

2. If your credit card company used the average-daily-balance with no new purchases included method of computing the finance charge, it would compute the charge on your average daily balance without including new purchases. Complete the statement below to determine the average daily balance with no new purchases included, the finance charge, and the new balance.

Billing Period 7/01–7/30					
PREVIOUS REFERENCE	PAYMENTS & CREDITS	UNPAID BALANCE	FINANCE CHARGE	NEW PURCHASES	NEW BALANCE

Simulation: Charge Accounts
(CONTINUED)

3. Assume that your credit card company computed the finance charge using the average-daily-balance method where new purchases *are* included.

   a. Complete the chart below to find the average daily balance.

DATES	PURCHASES OR PAYMENTS	END-OF-DAY BALANCE	NUMBER OF DAYS	SUM OF BALANCES
07/01–06				
07/07	$98.20			
07/08–16				
07/17	292.80			
07/18–21				
07/22	−100.00			
07/23–27				
07/28	84.80			
07/29–31				
Total				
Average Daily Balance				

   b. Complete the statement below to find the average daily balance, the finance charge, and the new balance.

BILLING PERIOD	PREVIOUS BALANCE	PERIODIC RATE	AVERAGE DAILY BALANCE	FINANCE CHARGE
07/01–07/30	$186.80	1.5%		
PAYMENTS & CREDITS	PURCHASES & ADVANCES	NEW BALANCE	MINIMUM PAYMENT	PAYMENT DUE
			$40.00	8/25

Student	Date
Class	Instructor

Career Path: Mathematician

Mathematics is the study of the relationship between numbers and the principles that govern numbers and their relationships. It is one of the oldest fields of science, originating thousands of years ago.

Professional mathematicians generally work in one of two broadly-defined fields: theoretical mathematics and applied mathematics. Theoretical mathematics, or abstract mathematics, is concerned with finding new principles or new relationships between existing ones. This is a purely theoretical approach to mathematics, without concern for its practical use. Theoretical mathematicians usually work in universities or colleges.

Applied mathematics is concerned with using mathematical principles to solve real-world problems. Applied mathematicians may be called engineers, computer scientists, economists, physicists, or statisticians. They often work for government agencies or businesses. In the insurance industry, for instance, actuaries calculate risk and probability to determine insurance premiums and dividends. In computer science, systems analysts and programmers apply mathematical principles to cryptanalysis—the science of devising and breaking codes. A doctoral degree is required for most of these positions.

Check Your Understanding

Professor Lemuel Jackson teaches theoretical physics at a state university. He knows everything there is to know about cosmic microwave background anisotropies, but he has trouble figuring out his credit card bill. In June, everything seemed to break down on his car and he charged the repairs on his credit card. Below is his credit card statement. Help Professor Jackson figure out his new balance. The finance charge is 1.75 percent of the unpaid balance.

DEPT.	DESCRIPTION	CHARGES	PAYMENT/CREDIT	DATE	REF. #
09	Battery	$84.39		6/02	9064
14	PAYMENT		$50.00	6/03	A345
03	Engine belt	27.83		6/16	11309
08	PAYMENT		27.83	6/19	3960
15	Misc. Repairs	239.95		6/24	11714

BILLING DATE: 6/30

PREVIOUS BALANCE	PAYMENTS & CREDITS	UNPAID BALANCE	FINANCE CHARGE	NEW PURCHASES	NEW BALANCE
$338.65					

1. What are the total payments and credits on Professor Jackson's credit card statement?

2. What is the unpaid balance?

3. What is the finance charge?

4. What is the total of new purchases?

5. What is the new balance?

Student _____ Date _____

Class _____ Instructor _____

SECTION 8-1 Single-Payment Loans

A single-payment loan is a loan that you repay with one payment after a specified period of time or term. Ordinary interest is calculated by basing the term on a 360-day year. Exact interest is calculated by basing the term on a 365-day year. The maturity value of the loan is the total amount you repay.

Maturity Value = Principal + Interest Owed

1. Tao Bergolt's bank granted him a single-payment loan of $4,400 at an interest rate of 12 percent. The term of the loan is 172 days. What is the maturity value of his loan at exact interest? _____

2. Jane Dimas obtained a single-payment loan of $420 to pay a repair bill. She agreed to repay the loan in 90 days at an interest rate of 12.75 percent ordinary interest. What is the maturity value of her loan? _____

3. Joyce Stein borrowed $8,460 from Merchants Trust to pay for some merchandise for her dress shop. The loan is for 45 days at 8.75 percent exact interest. What is the maturity value of the loan? _____

4. Gardening, Inc., borrowed $94,500 at 11.65 percent ordinary interest for 15 days. What is the maturity value? _____

5. Ruth and Juan Dimas would like to borrow $2,600 for 90 days to pay their real estate tax. State Savings and Loan charges 14.00 percent ordinary interest while Security Bank charges 14.25 percent exact interest.

   a. What is the maturity value of each loan? State _____

   Security _____

   b. Where should they borrow the money? _____

6. Walker Trust charges exact interest, while Farmers and Merchants Bank charges ordinary interest. You plan to borrow $9,000 for 60 days at 9 percent.

   a. What is the cost of interest at each bank? Walker Trust _____

   Farmers and Merchants _____

   b. Which bank offers you the better deal? _____

7. You have a chance to lend $6,500 at 12.65 percent interest for 95 days.

   a. If you charge ordinary interest, how much will you earn? _____

   b. If you charge exact interest, how much will you earn? _____

   c. If you were borrowing the money, would you prefer to pay ordinary interest or exact interest? Why?

   _____

   _____

Student _____ Date _____

Class _____ Instructor _____

SECTIONS 8-2, 8-3 Installment Loans and Simple Interest Loans

An installment loan is repaid in several equal payments over a specified amount of time. Usually, you make a down payment to cover a portion of the cash price of the item. The amount you finance is the portion of the cash price that you owe after making the down payment.

Amount Financed = Cash Price − Down Payment

Monthly Payment = (Amount of Loan ÷ 100) × Monthly Payment for $100 Loan

Total Amount Repaid = Number of Payments × Monthly Payment

Finance Charge = Total Amount Repaid − Amount Financed

---

1. Alan Lewis purchased a new computer for his office using the store's installment credit plan. The computer cost $5,991.64. What amount did he finance if he made a 40 percent down payment? _____

2. Lloyd and Linda Pearl want to remodel the dining room in their house. The estimated cost for the job is $6,890. They pay 30 percent of the cost up front and finance the rest at 15 percent interest for 48 months.

   a. What is the down payment? _____

   b. What is the amount financed? _____

   c. What is the monthly payment? _____

   d. What is the finance charge? _____

3. The Delgados obtained an installment loan of $12,000 from the credit union to pay for their son's tuition. They obtained the loan at an APR of 10 percent and agreed to repay the loan in 12 months. What is the finance charge?

   _____

4. Ann Nguyen would like an installment loan for $5,000. Her bank will loan her the money at 18 percent for 18 months. Her insurance company will loan her the money at 15 percent for 24 months. Which loan would cost her less?

MONTHLY PAYMENT ON A $100 LOAN				
Term in Months	\multicolumn{4}{c}{Annual Percentage Rate}
	10%	12%	15%	18%
6	$17.16	$17.25	$17.40	$17.55
12	8.79	8.88	9.03	9.17
18	6.01	6.10	6.24	6.38
24	4.61	4.71	4.85	4.99
30	3.78	3.87	4.02	4.16
36	3.23	3.32	3.47	3.62
42	2.83	2.93	3.07	3.23
48	2.54	2.63	2.78	2.94

5. You want to borrow $7,500 to buy a used boat. First Century Bank will lend you the money at 15 percent for 12 months. Fidelity Savings and Loan will lend you the money at 10 percent for 24 months.

   a. How much will each loan cost? _____

   b. Which loan would cost you less? _____

   c. How much less would it cost? _____

Student _____ Date _____

Class _____ Instructor _____

SECTIONS 8-4, 8-5 Installment Loans—Allocation of Monthly Payment and Paying Off

Part of each monthly payment is used to pay the interest on the unpaid balance of the loan and the remaining part is used to reduce the balance. To pay off a loan before the end of the term, you must pay the previous balance plus the current month's interest.

Payment to Principal = Monthly Payment − Interest

New Principal = Previous Principal − Payment to Principal

Final Payment = Previous Balance + Current Month's Interest

---

1. Ralph Phillips obtained a 12-month, $1,500 loan at 12 percent from his credit union. His monthly payment is $133.20. For the first payment:

   a. What is the interest? _____

   b. What is the payment to principal? _____

   c. What is the new balance? _____

2. Rita Rodriguez obtained a 24-month, $8,500 loan at 8 percent from Tri-County Savings & Loan. Her monthly payment is $384.20. For the first payment:

   a. What is the interest? _____

   b. What is the payment to principal? _____

   c. What is the new balance? _____

3. Complete the repayment schedule for a $2,400 loan at 12 percent for 6 months.

Payment Number	Payment	Amount for Interest	Amount for Principal	New Principal
1	$ 414.00	$ 24.00	$ 390.00	$ 2,010.00
2	414.00	20.10		
3	414.00			
4	414.00			
5	414.00			
6				

4. Patricia Nichols took out a $4,000 simple interest loan at 12 percent for 12 months. After 5 payments, the balance was $2,392.16. She pays off the loan when the next payment is due.

   a. What is the current month's interest? _____

   b. What is the final payment? _____

5. Chad Roth took out a $9,100 simple interest loan at 10 percent for 36 months. After 27 payments the balance is $2,526.85. He pays off the loan when the next payment is due.

   a. What is the current month's interest? _____

   b. What is the final payment? _____

Student _____ Date _____

Class _____ Instructor _____

SECTION 8-6 Determining the APR

If you know the number of monthly payments you will make and the finance charge per $100 of the amount financed, you can find the annual percentage rate (APR) of the loan from a table. You can use the APR to compare the relative cost of borrowing money.

Finance Charge per $100 = $100 × $\dfrac{\text{Finance Charge}}{\text{Amount Financed}}$

Use the APR table below to solve the problems.

	ANNUAL PERCENTAGE RATES										
APR	10.00%	10.25%	10.50%	10.75%	11.00%	11.25%	11.50%	11.75%	12.00%	12.25%	12.50%
Term	Finance Charge per $100 of Amount Financed										
6	$ 2.94	$ 3.01	$ 3.08	$ 3.16	$ 3.23	$ 3.31	$ 3.38	$ 3.45	$ 3.53	$ 3.60	$ 3.68
12	5.50	5.64	5.78	5.92	6.06	6.20	6.34	6.48	6.62	6.76	6.90
18	8.10	8.31	8.52	8.73	8.93	9.14	9.35	9.56	9.77	9.98	10.19
24	10.75	11.02	11.30	11.58	11.86	12.14	12.42	12.70	12.98	13.26	13.54

1. Ruby Crye obtained an installment loan of $3,870 to purchase new furniture. The finance charge is $378.10. She agreed to repay the loan in 18 monthly payments. What is the annual percentage rate? _____

2. Gordon Stewart obtained an installment loan of $10,900 to pay his daughter's tuition. The finance charge is $1,172. He agreed to repay the loan in 24 monthly payments. What is the APR? _____

3. The Gomez family has just purchased a $2,574.54 microcomputer. They made a down payment of $574.54. Through the store's installment plan, they have agreed to pay $121 per month for the next 18 months.

   a. What is the amount financed? _____

   b. What is the finance charge? _____

   c. What is the APR? _____

4. Ellen Andrzejewski purchased the car in the ad. She made a down payment of $775. She financed the remainder at $331.16 per month for 24 months. What is the APR?

   Used Sedan 4 Dr
   #6840–5 speed, alloy wheels, cloth seats, stereo prep,
   Was $8,925   NOW $7,775

   _____

5. You are buying a large screen TV set that costs $964.91. To use the installment plan available at the department store, you must make a down payment of 20 percent and make 12 monthly payments of $68.68 each.

   a. What is the amount financed? _____

   b. What is the finance charge? _____

   c. What is the APR for your loan? _____

Student   Date

Class   Instructor

Spreadsheet Application: Loans

DIRECTIONS:

1. Insert your *Student Activity Workbook CD* into your computer and click on Chapter 8 Loans. The spreadsheet will appear.
2. Key your name into cell B1. Key the date into cell G1.
3. Key the information below into the appropriate cells. The spreadsheet application will compute the data for you automatically.
4. Save your spreadsheet as Ch8XXX, where XXX are your initials.
5. Print out your spreadsheet.

Determine the monthly payment, total interest, and the monthly payment allocation, and answer any additional questions.

1. Used truck loan of $8,000.
   12 monthly payments.
   APR is 8 percent.
   What is the loan balance after payment 6?

   _____

2. Computer loan of $1,500.
   12 monthly payments.
   APR is 10 percent.
   What is the loan balance after payment 9?

   _____

3. Furniture loan of $2,360.
   24 monthly payments.
   APR is 12 percent.
   What is the loan balance after payment 16?

   _____

4. Used auto loan of $12,000.
   48 monthly payments.
   APR is 13.25 percent.
   What is the loan balance after payment 42?

   _____

5. New auto loan of $24,500.
   60 monthly payments.
   APR is 9 percent.
   What is the loan balance after payment 36?

   _____

6. Home repairs of $8,425.
   60 monthly payments.
   APR is 14.25 percent.
   What is the loan balance after payment 30?

   _____

7. Boat loan of $19,960.
   72 monthly payments.
   APR is 14.5 percent.
   What is the loan balance after payment 71?

   _____

8. Personal loan of $8,700.
   48 monthly payments.
   APR is 12.25 percent.
   What is the loan balance after payment 48?

   _____

   Is the loan paid off?

   _____

Student

Date

Class

Instructor

Career Path: Firefighter

Since the first fire brigade was organized in ancient Rome by the emperor Augustus, firefighters have worked to keep fires from occurring, limit the damage they do, and put them out once they start. Firefighters routinely risk their own lives to put out fires and save the lives of others. They also answer medical emergency calls, educate the public on fire safety, and inspect houses and buildings for conformance to fire codes.

Firefighters rely on both simple and sophisticated equipment. Ladders help them get to the people who need to be saved from a burning building, and axes let them put holes in roofs and walls to let heat and gases escape, preventing a dangerous buildup of pressure. A pumper truck increases the pressure of the water pumped out of a fire hydrant. Chemicals and specialized techniques are applied to hazardous materials in industrial and traffic accidents.

A firefighter needs a working knowledge of math, and even some physics, on the job. Calculations have to be made on the amount of water needed to put out a fire, based on the size of the blaze, the number of trucks and hoses on the scene, the diameter of a hose and its rate of water flow, and other factors. The bigger around the hose is, of course, the more water it can deliver in a given amount of time. The force of the water, combined with the angle of the spray, determine how far the water will go and where it will land. Pumper trucks typically deliver 750 gallons of water per minute at a pressure of 150 pounds per square inch.

Check Your Understanding

The mayor's office has approved an allocation of funds for Ladder Company 12 to buy new protective gear. The funds will not be available, however, until 90 days from now, in the new fiscal year. Company 12 needs the helmets and coats and boots immediately, so the mayor's office has also approved the interest on a 90-day loan at 9.5 percent. Use the formula below for Problems 1 and 2. Show your calculations for each problem.

Principal × Rate × Time = Interest

1. If the cost of the equipment is $16,800, how much exact interest will the city pay at the end of 90 days?

2. How much would the city save if the loan were at 4.5 percent?

3. Engine Company 12's pumper truck gets 6 miles to a gallon of fuel. Last month the truck was driven 1,176 miles on the way to fires and some school fire prevention events. The gas tank holds 52 gallons. How many tanks of fuel did the truck use?

4. Three firefighters are watering down a house near a forest fire to prevent it from igniting. Each one is spraying it with a hose that delivers 275 gallons of water per minute. Hose A waters the roof for 30 minutes. Hose B covers the walls for 20 minutes. Hose C soaks the bushes and vegetation around the house for 25 minutes. How much water did they use altogether?

SECTIONS 9-1, 9-2 — Purchasing a New Vehicle and Dealer's Cost

A vehicle's sticker price shows all charges for a vehicle, including the base price, all options, and the destination charge. The dealer pays less than the prices on the sticker for both the basic vehicle and the options.

Sticker Price = Base Price + Options + Destination Charge

$$\text{Dealer's Cost} = \text{Percentage of Base Price} + \text{Percentage of Options Price} + \text{Destination Charge}$$

1. Loren Weber wants to buy the sport sedan 4-door listed below. There is a 6 percent sales tax on the purchase price of the car in Weber's state. If Weber pays the full sticker price for the car, what is the total price?

CODE	DESCRIPTION	LIST PRICE
B19	SPORT SEDAN SE 4DR.	$15,580.00
C21	METALLIC TRI/STRIPE	65.95
IL1	AUTOMATIC TRANSMISSION	800.00
AC3	AIR-CONDITIONING	1,095.00
TG2	TINTED GLASS	99.60
S14	STEREO AM/FM CD	516.70
T14W	WHITE SIDEWALL RADIAL TIRES	152.90
E41	DESTINATION CHARGE	246.83

2. Hakeem Ellios wants to buy a sports utility vehicle (SUV). There is an 8 percent sales tax on the purchase price of the SUV in his state. If he pays the full sticker price for the SUV, how much is the total?

CODE	DESCRIPTION	LIST PRICE
A78	SUV	$48,680.00
C41	METALLIC BROWN	0.00
E30	LEATHER UPHOLSTERY	0.00
B45	AIR-CONDITIONING	0.00
P26	TINTED GLASS	129.90
L04	JBL SOUND SYSTEM	0.00
X-93	ENTERTAINMENT CENTER	864.75
M72	DESTINATION CHARGE	158.64

3. Lisa and Tomas Lopez are buying a new minivan that has a base price of $24,060. The options total $2,410.80 and the destination charge is $221.80. The dealer's cost is estimated to be 91 percent of the base price and 88 percent of the price of the options.

   a. What is the sticker price of the car?

   b. What is the estimated dealer's cost?

4. Kim Lee is buying a sedan that has a base price of $24,827. The options total $1,242, and the destination charge is $270. The dealer's cost is 90 percent of the base price and 85 percent of the price of the options. What will Lee pay if he can buy the vehicle for $200 over the dealer's cost?

Student _____ Date _____

Class _____ Instructor _____

SECTION 9-3 Purchasing a Used Vehicle

Vehicle dealers usually advertise used vehicles for prices that are higher than what they expect you to pay. Used-vehicle guides, published monthly, give the average prices for vehicles that were purchased from dealers during the previous month. This information can help you decide how much to offer for a used vehicle.

Average Retail Price = Average Retail Value + Additional Options − Options Deductions − Mileage Deduction

1. George Garcia owns a 3-year-old station wagon that he wants to sell in order to buy a new luxury car. One used-vehicle guide shows the average retail value of his station wagon is $13,000. He adds $50 for having tinted windows, $100 for air-conditioning, and $35 for power windows. He deducts $200 for excessive mileage. What is the average retail price he can ask for his station wagon? _____

2. Yolanda Lovelace owns a sports car. She wants to sell it in order to buy a new sports car. One used-vehicle guide shows the average retail value of her car is $16,900. She adds $50 for cruise control, $200 for stereo AM/FM radio/CD player, and $175 for leather seat covers. She deducts $100 for no air-conditioning and $100 for excessive mileage. What is the average retail price she can ask for her sports car? _____

3. The Tookesons want to trade in their station wagon on the purchase of a new station wagon. A used-vehicle guide shows the average trade-in value is $9,480. They add $150 for air-conditioning, $75 for anti-lock brakes, and $150 for the CD player. They subtract $100 for a manual transmission and $300 for excessive mileage. What is the average trade-in value of their wagon? _____

4. Atsuko Murakami is going to trade in her 5-year-old car for a new car. A used-vehicle guide shows the average trade-in value is $4,350, plus $100 for air-conditioning, and $50 for an automatic transmission. She deducts $175 for excessive mileage. What is the average trade-in value of her car? _____

Use the used-vehicle guide at the right for Problems 5 and 6.

5. You purchase a used V8 Spt Cpe with an AM/FM stereo/CD player, rear window defroster, and a tilt steering wheel. The car does not have air-conditioning. What is the average loan value of the car?

_____

6. You are going to trade in a Cpe 4D. Your car has a T-Top, power door locks, power windows, power seats, and cruise control. It has a 4-cylinder engine with manual transmission. What is the average trade-in value of your car?

_____

Average Trade-In	BODY TYPE	Average Loan	Average Retail
	SPORTS CAR		
$ 8,550	Spt Cpe 2D	$ 7,800	$ 9,670
9,450	Cpe 4D	8,620	10,575
10,350	V8 Spt Cpe	9,325	12,650
500	Add T-Top	450	550
125	Add AM/FM Stereo/CD	125	150
150	Add AM/FM Stereo/Tape/CD	150	250
75	Add Power Door Locks	75	100
100	Add Power Windows	100	125
100	Add Power Seats	100	150
75	Add Rear Window Defroster	75	150
75	Add Cruise Control	75	100
75	Add Tilt Steering Wheel	75	100
200	Deduct 4 Cy. Engine	200	200
375	Deduct Manual Transmission	350	375
550	Deduct w/out Air Conditioner	500	525

SECTION 9-4 Vehicle Insurance

Vehicle insurance protects you against financial losses if your vehicle is involved in an accident. Your annual premium depends on your base premium and your driver-rating factor. Your driver-rating factor depends on your age, your marital status, your gender, and the purpose for which you use your vehicle.

Annual Premium = Annual Base Premium × Driver-Rating Factor

LIABILITY PREMIUM FOR A PRIVATE PASSENGER VEHICLE

Property Damage Limits	\\ Bodily Injury Limits 25/50	25/100	50/100	100/200	100/300	300/300
$ 25,000	$ 206.40	$ 218.80	$ 213.20	$ 252.00	$ 258.00	$ 286.80
50,000	212.40	224.80	237.20	258.00	264.00	293.80
100,000	220.80	233.20	245.60	266.40	272.40	301.20

PHYSICAL DAMAGE PREMIUM

Coverage	Age Group	Insurance-Rating Group 10	11	12	13	14	15
Comprehensive $50-Deductible	A	$ 76.80	$ 81.60	$ 95.20	$ 108.00	$ 122.00	$ 135.60
	B	65.20	77.60	90.40	102.40	115.60	128.40
	C	62.00	74.00	86.00	98.00	110.40	122.80
	D	59.20	70.40	82.00	93.20	105.20	116.80
Collision $50-Deductible	A	$ 225.60	$ 246.00	$ 266.80	$ 287.20	$ 307.60	$ 328.00
	B	214.00	233.20	253.20	272.40	291.60	311.20
	C	204.00	222.80	241.60	260.00	278.40	296.80
	D	194.40	212.00	230.00	247.60	265.20	282.80

1. Julie Spiros, age 21 and unmarried, drives her vehicle to and from work. Her driver-rating factor is 1.85. Her vehicle is classified A-11. She has $25,000 property damage, 50/100 bodily injury, $50-deductible comprehensive, and $50-deductible collision coverages. What is her base premium? What is her annual premium?

2. Theo Norton is 18 years of age. His driver-rating factor is 2.30. The family car is classified C-15. The insurance the Nortons have is $50,000 property damage, 100/300 bodily injury, $50-deductible comprehensive, and $50-deductible collision. What is his annual premium?

3. Amy Schorling is age 24 and is unmarried. She uses her vehicle for business. Her driver-rating factor is 1.85. Her vehicle is classified D-14. Her insurance consists of $25,000 property damage, 25/50 bodily injury, $50-deductible comprehensive, and no collision coverage.

   a. What is her annual premium?

   b. How much is her annual premium if she includes $50-deductible collision coverage?

4. Julio Munoz is age 19 and unmarried. He drives his car to and from work. His car is classified C-11 and his driver-rating factor is 4.10. His insurance includes $25,000 property damage, 25/100 bodily injury, $50-deductible comprehensive, and $50-deductible collision.

   a. What is his annual premium?

   b. What is his annual premium if he raises his liability coverage to $100,000 property damage limits and 300/300 bodily injury limits?

Student _____ Date _____

Class _____ Instructor _____

SECTION 9-5 Operating and Maintaining a Vehicle

Many costs are involved in operating and maintaining a vehicle. Variable costs increase the more you drive, while fixed costs remain about the same no matter how many miles you drive.

Cost per Mile = $\dfrac{\text{Annual Variable Cost + Annual Fixed Cost}}{\text{Number of Miles Driven}}$

1. Tom Larson had fixed costs totaling $2,805.60 last year. His variable costs totaled $1,870.40. Larson drove his vehicle 16,700 miles last year. What was his cost per mile? _____

2. Jamila Simmons drove 9,910 miles last year. Her fixed costs totaled $1,754.07 last year. Her variable costs totaled $584.69. What was her cost per mile to the nearest tenth of a cent? _____

3. John and Evelyn each own a vehicle of the same model. John drove a total of 27,612 miles, while Evelyn drove 9,821 miles. Both had fixed costs totaling $2,357.04 each. John's variable cost totaled $4,822.03, and Evelyn's totaled $589.26.

   a. How much money did John spend to operate and maintain his vehicle on a cost-per-mile basis? _____

   b. How much did Evelyn spend per mile? _____

4. Luisa Diaz drove her vehicle about 7,200 miles last year. Her fixed costs totaled $1,058.40 and her variable costs were $1,965.60. How much did it cost per mile for Luisa to operate her vehicle? _____

5. Jim Spring maintained this record of vehicle expenses for last year: gas, $845.96; oil, lube, miscellaneous, $68.85; insurance, $418.50; and license, $35. He drove 8,280 miles last year.

   a. What were his total variable costs? _____

   b. What were his total fixed costs? _____

   c. What were his total costs? _____

   d. What was his cost per mile to the nearest tenth of a cent? _____

6. Last year, Ishiro Novato drove 21,986 miles and had these expenses: gas, $1,187.25; maintenance and miscellaneous, $118.80; parking and tolls, $125; tires, $300; wash and wax, $75; insurance, $614.80; license, $34.90; and depreciation, $1,780. What was his cost per mile last year? _____

7. Reka Maharis drove her vehicle to and from work last year. Her records show a total of $1,560 for fixed costs and $3,740 for variable costs. If it cost her $0.36 per mile to drive, how many miles did she drive last year? _____

8. You drove your vehicle to and from work last year. Your records show a total of $1,860 for fixed costs and $5,000 for variable costs. If it cost you $0.40 per mile to drive, how many miles did you drive last year? _____

62 • Mathematics with Business Applications ◆ Section 9-5   Copyright © Glencoe/McGraw-Hill

Student _____ Date _____

Class _____ Instructor _____

SECTION 9-6 Leasing a Vehicle

When you lease a vehicle you make monthly payments to the leasing agency. Your leasing costs include all the monthly payments, a security deposit, a title fee, and a license fee.

$$\text{Total Lease Cost} = \left[\text{Number of Payments} \times \text{Amount of Payment} \right] + \text{Deposit} + \text{Title Fee} + \text{License Fee}$$

1. Teresa Spaulding leased a pickup truck for use in her landscape business. She paid $120 per month for 60 months. She also paid a deposit of $1,000, a title fee of $90, and a license fee of $125. What is the total lease cost? _____

2. Sing-Chi Wah leased a sports car for $219.50 per month for 60 months. He paid a deposit of $250, a title fee of $95, and a license fee of $220. What is the total lease cost? _____

3. Abdul Muhal leased a sedan for business use as a salesperson. The lease cost $199 per month for 48 months. He paid a deposit of $750, a title fee of $95, and license fee of $135. What is the total lease cost? _____

4. Eva Truett had an open-end lease for a minivan for her home decorating business. The lease cost $315 per month for 60 months. She paid a deposit of $1,200, a title fee of $135, and a license fee of $85. At the end of the lease, she can buy the van for its residual value of $3,850.

   a. What is the total lease cost? _____

   b. What is the total cost if she buys the van? _____

5. Olathe Yiska had an open-end lease for a station wagon for the senior center. The lease cost $239 per month for 48 months. She paid a deposit of $550, a title fee of $65, and a license fee of $120. At the end of the lease, she can buy the station wagon for its residual value of $8,860.

   a. What is the total lease cost? _____

   b. What is the total cost if she buys the car? _____

6. Rashidi Zabka leased a 4-door sedan for $199.88 per month for 48 months. He paid a deposit of $1,515, a title fee of $95, and a license fee of $65. The lease carried a stipulation that there would be a $0.10 per mile charge for all miles over 60,000. He drove the car 67,640 miles. What is the total cost of leasing the vehicle? _____

7. Alejandro Yago leased a jeep for $209 per month for 60 months. He paid a deposit of $850, a title fee of $45, and a license fee of $60. The lease carried a stipulation that there would be a $0.12 per mile charge for all miles over 60,000. He drove the care 73,524 miles. What is the total cost of leasing the vehicle? _____

SECTION 9-7 Renting a Vehicle

When you rent a vehicle, the total cost may include a daily rate, a rate per mile, gasoline charged to you, and insurance.

$$\text{Cost per Mile} = \frac{\text{Total Cost}}{\text{Number of Miles Driven}}$$

---

1. Alicia Whitman rented a station wagon for her vacation. The wagon rented for $35.40 per day plus 21¢ per mile. She used the wagon for 7 days. She paid $54.20 for gasoline during her 620-mile drive. What is her cost per mile to the nearest cent? _____

2. The Browns plan to fly to their vacation spot and then drive through the mountains. They arranged to rent a sedan for $37.45 per day with no charge for mileage.

   a. What will it cost the Browns to rent the car for 10 days if they spend $78 for gasoline and $16.75 for miscellaneous items? _____

   b. What will it cost per mile if they drive 590 miles? _____

3. The Stocktons are moving into a new house this weekend. To transport all their household belongings, they will need to rent a truck for 1 day. The rental cost will be $45 per day plus 29¢ per mile. The collision waiver will cost $25.

   a. What will be their total cost if they pay $15.50 for diesel fuel and drive 68 miles? _____

   b. What will be their cost per mile? _____

4. Ruy Cortez rented a 14-foot truck to move into his new apartment. He rented the truck for 1 day at a cost of $37.50 per day plus 21¢ per mile. The collision waiver cost $10.00. Gasoline cost $44.60. Cortez drove 220 miles. What was his cost per mile? _____

5. Esther Zeeva flew to her vacation condominium and rented a convertible for 7 days. The car rents for $229 per week with no charge for mileage. Find her cost per mile if gasoline cost $31.64 and she drove 485 miles. _____

6. You fly to a weekend business conference and rent a vehicle for Friday, Saturday, and Sunday. You drive 115 miles and gasoline costs you $7.50. The weekend rental rate on the vehicle is $49.50 plus 25¢ per mile. What is the cost per mile? _____

7. You and 3 friends rent a limousine for the prom. The cost is $79.95 per day plus $0.38 per mile. Insurance costs $75. You rent the limo for 2 days and drive 48 miles. The limo gets 8 miles per gallon. Gas costs $1.23 per gallon.

   a. What is the total cost of renting the limo? _____

   b. What is the cost per mile? _____

   c. What is the cost per person? _____

Student _____ Date _____

Class _____ Instructor _____

Simulation: Vehicle Expenses

According to the American Automobile Association, the average vehicle owner spends approximately $4,000 per year in operating and maintaining a vehicle. The costs of owning a vehicle include fixed costs, such as finance charges, depreciation, insurance, and license fees. You also have variable costs, such as gasoline, maintenance, repairs, parking fees, and tolls. As a vehicle owner, you may want to calculate the cost per mile. If you drive to work, you may want to know the cost per day.

1. Suppose you drove your 4-year-old vehicle 12,600 miles and the vehicle gets 26 miles per gallon. How many gallons of gasoline did you use? At $1.499 per gallon, how much will it cost?

2. In addition to gasoline, your variable costs include 5 oil changes at $29.50 each, $89.00 for a tune-up, $225 for brake repairs, $185 for motor repairs, $49.40 for a tire, and $117 for parking and tolls. Your fixed costs include depreciation of $900 and an $85.50 registration fee. What is the total of these expenses?

3. The rating factor for your vehicle insurance is 2.3. Your vehicle is classified D-12. You have $50,000 property damage, 100/200 bodily injury, $50-deductible comprehensive, and $50-deductible collision. Using the tables at the beginning of Section 9-4, find your annual premium.

4. What is the total annual cost for gasoline, maintenance, repairs, tires, parking, depreciation, registration, and insurance?

5. What is your cost per mile?

6. Suppose you drive 12 miles round-trip to work each day, 5 days per week, 50 weeks per year. How much does it cost you to drive to work each day? Each week? Each year?

Find the cost per mile and the cost to drive to work for each of these cases. Use a driver-rating factor of 3.0.

	Annual Miles	Miles per Gallon	Cost per Gallon	Variable Cost	Fixed Cost	Base Insurance Premium	Cost per Mile	Daily Miles	Cost per Day to Go to Work
7.	12,160	40	$1.399	$690	$1,200	$520		45	
8.	11,950	25	1.899	460	600	660		30	
9.	13,689	27	1.599	330	1,400	672		26	
10.	21,300	15	1.499	850	1,200	672		63	

Student _____ Date _____

Class _____ Instructor _____

Simulation: Vehicle Expenses
(CONTINUED)

PURCHASE PRICE AND FINANCING

You have decided to buy a vehicle. One choice you have to make is whether to buy a new vehicle or a used vehicle. A new vehicle has a higher purchase price and greater depreciation. Comprehensive and collision insurance are more expensive for a new vehicle. A used vehicle can be expected to have higher maintenance and repair costs.

There are two vehicles you are considering: a new compact car and a used sedan. To help choose which one to buy, you calculate how much it would cost per month to run each vehicle for the next 3 years.

Code	Description	List Price
CC2	Compact Car 2-door	$14,400.00
SRM	Sunset Red Metallic	145.00
CDT	AM/FM CD Tape Deck	475.00
PPS	Power Passenger Seat	260.00
ATR	Automatic Transmission	780.00
AC	Air-Conditioning	750.00
DChg	Destination Charge	425.00

MONTHLY PAYMENT ON A $100 LOAN

Term in Months	Annual Percentage Rate			
	8.00%	10.00%	12.00%	14.00%
6	17.06	17.16	17.25	17.35
12	8.70	8.79	8.88	8.98
18	5.91	6.01	6.10	6.19
24	4.52	4.61	4.71	4.80
30	3.69	3.78	3.87	3.97
36	3.13	3.23	3.32	3.42
42	2.74	2.83	2.93	3.03
48	2.44	2.54	2.63	2.73

11. A portion of the sticker price for the compact car is shown. What is the total sticker price? _____

12. The dealer's cost for the compact car is about 94 percent of the base price and 85 percent of the price of the options. If the dealer accepts your offer of $200 over the dealer's cost, what would the compact car cost you, including the destination charge and 6 percent sales tax? _____

13. You would make a $2,000 down payment for the compact car and finance the rest of the cost with a simple interest installment loan at 8 percent for 48 months.

   a. What is the amount financed? _____

   b. Use the monthly payment table above to find the monthly payment. _____

   c. What is the total amount repaid? _____

   d. What is the finance charge? _____

Student _____ **Date** _____

Class _____ **Instructor** _____

Simulation: Vehicle Expenses
(CONTINUED)

14. The used-vehicle guide entry for the sedan is shown. You are interested in a 4-door sedan with power windows, AM/FM CD, and cruise control. If you bought the sedan for its average retail value, what would it cost, including 6 percent sales tax? _____

Average Trade-in	Body Type/ Model	Average Loan	Average Retail
$3,875	4-door Sedan	$3,500	$4,800
125	AM/FM CD	125	125
75	Pwr Dr Locks	75	75
100	Pwr Windows	100	100
100	Pwr Seats	100	100
75	Cruise Ctrl	75	75
600	A/C	600	600
500	Sunroof	500	500

15. You make a $2,000 down payment for the sedan and finance the rest of the cost at 12 percent for 36 months. Using the monthly payment table on page 66, find the monthly payment and the finance charge.

_____

INSURANCE

To choose the best vehicle insurance company, you read articles in consumer and automotive magazines, talk with relatives and friends, and ask insurance companies about their coverage and premiums. Use the tables in Section 9-4 of this workbook to find the base premiums.

16. For either vehicle you choose, you plan to have 50/100 bodily injury and $50,000 property damage coverage. What is the annual base premium for liability coverage? _____

17. You plan to have $50-deductible comprehensive and $50-deductible collision insurance coverage. The compact car is in age group A and rating group 12. What is the annual base premium for physical damage coverage? _____

18. The sedan is in age group B and driver-rating group 10. What is the annual base premium for comprehensive and collision insurance? _____

19. Assume you are under 21, unmarried, and the principal operator of a car you drive for pleasure. Your driver-rating factor is 4.10. For each car, what is the total cost per month for insurance?

_____

Copyright © Glencoe/McGraw-Hill

Student _____ Date _____

Class _____ Instructor _____

Simulation: Vehicle Expenses
(CONTINUED)

MAINTENANCE, DEPRECIATION, AND OTHER COSTS

A vehicle depreciates in value most quickly when it is new. You can estimate how a vehicle will depreciate by looking at the values of older vehicles of the same model. Depreciation is often expressed as a percentage of the purchase price.

Maintenance and repair costs tend to increase as a vehicle ages. You can estimate these costs by talking with mechanics and with people who own the same model. Consumer and automotive magazines sometimes have articles comparing these costs for various models.

20. The compact car should lose 23 percent of its purchase price (less tax) the first year, 19 percent of its purchase price (less tax) the second year, and 15 percent of its purchase price (less tax) the third year. What is the total percentage? How much less will the compact car be worth in 3 years? What is the average depreciation per month?

    _____

21. The sedan can be expected to have a value of $2,094 in 3 years. What is the depreciation per month? _____

22. For the compact car, you expect to spend $100 the first year, $160 the second year, and $480 the third year for maintenance and repairs. What is the average cost per month? _____

23. You expect the sedan to have maintenance and repair costs of $440 the first year, $560 the second year, and $750 the third year. It will also need tires for $250 plus 6 percent sales tax. What is the average cost per month? _____

24. You plan to drive 12,000 miles per year. Gasoline costs $1.499 per gallon.

    a. The compact car gets 30 miles per gallon. What is the cost of gasoline per month? _____

    b. The sedan gets 25 miles per gallon. What is the cost of gasoline per month? _____

Simulation: Vehicle Expenses   Copyright © Glencoe/McGraw-Hill

Student _____ Date _____

Class _____ Instructor _____

SECTIONS 10-1, 10-2 Mortgage Loans, Monthly Payment and Total Interest

When you purchase a home, you will probably make a down payment and finance the remaining portion of the selling price with a mortgage loan from a bank, a savings and loan association, a credit union, or a mortgage company. A mortgage loan is usually repaid with interest in equal monthly payments. If you know the annual interest rate, the amount of the loan, and the length of the loan, you can use a table to find the monthly payment, the total amount paid, and the interest charged.

Mortgage Loan Amount = Selling Price − Down Payment

Monthly Payment = $\dfrac{\text{Amount of Mortgage}}{\$1,000}$ × Monthly Payment for a $1,000 Loan

Amount Paid = Monthly Payment × Number Of Payments

Total Interest Charged = Amount Paid − Mortgage Amount

1. Kung and So Lee offered $87,000 on a home that had been priced at $96,500. The seller agreed to the offer. A 20 percent down payment is required. What is the amount of the down payment? What is the amount of the mortgage loan needed to finance the purchase?

   _____

   _____

MONTHLY PAYMENT FOR A $1,000 LOAN			
Annual Interest Rate	Length of Loan in Years		
	20	25	30
5.00%	$6.60	$5.85	$5.37
5.50%	6.88	6.14	5.68
6.00%	7.16	6.44	6.00
6.50%	7.46	6.75	6.32
7.00%	7.75	7.07	6.65
7.50%	8.06	7.39	6.99
8.00%	8.36	7.72	7.34
8.50%	8.68	8.05	7.69

2. Mary Cunningham offered $156,500 for a home that had been priced at $169,500. The seller agreed to the offer. A bank is willing to finance the purchase if she can make a down payment of 20 percent. What is the amount of the mortgage loan? _____

3. Danelle and Jim Baraka have obtained a $70,000 mortgage loan at an annual interest rate of 8.00 percent for 30 years.

   a. What is the monthly payment? _____

   b. What is the total amount paid? _____

   c. What is the total interest? _____

4. Lee Hays has obtained a $240,000 mortgage loan at 7.00 percent interest for 25 years.

   a. What is the monthly payment? _____

   b. What is the total amount paid? _____

   c. What is the total interest? _____

5. How much can be saved in total interest by financing $120,000 at 7.50 percent for 20 years rather than 25 years? _____

6. How much can be saved in total interest by financing $120,000 at 8.00 percent for 25 years rather than 8.50 percent interest for 25 years? _____

Student _____ Date _____

Class _____ Instructor _____

SECTION 10-3 Closing Costs

At the time you sign the documents to transfer ownership of your new home, you must pay any closing costs that the lender charges. Your closing costs may include fees for lawyers, credit checks and title searches, taxes, and the preparation of the documents.

Closing Costs = Sum of Bank Fees

Use the list of closing costs at the right to solve Problems 1 and 2.

1. Al and Viola Speer were granted an $80,000 mortgage. At the closing, they will have to pay the closings costs shown plus real estate taxes of $1,230. What are the total costs?

   _____

Credit report:	$ 55.00
Appraisal report:	425.00
Title search:	230.00
Survey:	325.00
Recording & transfer fee:	120.00
Legal fees:	360.00
Loan origination fee:	2% of mortgage

2. Pablo and Maria Rivera were granted a $128,000 mortgage. At the closing, they will have to pay the closing costs shown plus real estate taxes of $1,920. What are the total costs?

   _____

3. Joy and John MacAllister have agreed to purchase a house for $79,900. First National Savings & Loan is willing to lend the money at 10.75 percent for 25 years, provided the MacAllisters can make a $19,900 down payment. The total closing cost is 3.5 percent of the amount of the mortgage. What is their total closing cost?

   _____

4. You are interested in purchasing a $144,000 home. You plan to make a 25 percent down payment and obtain a 12 percent mortgage for 20 years for the remaining amount through City Savings and Loan. Complete the form below to determine the total closing cost.

CITY SAVINGS AND LOAN ASSOCATION
DISCLOSURE OF CLOSING COSTS

AMOUNT OF MORTGAGE: _____ DATE: 3/1/20—

Appraisal report	$ 455.00
Credit report	65.00
Loan origination fee: 2% of mortgage	_____
Recording costs	145.85
Survey and photos	345.60
Title search & insurance	160.00
Legal fees	425.00
Property taxes	857.25
Interest on the mortgage from 1st of the month to the closing date 3/16 (exact interest)	_____
Total	_____

---

70 Mathematics with Business Applications ◆ Section 10-3

Student _____ Date _____

Class _____ Instructor _____

SECTIONS 10-4 The Monthly Payment

Most mortgage loans are repaid in equal payments. Each payment includes an amount for interest and an amount for the principal of the loan. The amount of interest is calculated using the simple interest formula. Each payment you make decreases the amount of the principal you owe.

Principal Payment = Monthly Payment − Interest Payment

New Principal = Previous Principal − Principal Payment

Complete the table below.

	Mortgage Amount	Interest Rate	First Monthly Payment	Amount for Interest	Amount for Principal	New Principal
1.	$86,000	8.00%	$663.92	$573.33	$90.59	
2.	165,000	12.50%	1,762.20			
3.	42,500	10.00%	410.55			

4. Julie and Barry Spinos purchased a house for $96,400. They made a 25 percent down payment and financed the remaining amount at 13 percent for 30 years. Their monthly payment is $800.36. How much of the first monthly payment is used to reduce the principal? _____

5. Jim and Julie Speer purchased a home for $137,400. They made a down payment of $17,400 and financed the remaining amount at 11.00 percent for 25 years. Their monthly payment is $1,177.20. What is the new principal after the first monthly payment? _____

6. The Harrises purchased a home for $287,000. They made a $31,000 down payment and financed the remaining amount at 6.00 percent for 30 years. Their monthly payment is $1,722.00.

   a. How much of the first monthly payment is used to reduce the principal? _____

   b. What is the new principal after the first monthly payment? _____

7. You purchase a home for $87,500. After a 20 percent down payment, you finance the remaining amount for 25 years at 11 percent. Your monthly payment is $686.70. Complete the repayment schedule below for the first 6 months of your loan.

	Monthly Payment	Amount for Interest	Amount for Principal	New Principal
a.				
b.				
c.				
d.				
e.				
f.				

Student _____ Date _____

Class _____ Instructor _____

SECTION 10-5 Real Estate Taxes

When you own a home, you will have to pay city or county real estate taxes. The amount of real estate tax that you pay in 1 year depends on the assessed value of your property and the tax rate. The assessed value is found by multiplying the market value of your property by the rate of assessment. Your tax rate may be expressed in mills per dollar of valuation. A mill is $0.001.

Assessed Value = Rate of Assessment × Market Value

Real Estate Tax = Tax Rate × Assessed Value

---

1. The Mariaskis' home is located in a community where the rate of assessment is 45 percent of the market value. The tax is $65 per $1,000 of assessed value. The Mariaskis' home has a market value of $97,400.

   a. What is the assessed value? _____

   b. What is the yearly real estate tax? _____

2. The rate of assessment in Fulton County is 35 percent. The tax rate is 81.31 mills. What is the real estate tax on a piece of property that has a market value of $238,500? _____

3. Ron and Barbara Lugo live in a city where the tax rate is 83.21 mills. The rate of assessment is 30 percent. The property that the Lugos own has a market value of $367,500. What is their real estate tax for a year? _____

4. Peter and Camilla Myers live in a home with a market value of $124,750. The rate of assessment is 40 percent and the tax rate is 112.8 mills. What is the Myers's real estate tax for a year? _____

5. You live in a home in Bloom County. Your home has a market value of $80,000. Your rate of assessment is 45 percent. You pay total property taxes of 56.79 mills. Complete the form below to see how your property tax bill is distributed.

Purpose of Tax	Tax Rate in Mills	Real Estate Tax
County:		
County general fund	2.35	$ _____
County parks	.50	_____
Mental health levy	1.20	_____
Children's health program	1.55	_____
Transportation system	2.14	_____
Schools:		
Local school	32.50	_____
Vocational school	3.20	_____
School building bonds	9.95	_____
Others:		
Corporation—city	2.40	_____
Police/fire pension fund	1.00	_____
	Total _____	Total $ _____

Student _____ Date _____

Class _____ Instructor _____

SECTIONS 10-6, 10-7 — Homeowners Insurance and Insurance Premium

When you own a home, you will probably purchase homeowners insurance as protection against losses due to fire, theft of contents, and personal liability. To receive full payment for any loss up to the amount of the policy, you must insure your home for at least 80 percent of its replacement value. Insurance companies use the amount of coverage on your home to calculate the amount of coverage on your garage, on your personal property, and for loss of use. The amount of your premium depends on the amount of insurance, the location of your property, and the type of construction of your home.

Amount of Coverage = Percent × Amount of Coverage on Home

Use the table at the right to answer Problems 1 and 2.

Coverage	Percent of Coverage
Personal Property	50%
Loss of Use	20%
Garage and Other Structures	10%

1. The Kimbroughs' home has a replacement value of $82,700. They are insuring it for 80 percent of the replacement cost.

   a. What is the amount of insurance? _____

   b. What is the amount of coverage for personal property? _____

2. The Lugos's home has a replacement value of $287,000. It is insured for 90 percent of the replacement cost.

   a. What is the amount of insurance? _____

   b. What is the amount of coverage for loss of use? _____

3. The Ellisons have insured their home for $90,000. Their personal property coverage is 50 percent of the amount of their home coverage, personal liability coverage is 45 percent, and loss of use coverage is 20 percent.

   a. What is the amount of coverage for personal liability? _____

   b. What is the amount of coverage for personal property? _____

   c. What is the amount of coverage for loss of use? _____

Use the table at the right for Problems 4 and 5.

4. Your brick home has a replacement value of $100,000 and is insured for 80 percent of the replacement value. You live in an area that has been designated fire protection class 3. Find the annual premium.

   _____

5. Your brick home has a replacement value of $150,000 and is insured for 80 percent of the replacement value. You live in an area that has been designated fire protection class 9. Find the annual premium.

   _____

Amount of Insurance Coverage	ANNUAL PREMIUMS Brick/Masonry Veneer Fire Protection Class				
	1–6	7–8	9	10	11
$ 50,000	178	183	241	254	290
60,000	191	196	259	273	313
70,000	213	216	285	299	343
80,000	241	248	328	343	394
90,000	268	276	365	384	441
100,000	298	307	407	426	490
120,000	354	364	484	508	584
150,000	459	471	625	657	755

Student _____ Date _____

Class _____ Instructor _____

SECTION 10-8 Other Housing Costs

In addition to your monthly mortgage payment, real estate taxes, and insurance payment, you will have other expenses for utilities, maintenance, and home improvements. The Federal Housing Administration (FHA) recommends that your total monthly housing cost be less than 35 percent of your monthly net pay.

---

1. Mario Orozco's monthly net pay is $3,245. Housing expenses for November were:

Mortgage Payment	$ 636.30
Real Estate Taxes	172.00
Insurance	29.50
Electricity	87.50
Heating Fuel	60.50
Telephone	39.50
Cable Service	39.99

   Total Housing Costs _____

   Is it within the FHA recommendation?

   _____

2. Kamil Saleb's monthly net pay is $2,150. Housing expenses for March were:

Mortgage Payment	$502.32
Real Estate Taxes	180.91
Insurance	29.50
Electricity	126.30
Gas	56.32
Telephone	44.25
Water/Sewer Service	25.60

   Total Housing Costs _____

   Is it within the FHA recommendation?

   _____

3. The Miquels had the following housing expenses for September: mortgage payment of $396.80, $34.15 for insurance premium, $139.40 for real estate taxes, $44.75 for home improvements, $51.20 for electricity, $29.75 for telephone service, $63.84 for natural gas, and $18.50 for water. Their monthly net pay is $2,478.60.

   a. What is their monthly housing cost? _____

   b. Based on their monthly net pay, what is the recommended FHA maximum for their housing expenses? _____

   c. Is their monthly housing cost within the FHA recommendation? _____

4. Lori and Mike Boyd have a combined monthly net income of $3,395. Their records show that last year they paid $5,484.60 in mortgage payments, $356 for insurance premiums, and $2,240 in annual real estate taxes. They also had the annual expenses shown. Did they stay within the FHA recommendation?

Electricity	$1,960.00
Water	194.50
Telephone	275.28
Washer/dryer	941.76
Painting	857.60
New carpeting	1,231.75

5. You purchased a brick home for $162,500. You had a 20 percent down payment and financed the remainder at 8.00 percent for 25 years. Your property tax rate is 86.41 mills with an assessment rate of 25 percent. You had the housing expenses shown. How much net income do you need to be within the FHA recommendation?

Insurance	$ 645.00
Electricity	1,140.37
Water	438.70
Telephone	507.96
Heating fuel	1,297.74
Repairs	446.20

Student _____ Date _____

Class _____ Instructor _____

Simulation: Energy Savings—Home Weatherization

Many homes have been constructed with insufficient insulation and without proper weatherization. Homes can be made more energy efficient by adding attic or sidewall insulation, by sealing air leaks around windows, doors, and foundations, and by putting on storm windows or installing new windows.

To conserve energy and save money on fuel bills, you've conducted a "Home Energy Audit" of your house. You hired an energy consultant, who did an analysis of your house including a blower door test to check how air tight your house is. The test showed that you had air leaks around doors, windows, and the foundation sill plate. Your house was also checked for heat loss through the floors, ceiling, sidewalls, and windows.

Your consultant furnished the following energy savings guide:

ESTIMATE OF ANNUAL ENERGY SAVINGS

Type of Heat Loss	Proposed Remedies	Heat to Be Saved (Million BTUs)
Infiltration	Caulk and weather strip all doors and windows. Seal foundation leaks.	25.1
Conduction through:		
Floors	Insulate upper portion of basement walls.	2.5
Ceilings	Add 6 inches of insulation to attic floor.	15.0
Windows	Add storm windows.	7.9
	TOTAL	50.5

To save energy, you make the proposed changes. Complete the chart below to estimate the cost of each change. You plan to do the work yourself, so there will be no labor charge.

	Type of Material	Number of Units	Cost per Unit	Total Cost
1.	Caulking	8 tubes	$3.85 each	
2.	Foam crack filler	4 cans	$7.95 each	
3.	Weather stripping	45 feet	$7.95 per 6-foot section	
4.			SUBTOTAL	
5.	Storm windows	12	$105.50 per window	
6.	Storm doors	2	$159.95 per door	
7.			SUBTOTAL	
8.	Foam panel for basement walls	480 sq ft	$6.85 for a 32-square-foot panel	
9.	Ceiling insulation	900 sq ft	$25.58 per 77-square-foot roll	
10.			SUBTOTAL	
11.			TOTAL	

Copyright © Glencoe/McGraw-Hill

Student		Date	
Class		Instructor	

Simulation: Energy Savings—Home Weatherization
(CONTINUED)

After estimating the cost of each improvement, you want to determine the number of heating seasons it will take to recover the cost of the improvements. The pay-off time for an improvement is found by using the formula:

$$\text{Pay-off Time} = \frac{\text{Cost of Improvement}}{\text{Million BTUs Saved Annually} \times \text{Cost per Million BTUs}}$$

Type of Heat	Cost per Million BTUs
Natural Gas	$ 8.41
Propane Gas	12.25
Fuel Oil	10.33
Electric	29.16

Find the pay-off for each improvement and the total of all improvements for each type of heating. Round answers to the nearest hundredth.

The example below shows the formula for caulking/weather stripping and natural gas.

$$\text{Pay-off Time} = \frac{126.20}{25.1 \times 8.4} = \frac{126.20}{210.84} = 0.5986 = 0.60$$

	Improvement	Natural Gas	Propane Gas	Fuel Oil	Electricity
12.	Caulking/weather stripping				
13.	Storm windows/doors				
14.	Foam panels				
15.	Ceiling insulation				
16.	TOTAL				

You might consider other energy savings strategies such as:

- turning back your thermostat. In the Midwest, turning the thermostat back 1°F, could save as much as 3.89 percent of the natural gas used.

- installing a programmable thermostat. You can save as much as 10 percent per year on your heating and cooling bills by simply turning your thermostat back 7 degrees for 8 hours.

17. If your natural gas bill is $1,200 for the year, how much do you save by turning the thermostat back 1°F?

18. Suppose you pay $95.00 for a programmable thermostat and you lower your nighttime temperature 7 degrees. Your heating bills for the year are $1,200. Did you save enough to pay for the thermostat?

Student _____ Date _____

Class _____ Instructor _____

SECTION 11-1 Health Insurance Premiums

An accident or illness could cut off your income, wipe out your savings, and leave you in debt. To protect against overwhelming medical expenses, many people have health insurance. One way to get health insurance is by joining a group plan where you work. Your employer may pay part or all of the premium. Health insurance companies also offer non-group plans for people not enrolled in a group plan.

Employee's Percent = 100% − Employer's Percent

Employee's Contribution = Total Premium × Employee's Percent

---

1. Paul Woonan, a self-employed accountant, is married and enrolls in a non-group health insurance plan. The plan costs $7,710 per year for the family coverage. What will he pay each month in premiums? _____

2. Donna Ray is employed at Stone Manufacturing. Her total annual health insurance premium is $5,976. Her employer pays 70 percent of the premium. How much does she pay per month? _____

3. Chandara and Kobe Martin are self-employed motel operators. They pay 100 percent of the PPO insurance premium of $6,510 annually. They also have a dental plan that costs $546 annually and a vision plan that costs $244 annually. The premiums are paid quarterly (every 3 months). How much do they pay each quarter? _____

4. Hermosa Menendez is employed by Chemical Industries. She has a family membership in the group preferred provider organization (PPO). The annual premium is $6,180. Her employer pays 75 percent of the premium.

   a. How much does the employer pay annually? _____

   b. How much does she pay annually? _____

   c. How much is deducted each week from her paycheck? _____

5. Oscar Ankebrandt is employed by Bargain Department Store. He has a single membership in a commercial health maintenance organization (HMO) and is enrolled in the company sponsored life insurance program. The annual premium is $4,880 for the HMO and $940 for the life insurance. The company pays 60 percent of the HMO premium and 80 percent of the life insurance premium. How much is withheld from Ankebrandt's bi-weekly paycheck for insurance? _____

6. You are employed by Research Laboratories as a chemical technician. You are single and pay into the Research Laboratories Super Med Plus HMO. The total cost is $5,175 annually. The employer pays 90 percent of the total cost. You also pay 60 percent of the optional annual dental premium of $462 and 55 percent of the optional vision premium of $188.

   a. How much is deducted weekly for the HMO? _____

   b. How much is deducted each week for dental coverage? _____

   c. How much is deducted each week for vision coverage? _____

   d. What is the total weekly insurance premium? _____

Student _____ Date _____

Class _____ Instructor _____

SECTION 11-2 Health Insurance Benefits

Most insurance plans, whether they are traditional, preferred provider organization (PPO), or health maintenance organization (HMO) plans, do not pay for all services. Health insurance policies have an annual deductible clause, which is the amount of money you must pay each year before your insurance company pays anything. Health insurance policies also have a co-payment clause, which is a way of sharing medical costs. You might pay $10.00 every time you receive a medical service, such as a visit to your physician. Some policies also have a co-insurance clause. An 80 percent co-insurance clause means your insurance company pays 80 percent of the bill and you pay 20 percent.

Amount Paid by Patient = Deductible + Co-payments + Co-insurance Amount + Other Charges

Complete the table.

	Deductible Amount	Number of Co-payments at $10.00 Each	Amount of the Co-payments	Amount Subject to Co-insurance	Insured Co-insurance Rate	Amount Paid by Insured Co-insurance	Amount Paid by Insured Total
1.	$500	20		$20,000	20%		
2.	200	24		30,000	20%		
3.	250	35		25,500	30%		
4.	700	26		84,000	25%		

Use the table at the right for Problems 5 and 6.

5. Sharon Wilson is single and has health insurance benefits as shown in the table. Her recent network health care costs include co-payments for 9 physician visits and 10 specialist visits. Following hospital surgery, she made co-payments for 15 physical therapy visits. Her hospital admission charge was $240 and she had a hospital bill for $54,860. What amount did she pay:

   a. for the deductible? _____

   b. in total co-payments? _____

   c. in hospital charges? _____

   d. in total costs? _____

6. When we calculated Sharon Wilson's health care costs in Problem 5, we did not consider her maximum out-of-pocket expenses of $800. She must pay the deductible and the co-payments. What is the total for these items?

_____

	Network
Annual Deductible	
Single	$300
Family	$900
Out-of-Pocket Maximum	
Single	$800
Family	$1,200
Hospital Charges	90%
Co-payments	
Physicians Visit	$10
Specialist	$20
Physical Therapy	
First 15 Visits	$15
Over 15 Visits	80%
Emergency Room	$50
Ambulance	$25

Student _____ Date _____

Class _____ Instructor _____

SECTIONS 11-3, 11-4 Life Insurance—Term and Other Types

The main purpose of life insurance is to provide financial protection for your dependents in case of your death. You may purchase term insurance, whole life insurance, or limited payment life insurance.

Annual Premium = Number of Units Purchased × Premium per $1,000

Use the tables below to solve the problems.

ANNUAL PREMIUMS PER $1,000 OF LIFE INSURANCE: 5-YEAR TERM*		
Age	Male	Female
18–30	$2.47	$2.13
35	2.70	2.29
40	3.27	2.67
45	4.17	3.54
50	5.84	4.82
55	8.81	6.60
60	13.22	9.71

*Minimum amount is $50,000

ANNUAL PREMIUMS PER $1,000 OF LIFE INSURANCE				
	Paid Up at Age 65		Whole Life	
Age	Male	Female	Male	Female
20	$11.75	$9.75	$8.00	$6.25
25	13.75	11.50	9.50	7.50
30	17.00	14.50	11.75	9.25
35	21.50	18.00	15.00	11.50
40	29.75	25.00	19.50	14.50
45	39.50	32.50	25.50	18.75
50	56.25	45.75	34.00	24.25

Complete the table below.

	Insured	Sex	Age	Type of Insurance	Annual Premium per $1,000	Coverage	Number of Units	Annual Premium
1.	Ricardo Oro	M	25	5-Year Term		$ 50,000		
2.	Doris Stelnick	F	35	Whole Life		25,000		
3.	Marylin Wilson	F	45	5-Year Term		100,000		
4.	Perry Zamora	M	20	Whole Life		50,000		
5.	Tara McIntosh	F	50	Paid Up at 65		60,000		

6. Frederico Ortiz wants to purchase a $50,000 5-year term life insurance policy. He is 18 years old. What is his annual premium? _____

7. Alicia Bitman, age 30, plans to purchase a $50,000 whole-life policy. What is the annual premium? _____

8. Ten years ago, you purchased a $70,000 Paid-Up-at-Age-65 life insurance policy. At that time you were 30 years old.

   M _____ F _____

   a. What is your annual premium? _____

   b. How much have you paid in the last 10 years? _____

Student _____ Date _____

Class _____ Instructor _____

Career Path: Psychologist

A psychologist is not the same as a psychiatrist. A psychiatrist is a physician. He or she has gone through medical school and has graduated with a medical degree. A psychologist has a degree in psychology. Psychologists study and treat the mental and behavioral characteristics of individuals and groups. Some psychologists work in private practice, meeting and treating patients. Others work in schools, counseling students; in industrial and organizational settings, working with employees; in clinical settings, studying and treating patients in a hospital or clinic; in the military; and in consumer psychology, studying the ways people behave as consumers of goods and services.

Psychologists performing research in university or clinical settings often conduct experiments. When they perform an experiment on a number of subjects, they often measure their reaction to stimuli, their behavior in situations, or whatever is being studied. The data from the experiments often take the form of numbers—the number of subjects who reacted in each of several possible ways, for instance, or the ratings on a number scale of the answers the subjects gave in a survey. Psychologists often perform statistical calculations on their data to determine what the results of their observations mean. These calculations can be anything from simple averages to complex calculus-based formulas.

Check Your Understanding

Dr. Selma Fried is a psychologist in private practice. She is also an adjunct professor at the state university, through which she gets her insurance coverage. The table below shows the premiums she paid this year and will pay next year for her coverage.

Type of Insurance	Bi-weekly Premium This Year	Bi-weekly Premium Next Year
Major medical	$62.49	$71.25
Dental	11.82	12.12
Term life	12.94	14.51

1. How much will Dr. Fried pay next year for her major medical coverage?

   _____

2. This year Dr. Fried went to the dentist 3 times. Two visits were for routine checkups. Her dentist charges $80.00 per visit and her insurance pays 80 percent of that. She also had a filling replaced, for which her dentist charged $225.00, and the insurance paid 100 percent. Did she spend more or less for dental coverage last year than she would have spent if she had had no coverage and paid the dentist herself? Show your calculations.

   _____

   _____

   _____

   _____

   _____

3. How much will Dr. Fried pay next year for term life insurance? How much more will it cost than it did last year?

   _____

4. What is the percentage increase in Dr. Fried's major medical coverage? Show your calculations.

   _____

Student
Date

Class
Instructor

SECTIONS 12-1, 12-2   Certificates of Deposit and Effective Annual Yield

Your money earns interest at a higher rate when you buy a certificate of deposit than it does when you invest it in a regular savings account. Most certificates earn interest compounded daily. The annual yield is the rate at which your money earns simple interest in one year.

Interest Earned = Amount − Original Principal

Annual Yield = Interest for One Year / Principal

Use the table below to solve the problems.

AMOUNT PER $1.00 INVESTED, DAILY COMPOUNDING						
Annual Rate	3 Months	1 Year	2.5 Years	4 Years	6 Years	8 Years
5.75%	1.014278	1.059180	1.154458	1.258577	1.411952	1.584017
6.00%	1.014903	1.061831	1.161820	1.271224	1.433287	1.616011
6.25%	1.015529	1.064489	1.169103	1.283998	1.454945	1.648651
6.50%	1.016155	1.067153	1.176431	1.296900	1.476930	1.681950
6.75%	1.016782	1.069824	1.183806	1.309932	1.499246	1.715921
7.00%	1.017408	1.072501	1.191226	1.323094	1.521900	1.750579
7.25%	1.018036	1.075185	1.198693	1.336389	1.544896	1.785936
7.50%	1.018663	1.077876	1.206207	1.349817	1.568240	1.822006
7.75%	1.019291	1.080573	1.213768	1.363380	1.591936	1.858806
8.00%	1.019920	1.083278	1.221376	1.377079	1.615989	1.896348

1. Alicia Cox purchased a 2½-year certificate of deposit for $15,000. The certificate earns interest at a rate of 7.00 percent compounded daily.

   a. What is the amount of the certificate at maturity? _____

   b. What is the interest earned? _____

2. Charles Demaize purchased an 8-year certificate of deposit for $45,000. The certificate earns interest at 8.00 percent compounded daily.

   a. What is the certificate worth in 8 years? _____

   b. What has the certificate earned in those 8 years? _____

3. The Nakatas have $30,000 they want to invest in a certificate of deposit. They can purchase a 4-year certificate that earns interest at a rate of 5.75 percent or a 2½-year certificate that earns interest at a rate of 8.00 percent

   a. Which certificate offers a higher maturity value? _____

   _____

   b. What is the difference in the maturity values of the 2 certificates? _____

4. What is the annual yield on a 1-year $15,000 certificate of deposit that earns interest at a rate of 7.50 percent compounded daily? _____

5. You invest $25,000 in an 8-year certificate of deposit that earns interest at 8.00 percent compounded daily. What is the annual yield? _____

Student _____ Date _____

Class _____ Instructor _____

SECTIONS 12-3, 12-4 Stocks and Stock Dividends

When you purchase a share of stock, you become part owner of the corporation that issues the stock. The total amount you pay for the stock depends on the cost per share, the number of shares you purchase, and the stockbroker's commission. You can use the annual yield to compare different stocks as investments.

Cost of Stock = Number of Shares × Cost per Share

Total Paid = Cost of Stock + Commission

Annual Yield = $\dfrac{\text{Annual Dividend per Share}}{\text{Cost per Share}}$

1. Tania Elliot purchased 400 shares of Frontier Oil at $19.00 per share and paid a $29.95 commission.

   a. What was the cost of the stock? _____

   b. What was the total paid? _____

2. Arthur McGrag purchased 320 shares of Auto Zone. He paid a 3 percent commission to the stockbroker. The stocks cost him $78.50 per share.

   a. What was the cost of the stock? _____

   b. What was the total paid? _____

3. Warisaro Kaierithorn owns 90 shares of Allegheny Energy for which he paid $41.56 per share. The company paid annual dividends of $1.72 per share. What is the annual yield? _____

4. Kaiori Hayashi owns 60 shares of Comerica, Inc., for which he paid $3,945.90, including a commission of $113.40. Comerica pays annual dividends of $1.92. What is the annual yield? _____

5. You are considering the purchase of either 100 shares of Health Care Right at $28.06 per share or 80 shares of Health Care Provider at $40.90 per share. Health Care Right is expected to pay a dividend of $2.34 per share, and Health Care Provider is expected to pay a dividend of $3.24 per share.

   a. If you bought the 100 shares of Health Care Right, what would you receive in annual dividends? _____

   b. What would your annual yield be? _____

   c. If you bought the 80 shares of Health Care Provider, what would you receive in annual dividends? _____

   d. What would your annual yield be? _____

6. Mario Gillespie owns 200 shares of Asset Investment Corporation for which he paid $32.75 per share. The broker's commission was $19.95 or 2¢ per share over 1,000. Asset Investment paid a $5.00 per share dividend. What was the annual yield? _____

82 Mathematics with Business Applications ♦ Sections 12-3, 12-4   Copyright © Glencoe/McGraw-Hill

Student   Date

Class   Instructor

SECTION 12-5 Selling Stocks

When you sell your stocks, the sale can result in either a profit or a loss. If the amount you receive for the sale minus the sales commission is greater than the total amount you paid for the stocks, you have made a profit. If the amount you receive minus the sales commission is less than the total paid, your sale has resulted in a loss.

   Net Sale = Amount of Sale − Commission

   Profit = Net Sale − Total Paid

   Loss = Total Paid − Net Sale

Round each answer to the nearest cent.

1. Kado Kato owned 400 shares of stock in a car company, for which he paid a total of $11,580. He sold the stock for $29.50 per share and paid a commission of 1 percent of the selling price.

   a. What was the amount of the sale? _____

   b. What was the net sale? _____

   c. What was the profit or loss? _____

2. Marty and Irene Benefield purchased 400 shares of airline stock 2 years ago. They paid a total of $8,484.55 for the stock. Last week they sold the stock for $19.50 per share and paid an online commission of $19.95.

   a. What was the amount of the sale? _____

   b. What was the net sale? _____

   c. What was the profit or loss? _____

3. Jose Rodriguez recently sold 1,320 shares of oil stock for $31.70 per share plus a commission of $29.95 plus 3¢ per share. He paid a total of $56,166.00 for the stock.

   a. What was the amount of the sale? _____

   b. What was the selling commission? _____

   c. What was the net sale? _____

   d. What was the profit or loss? _____

4. Emma Kishketon recently sold 300 shares of stock in a fast food company for $46.54 per share plus a commission of $49.95 plus 2¢ per share. She purchased the stock for $39.22 plus a 1 percent commission.

   a. What was the cost of the stock? _____

   b. What was the total paid? _____

   c. What was the amount of the sale? _____

   d. What was the net sale? _____

   e. What was the profit or loss? _____

Student _____ Date _____

Class _____ Instructor _____

SECTION 12-6 Bonds

Bonds are issued by governments and large corporations to raise money. When you invest in bonds, you lend money to the corporation or government, and you are paid interest. When the bond matures, you receive the face value of the bond.

Annual Interest = Interest Rate × Face Value

Bond Cost = Percent × Face Value

Annual Yield = Annual Interest / Bond Cost

Complete the table below. Round each percent to the nearest hundredth.

	Face Value of Bond	Quoted Price	Cost of Bond	Interest Rate	Annual Interest	Annual Yield
1.	$10,000	98		8%		
2.	12,000	77		7½%		
3.	5,000	85½		8¼%		
4.	20,000	91⅜		10⅛%		
5.	40,000	85¼		12%		

6. Ralph Suarez purchases a $9,000 bond at 88¼. It pays 6 percent annual interest.

   a. What is the cost of the bond? _____

   b. What is the annual interest earned? _____

   c. What is the annual yield? _____

7. Eva Rhodes purchases a $14,000 bond at 96¾. It pays 12⅝ percent annual interest.

   a. What is the cost of the bond? _____

   b. What is the annual interest earned? _____

   c. What is the annual yield? _____

8. You use your savings to buy a $1,500 bond at 82⅞. It pays 8¾ percent annual interest.

   a. What is the cost of the bond? _____

   b. What is the annual interest earned? _____

   c. What is the annual yield? _____

Student _____ Date _____

Class _____ Instructor _____

Simulation: Selecting a Stock

There are many different methods investors use to select a stock to purchase. Many follow the advice of their full-service broker. Others invest in a stock mutual fund and let the administrator of that fund decide which stocks to buy. Still others, either individually or as part of a group, study and analyze a stock before deciding whether it should be purchased.

When studying a stock, the usual procedure is to examine its historical performance in attempting to predict its future potential. Generally, both income from the stock purchase in the form of dividends and an increase in the value of the stock are considerations.

In this activity you will be primarily interested in the potential increase in the value of the stock. You will use a modified and simplified version of the *Stock Selection Guide and Report* prepared by The National Association of Investors Corporation.

You are asked to examine the price per share, the earnings per share, and the price earnings ratio for the past 10 years in order to determine if the present price per share is in the *buy, maybe,* or *sell* range. The information you will need can be found in *Standard and Poor's Stock Reports,* in *Value Line,* or on the Internet Web site for various stocks. Check in your school or local public library.

First, complete this table for the stock you are studying.

Stock Name:				Present Price: $	
	Price		Earnings per Share	Price Earnings Ratio	
	High	Low		High (A ÷ C)	Low (B ÷ C)
Year	(A)	(B)	(C)	(D)	(E)
1.					
2.					
3.					
4.					
5.					
6.					
7.					
8.					
9.					
10.					
11. Total					
12. Average					

Note that the columns are labeled (A), (B), (C), (D), (E), and the rows are numbered 1–12.

Simulation: Selecting a Stock
(CONTINUED)

Use your table to answer these questions to determine whether or not to buy the stock in question.

1. Graph the earnings per share based on the ten-year history in the table.

Earnings per Share

Price

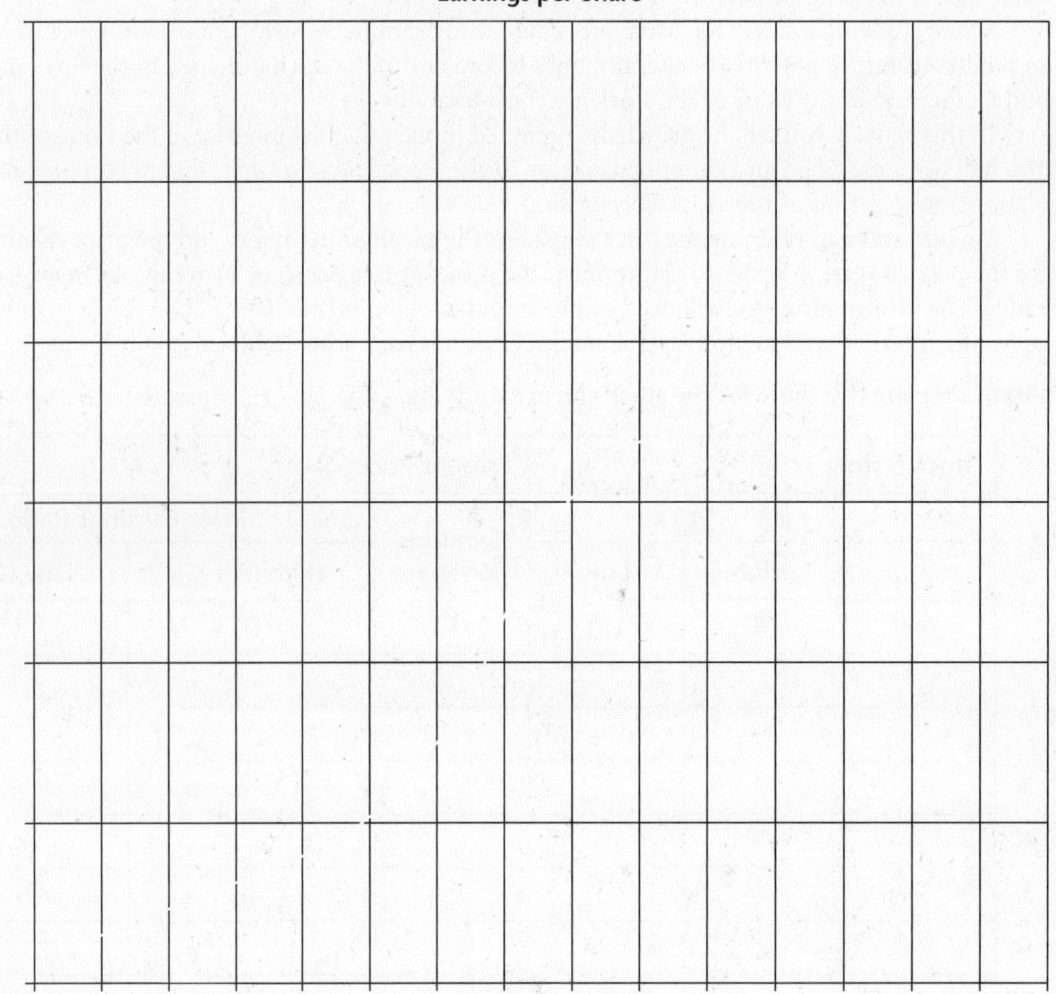

Year

Use your graph to make your best estimate of what the high earnings per share will be in 5 years. _____

2. To find the Forecasted High Price, take your best estimate in Problem 1 and multiply it by the Average High Price per Earnings Ratio (D-12). _____

3. To find the Forecasted Low Price, sometimes the Average Low Price for the past 10 years (B-12) is used. Multiply the Average Low Price per Earnings Ratio (E-12) by the most recent Earnings per Share (C-10). This is your Forecasted Low Price. _____

Simulation: Selecting a Stock
(CONTINUED)

4. The *buy* range is the lower third of the range between your Forecasted High Price and your Forecasted Low Price.

   a. Find the difference between your answers to Problems 2 and 3. _____

   b. Divide the answer to Problem 4a by 3. _____

   c. Add the answer to Problem 4b to your Forecasted Low Price from Problem 3. This is the upper limit of the *buy* range. Your *buy* range is, therefore, from: _____

5. Add the answer to Problem 4b to the upper limit of the *buy* range. This is the upper limit of the *maybe* range. _____

6. Add the answer to Problem 4b to the upper limit of the *maybe* range. This is the upper limit of the *sell* range. _____

7. Determine if the present price per share of the stock you are studying is in the *buy, maybe,* or *sell* range. Your recommendation is: _____

8. The ratio of the difference between your Forecasted High Price (Problem 2) and the Present Price per Share, and the difference between the Present Price per Share and your Forecasted Low Price (Problem 3) is viewed by some as the ratio of potential gain to risk of loss. This ratio should be 3.0 to 1 or greater if you are going to buy the stock. Compute this ratio for the stock you are studying.

   Forecasted High Price per Share − Present Price per Share
   Present Price per Share − Forecasted Low Price per Share

Student _____ Date _____

Class _____ Instructor _____

Career Paths: Stockbroker

A stockbroker is a financial professional who buys and sells stocks, bonds, and other financial instruments on behalf of his or her clients. With Internet access and an online brokerage account, it is now possible for investors to trade their stocks themselves. Many still choose, for a variety of reasons, to do so through a broker.

A stockbroker can provide a number of services that are not available to the investor trading in an online account. For one, the broker has a direct connection to the stock exchange, which can make for a faster and instantly verifiable trade. For another, the broker, who works full time in the industry along with financial researchers and analysts, often has valuable information about the companies being traded that investors would have to spend considerable time finding on their own.

How do stockbrokers earn their pay? Some of it comes in the form of commissions. Each time the investor sells or buys a stock, the order is for a certain number of shares. With stocks, usually traded in groups of 100 shares (called *lots*), the commission typically depends on the price of the share of stock and the number of shares being bought or sold.

Check Your Understanding

Type of Investment	Percent of Holdings	Amount
Certificate of Deposit	10%	$14,500.00
Stocks	60%	87,000.00
Bonds	20%	29,000.00
Money Market	10%	14,500.00
	TOTAL	145,000.00

1. A broker advised his client to divide his holdings as shown above. The certificate of deposit paid 7.25 percent interest, compounded daily. How much interest did the CD earn after one year? (See the Amount per $1.00 Invested, Daily Compounding table on page 81.)

2. The client decided to put half his stock money in BigCo, which was selling for $62.50 per share. How many shares did he buy?

3. The broker charged him a commission of $8.95 per 100 shares. How much was the commission?

4. BigCo pays an annual dividend of $0.48 per share. What is the client's total annual dividend? What is the annual yield?

88 Career Paths: Stockbroker Copyright © Glencoe/McGraw-Hill

SECTION 13-1 Hiring New Employees

To fill openings in your business, you can either recruit new employees or pay an employment agency to locate a candidate for you. The cost of recruiting may include advertising fees; interviewing expenses, such as travel costs for job candidates; and hiring expenses, such as moving costs for new employees.

$$\text{Total Recruiting Cost} = \text{Advertising Expenses} + \text{Interviewing Expenses} + \text{Hiring Expenses}$$

Fill in the total recruiting costs in the table below.

	Position	Advertising Expenses	Interviewing Expenses	Hiring Expenses	Total Recruiting Cost
1.	Statistician	$ 212.50	$ 56.80	$ 3,952.00	
2.	Analyst	350.50	762.20	5,012.90	
3.	Instructor	615.84	8,262.48	7,467.97	
4.	Director	68.40	396.42	2,147.80	
5.	Accountant	253.82	910.48	4,697.80	

6. Commerce Bank hired Pete Drexel as its new branch office manager, at an annual salary of $39,500.

   Advertising Costs: $421.27
   Interview Expenses:
      P. Drexel $85.25
      L. Lindsay $94.60
   Search Agency Fee: 15 percent of first year's annual salary

   What was the total cost of recruiting Pete Drexel for this position? _____

7. To search for a new vice president, your company hired the Executive Placement Agency to locate candidates for the position. The agency's fee is 25 percent of the first year's salary, if you hire one of its candidates. You have also run advertisements in professional magazines for a total cost of $849.04. You interviewed 3 people:

   Denise Hoffman   Omarr Kalifa   Magena Hurit
   Applied through   Answered ad   Applied through
   the agency   Travel Cost: $104   the agency
   Travel Cost: $490   Travel Cost: $229

   You hired Magena Hurit at an annual salary of $44,600. Your company paid her moving expenses of $1,564.80, plus relocation expenses of $8,100. What was your total recruiting cost? _____

8. A major Midwestern university hired Executive Search Consultants to assist in finding a new president. The consultant's fee is a flat $68,000. Advertisements cost $3,160.96. The search committee brought 3 finalists to the campus for interviews.

	Delmar Alfred	June Day	Leonides Reyes
Transportation	$410.25	$ 42.50	$694.30
Lodging and meals	118.80	197.46	212.40

   The university selects Delmar Alfred as its new president. Moving expenses of $914.40 plus relocation costs of $5,500 were paid by the university. What was the total recruiting cost?

SECTION 13-2 Administering Wages and Salaries

Your business may have a wage and salary scale for the positions in the company. A cost-of-living adjustment is a raise in your salary to help you keep up with inflation. A merit increase is a raise in your salary to reward you for the quality of your work.

New Salary = Present Salary + Cost-of-Living Adjustment + Merit Increase

Find the new salary in the table below.

	Job Title	Present Salary	Cost-of-Living Increase	Merit Increase	New Salary
1.	Clerk	$13,520.00	$ 301.30	$ 452.60	
2.	Manager	32,400.00	1,580.00	2,517.00	
3.	Programmer	22,500.00	1,283.00	658.47	
4.	Accountant	34,640.00	1,232.00	1,232.00	

5. Jalen Russell is the credit manager at Value Line Shops. His annual salary is $34,650. Next month he will receive a 5.5 percent cost-of-living adjustment and a 4.0 percent merit increase. What will be his new annual salary? _____

6. Sherry Spencer is the Senior Vice President for her company. Her annual salary is $76,425. She received a 6.4 percent merit increase this month. What is her new annual salary? _____

7. Andres Carillo will receive a promotion next month. He will receive a 12.5 percent salary increase, in addition to a 5.5 percent cost-of-living adjustment and a 6.8 percent merit increase. His present annual salary is $26,990. What will be his new annual salary? _____

8. Atsuko Nagayama is the head computer analyst for Data Program Controls, Incorporated. She will receive a 5.5 percent cost-of-living adjustment in her salary this month. Her present annual salary is $42,000. What will be her new annual salary? _____

9. After working at a company for 8 months, you received your first performance review last week. As a result, you have been given a 7.5 percent merit increase based on your present annual salary of $21,640. What is your new salary? _____

10. Killian Manufacturing awards merit increases based on performance and uses a sliding scale for cost-of-living adjustments. Employees at Killian who earn less than $18,000 receive a cost-of-living adjustment of 7.5 percent. Employees who earn $18,000 to $25,000 receive a cost-of-living adjustment of 6.5 percent. Employees who earn $25,000 or more receive a cost-of-living adjustment of 6.3 percent. Find the new annual salary for these 5 Killian employees. Their merit increases are given.

	Jim Spar	Tama Beggins	Ralph Stokes	Doug Garcia	Janice Stites
Annual Salary	$18,000	$21,750	$31,860	$14,615	$27,916
Merit Increase	6%	3½%	5.1%	0.7%	6¼%
New Annual Salary					

Student Date

Class Instructor

SECTION 13-3 Employee Benefits

Employee benefits are offered in the form of various types of insurances, pension plans, and paid vacations. The total of your benefits is often figured as a percentage of your annual gross pay.

Rate of Benefits = $\dfrac{\text{Total Benefits}}{\text{Annual Gross Pay}}$

Find the rate of benefits in the table below. Round to the nearest tenth of a percent.

	Job Title	Annual Gross Pay	Total Benefits	Rate of Benefits
1.	Administrator	$23,140	$7,520	
2.	Clerk	18,600	2,790	
3.	Programmer	19,750	2,070	
4.	Receptionist	15,600	1,844	
5.	Assistant	24,416	3,489	
6.	Vice President	92,412	9,867	

7. Juan Fuentes is a computer processing supervisor. His annual salary is $32,190. Benefits consist of $1,881.73 in vacation time, holidays worth $1,287.60, health insurance premiums of $2,300 paid by the employer, Social Security of $1,995.78, Medicare of $466.76, and unemployment insurance of $541.06.

   a. What are the total benefits?

   b. What is the rate of benefits?

8. Teri Schenk is employed as a supermarket cashier. Her annual salary is $17,470. Benefits consist of 1 week paid vacation, 8 paid holidays, 80 percent of a total health insurance package consisting of $2,100, 3 percent unemployment insurance, 6.2 percent Social Security, and 1.45 percent Medicare.

   a. What are the total benefits?

   b. What is the rate of benefits?

9. You work in a payroll office. Complete the form below. Remember 6.2 percent of the first $84,900 of the annual salary is deducted for Social Security and 1.45 percent of all income is deducted for Medicare.

Position	Annual Salary	Vacation	3% Health Ins.	3.6% Unemp. Ins.	6.2% Soc. Sec.	1.45% Medical	Total Benefits
Manager	$82,100	3 wk:					
Receptionist	18,600	2 wk:					
Clerk I	17,900	2 wk:					
Clerk II	15,400	2 wk:					

   a. What is the rate of benefits for the manager?

   b. What is the rate of benefits for the receptionist?

   c. What is the rate of benefits for clerk I?

   d. What is the rate of benefits for clerk II?

SECTION 13-4 Disability Insurance

Disability Insurance pays benefits to individuals who must miss work because of an illness or injury. Most independent retirement systems compute long term disability benefits based on a percent of the final average salary.

$$\text{Annual Disability Benefit} = \left[\text{Years Worked} + \text{Expected Retirement Age} - \text{Present Age} \right] \times \text{Rate of Benefits} \times \text{Final Average Salary}$$

Disability Insurance under Social Security is based on your inability to work and is available from the Social Security Administration. Supplemental Security Income (SSI) is a program run by the Social Security Administration for the elderly, the blind, and people with disabilities. The basic monthly SSI benefit is $531 for one person and $796 for a couple. This may vary if the state adds to the SSI benefit.

In the table below, find the annual and the monthly disability benefit using the independent retirement system formula given above.

	Name	Years Worked	Expected Ret. Age	Present Age	Rate of Benefits	Final Average Salary	Annual Disability Benefit	Monthly Disability Benefit
1.	A. Brown	18	60	48	2.0%	$49,860		
2.	R. Garcia	9	55	32	1.8%	32,500		
3.	T. Mustafi	28	62	59	2.1%	48,830		
4.	P. Pappas	16	65	39	1.9%	45,800		
5.	S. Stein	33	60	57	2.0%	52,848		
6.	W. Moore	14	55	46	1.7%	33,850		

7. Thomas Johnson has contributed to Social Security for the past 22 years. He becomes disabled while working and qualifies for Supplemental Security Income (SSI). Find the monthly SSI benefit for Johnson and his wife.

8. Alice Walker has worked for Extended Care Facility for the past twelve years. Her employment is covered by Social Security. She becomes disabled and qualifies for SSI. If she is single with no dependents, how much will she receive monthly in SSI benefits?

9. Mario Ramirez had worked for the Western State University system for 21 years when he suffered a stroke and became disabled. Ramirez is 58 years of age and planned to retire at the age of 62. His final average salary is $74,820. Western State has a rate of benefit of 1.9 percent. What is his monthly disability benefit?

10. Sheronda Williams, age 43, was an employee of Transcontinental Rail System for 20 years when she became permanently disabled. Normal retirement age for Transcontinental is 55. The rate of benefit is 2.1 percent. Williams' final average salary was $47,485. Find her monthly disability benefit.

Student _____ Date _____

Class _____ Instructor _____

SECTION 13-5 Workers Compensation and Unemployment Insurance

Workers compensation insurance covers employees' medical expenses and lost wages if they're hurt on the job. The premiums are paid by the employer and vary by state, total payroll, and type of business. The premium for workers compensation insurance is computed by multiplying a base rate, normally per $100, by the total payroll.

Premium for Workers Compensation Insurance = Base Rate × Total Payroll

Unemployment insurance is a federal and state program that provides financial aid to qualified persons who, through no fault of their own, become unemployed. These premiums are also paid by the employer. The federal unemployment tax (FUTA) rate is 6.2 percent of the first $7,000 of taxable wages. Normally, 5.4 percent of that goes for the state unemployment tax (SUTA), leaving 0.8 percent for federal. If the state rate is 2.0 percent, then 4.2 percent would be left for the federal.

1. The base rate for workers compensation insurance for roofers in one state is $16.95 per $100 paid to employees. The total monthly payroll for Certified Roofing Contractors is $15,738. What is the monthly premium for workers compensation insurance? _____

2. In the same state as Problem 1, the owner of Variety Store pays the base rate of only $2.24 per $100 paid in wages. The payroll for the store for the month of October is $14,830. What is the monthly premium for workers compensation insurance? _____

3. The Landscape Company has 6 employees. It has some unemployment during the winter months and, therefore, must pay a state unemployment tax (SUTA) of 5.4 percent. That leaves 0.8 percent for the federal unemployment tax (FUTA). Compute the federal and state unemployment tax if their annual wages are as given:

Employee	Annual Wage	Amount Taxed	FUTA (0.8%)	SUTA (5.4%)
Andy Cole	$34,750	$7,000		
Tricia Gomez	29,268	7,000		
Ben Abdulmin	25,000	7,000		
Tom Smith	7,575	7,000		
Mary Beans	6,836	6,836		
Sam Cook	5,194	5,194		

4. The law offices of Jones and Jones has good experience with respect to layoffs and, as a result, pays a SUTA rate of only 1.1 percent on the first $7,000 of each employee's annual wage. The FUTA rate would, therefore, be 5.1 percent (6.2% − 1.1%). Find the federal and state unemployment insurance tax paid on the wages of these 4 employees.

Employee	Annual Wage	Amount Taxed	FUTA (5.1%)	SUTA (1.1%)
Malik Jones	$125,000	$7,000		
Ahmad Jones	135,000	7,000		
Tamika Sams	24,800	7,000		
Thomas Links	4,685	4,685		

SECTION 13-6 Travel Expenses

If you travel for your business, you will be reimbursed for your authorized expenses. Travel expenses usually include transportation, lodging, and meals.

Total Travel Expense = Cost of Transportation + Cost of Lodging + Cost of Meals + Additional Cost

Fill in the table below.

	Name	Miles Traveled	Cost at $0.345/mile	Meals	Lodging	Total Travel Expense
1.	H. Salkowski	240.5	$ 82.97	$ 67.71	$ 98.60	
2.	O. Wines	1,980.9	683.41	71.04	168.40	
3.	S. Irelan	410.5	141.62	51.60	64.90	
4.	J. Jablonski	1,070.2	369.22	80.40	148.10	
5.	T. Mears	2,540.6	876.51	180.41	260.80	

6. Tom Maxwell is a consultant. This month his travel expenses include: airfare, $2,690; taxi fares, $98.60; meals, $290; hotels, $590; miscellaneous, $38.00. What is Tom's total travel expense? _____

7. Tamika Clark is the County Superintendent. She travels to the 3 schools in her district every month. This month her travel expenses include: 246 miles traveled at $0.31 per mile; meals, $180.70; miscellaneous, $46.90. What is her total travel expense this month? _____

8. You went to Kansas City for a 3-day conference last week. Your travel expenses include the following: airfare, $220; taxi fare, $26.80; meals, $127.80; hotel, $89.90 per night for 2 nights; conference registration fee, $150. What is your total travel expense? _____

9. Rosa Jiminez, a systems engineer, spent 3 days at the Education Center doing bench marks on a bill-calc program. Her expenses included $289 airfare, $40 taxi fare plus 15 percent tip, $75 per night at a hotel for 2 nights, 2 dinners at $19.60 and $27.90 plus 20 percent tip for each, and $12.50 each for 2 breakfasts including tip. What is her total travel expense? _____

10. James Pappas drove to a 1-day business conference. He drove 224 miles round trip. His meals cost $21.90 plus 5.5 percent tax and 20 percent tip. Registration at the conference cost $55. He is reimbursed at $0.32 per mile plus gas. His car gets 28 miles per gallon and gas cost $1.499 per gallon. What is his total travel expense? _____

SECTION 13-7 Employee Training

In-service training is often available to employees. Your company may grant you release time to attend these special classes. Release time allows you to attend the training sessions and still receive your regular wages while you are away.

Total Training Cost = Cost of Release Time + Cost of Instruction + Additional Cost

Find the total trainings costs in the table below.

	Purpose of Training	Number of Days	Daily Cost of Release time	Daily Cost of Instruction	Daily Cost of Supplies	Total Training Cost
1.	Marketing New Products	3	$486.00	$132.60	$78.40	
2.	Fuel Saving Tips	4	359.00	29.40	77.90	
3.	Management Training	2	794.00	1,240.00	48.96	
4.	New Phone System	2	176.04	150.00	87.90	

5. Two orthopedic surgeons attend a 3-day conference on minimally invasive knee surgery. Release time costs $890 per person per day, registration fee is $1,060 per person, lodging and meals cost $175 per person per day, and supplies cost $194.60 per person. What is the total training cost? _____

6. The Graphics Company is sending 4 of its designers to attend a 3-day workshop on computer assisted graphics (CAG). The daily cost of release time is $173 per person. The registration fee is $68 per person. Each designer is also given a $50 per day miscellaneous allowance. What is the total training cost for the company? _____

7. You are going to a 7-day conference. The cost for release time will be $94.90 per day. The registration fee will be $580. Your travel expenses for these 7 days will be $764.80. What will be the total cost of your training? _____

8. Six supervisors attend an in-service training session on better interpersonal communications. The 1-day session is conducted by a licensed psychologist at a cost of $670. Release time for 3 of the supervisors is $85 each; release time of the other 3 is $78.90 each. Supplies cost $21.50 per person. What is the total training cost? _____

9. Nine salespersons at Corner Furniture attended an 8-hour new products conference. The average hourly rate of pay for the 9 salespersons is $9.86. The sales manager, who has an annual salary of $44,800, conducted the 1-day session after a 1-day prep period. Lunch was provided for the 9 salespersons and the sales manager at a cost of $11.80 per person. What is the total training cost? _____

Student _____ Date _____

Class _____ Instructor _____

Spreadsheet Application: Personnel

DIRECTIONS:

1. Insert your *Student Activity Workbook CD* into your computer and click on Chapter 13 Personnel. The spreadsheet will appear.
2. Key your name into cell B1. Key the date into cell G1.
3. Key the information below into the appropriate cells. The spreadsheet application will compute the data for you automatically.
4. Save your spreadsheet as Ch13XXX, where XXX are your initials.
5. Print out your spreadsheet.

Input the information below to find the individual benefits, total benefits, and rate of benefits. Then answer the questions that follow.

Title	Annual Wage	Vacation	Vacation Benefit Value	3.6% Unemp. Ins.	8-Day Sick Leave	6.2% Soc. Sec.	1.45% Medicare	Total Benefits	Rate of Benefits
Dir.	$72,600	(3 wks.)							
Asst. Dir.	48,900	(3 wks.)							
Adm. Asst.	42,300	(2 wks.)							
1st Clerk	27,650	(2 wks.)							
2nd Clerk	18,540	(2 wks.)							
Total									

1. What are the total benefits for the director? _____
2. What is the rate of benefits for the assistant director? _____
3. What is the total compensation insurance collected for these 5 employees? _____
4. How much Social Security is withheld from the 1st clerk's pay? _____
5. How much more would it cost to give the administrative assistant a 3-week vacation? _____

Title	Annual Wage	Vacation	Vacation Benefit Value	3.6% Unemp. Ins.	8-Day Sick Leave	6.2% Soc. Sec.	1.45% Medicare	Total Benefits	Rate of Benefits
Mgr.	$45,000	(4 wks.)							
Asst. Mgr.	37,500	(4 wks.)							
Ser. Tech.	28,500	(3 wks.)							
Ser. Tech.	24,000	(2 wks.)							
Janitor	18,540	(2 wks.)							
Total									

6. What is the rate of benefits for the manager? _____
7. What are the total benefits for the janitor? _____
8. What does vacation time cost for these 5 employees? _____
9. What is the total unemployment insurance collected for these 5 employees? _____
10. How much Social Security was withheld from the service technician earning $28,500 per year? _____

Student _____ Date _____

Class _____ Instructor _____

SECTION 14-1 Manufacturing

The cost of manufacturing an item depends, in part, on the direct material cost and the direct labor cost.

$$\text{Prime Cost per Item} = \text{Direct Material Cost per Item} + \text{Direct Labor Cost per Item}$$

Fill in the table below.

	Cost per Unit	Pieces per Unit	Direct Material Cost per Item	Labor Cost per Hour	Units per Hour	Direct Labor Cost per Item	Prime Cost
1.	$0.72	48		$8.50	340		
2.	0.12	4		13.60	170		
3.	11.88	25		10.40	270		
4.	3.85	10		36.90	28		

5. General Plastics manufactures plastic picture frames. Each sheet of plastic yields 184 frames. Each sheet costs $78.40. The direct labor charge is $9.60 per hour. The machine operator can cut 1 sheet per hour. What is the prime cost of manufacturing 1 frame? _____

6. A machine operator at The Can Company stamps labels on sheets of metal that are later made into cans. Each sheet can make 118 cans. The cost per sheet of metal is $10.60. The operator is paid $9.40 per hour and stamps labels on 120 sheets per hour. What is the prime cost of labeling 1 can? _____

7. Charlie Dakin, an industrial engineer, estimates the prime cost of manufacturing a staple remover. What is the prime cost per staple remover?

_____

STAPLE REMOVER Cost Element	Cost per Item Material	Labor
Retractor	$0.017	$0.003
Wedge	0.005	0.002
Housing	0.005	0.014
Screw	0.005	0.003
Spring	0.004	0.002
Assembly	—	0.068
Tooling cost	0.002	0.053
Total		

8. Cooking Products manufactures a garlic press. What is the prime cost of manufacturing 1,000,000 garlic presses?

_____

GARLIC PRESS Cost Element	Cost per Item Material	Labor
Top handle	$0.099	$0.095
Bottom handle	0.079	0.007
Basket	0.034	0.019
Press plate	0.008	0.002
Sleeve	0.042	0.084
Assembly	0.038	0.195
Tooling cost	—	0.164
Total		

Student _____ Date _____

Class _____ Instructor _____

SECTION 14-2 Break-Even Analysis

A break-even analysis tells you how many units of a product must be made and sold to cover the cost of production. Any item sold beyond the break-even point results in a profit for your business.

$$\text{Break-Even Point in Units} = \frac{\text{Total Fixed Costs}}{\text{Selling Price per Unit} - \text{Variable Costs per Unit}}$$

1. The Johnstowne Company manufactures porcelain figurines. The fixed costs of the product total $124,362.88. The average selling price per figurine is $210.10. The variable cost per figurine is $54.65. What is the break-even point in number of figurines? _____

2. Whisk-Off dog collar is produced by Pet Mart. It has total fixed costs of $12,000,000 in the manufacture of the collar. The selling price of each collar is $6.95. The variable cost per collar is $4.55. What is the break-even point in number of collars? _____

3. Tobby Toy manufactures teddy bears. It has total fixed costs of $232,552 in the production of the bears. The selling price of each bear is $19.16. The variable cost per bear is $15.15. What is the break-even point in number of bears? _____

4. Your company produces In-A-Stick glue in 8-oz tubes. The total fixed costs for the production of the glue are $477,999.50. The variable cost per tube is $0.38. The selling price is $1.16 per tube. What is the break-even point in tubes of In-A-Stick glue? _____

5. Forever Green Plastics manufactures garden tool sets for cultivating. Total fixed costs are estimated at $64,800. The variable cost per set is $2.95 and the selling price is $8.60. What is the break-even point? _____

6. Fleckston Rubber manufactures hood release levers for a car manufacturer. The fixed costs are $53,090. Each lever is sold for $3.76. The variable cost per lever is $1.77. What is the break-even point? _____

98 Mathematics with Business Applications ◆ Section 14-2   Copyright © Glencoe/McGraw-Hill

Student _____ Date _____

Class _____ Instructor _____

SECTION 14-3 Quality Control

You can control the quality of items being mass produced by using a quality control chart. If too many items are defective, the situation is "out of control."

Percent Defective = $\dfrac{\text{Number Defective}}{\text{Total Number Checked}}$

1. Rita DeVane, a quality control inspector for The Sock Company, checked a sample of 875 socks. She found 94 defective samples. If more than 7 percent of the samples is defective, the process is out of control. What percent of the sample is defective? Is the process in or out of control?

   _____

2. Lamar Watson checks 400 samples per hour of calculators produced by The Math Company. The production process is in control if 1 percent or less of the samples is defective. At 6:00 A.M. Watson found 3 of the 400 samples defective. At 7:00 A.M. he found 6. At 8:00 A.M. he found 1. What percent of each inspection was defective? Was the process in or out of control each hour?

   6 A.M. _____ 7 A.M. _____ 8 A.M. _____

3. Quality control inspectors at Glass Works recorded the following data during one 8-hour shift. Compute the percent defective. Record the information on the quality control chart on the following page.

   ITEM:
   GLASS GOBLETS #131

TIME:	8 A.M.	9 A.M.	10 A.M.	11 A.M.	12	1 P.M.	2 P.M.	3 P.M.
Number Checked	25	40	20	25	25	25	40	25
Number Defective	1	1	2	1	1	1	3	1
Percent Defective	___	___	___	___	___	___	___	___

4. You work as a quality control inspector at Glass Works. You recorded the data for the midnight to 7 A.M. shift. Compute the percent defective. Record the information on the quality control chart on the following page.

   ITEM:
   GLASS GOBLETS #131

TIME:	12	1 A.M.	2 A.M.	3 A.M.	4 A.M.	5 A.M.	6 A.M.	7 A.M.
Number Checked	40	25	40	20	25	40	40	20
Number Defective	2	1	1	1	2	2	1	2
Percent Defective	___	___	___	___	___	___	___	___

3.

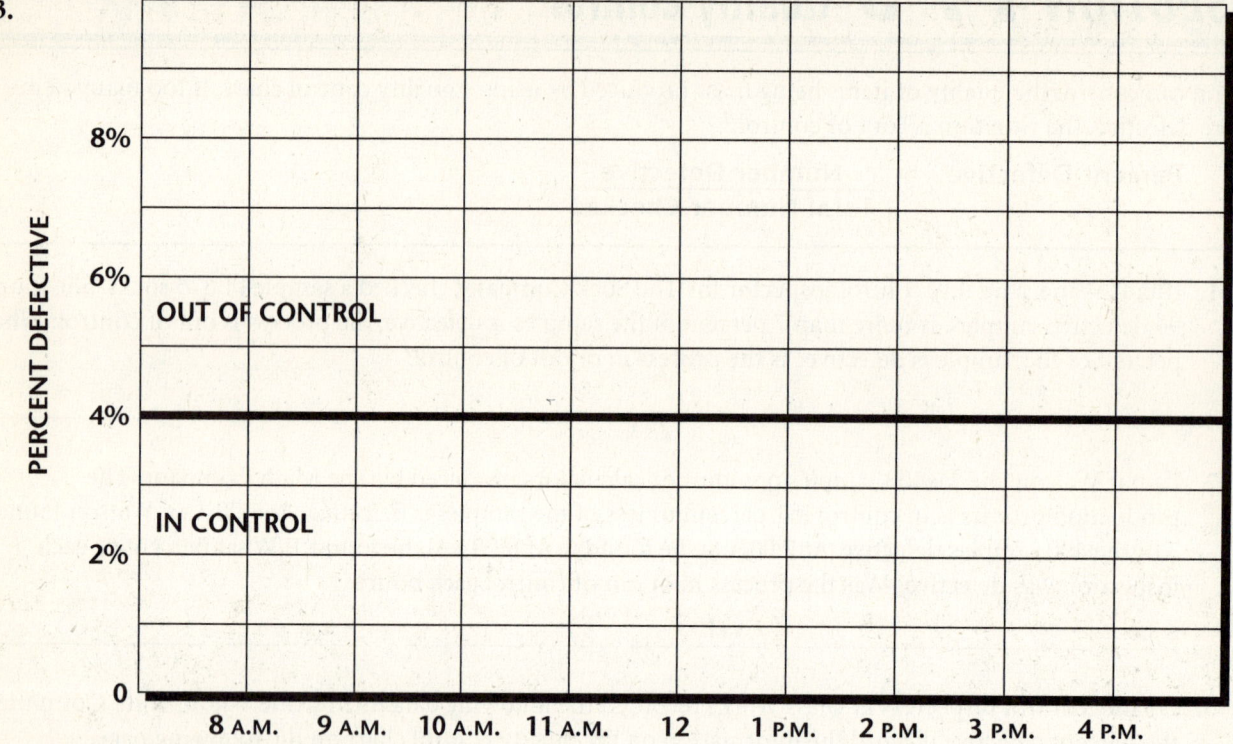

PERCENT DEFECTIVE

8%

6% OUT OF CONTROL

4%

2% IN CONTROL

0

8 A.M. 9 A.M. 10 A.M. 11 A.M. 12 1 P.M. 2 P.M. 3 P.M. 4 P.M.

4.

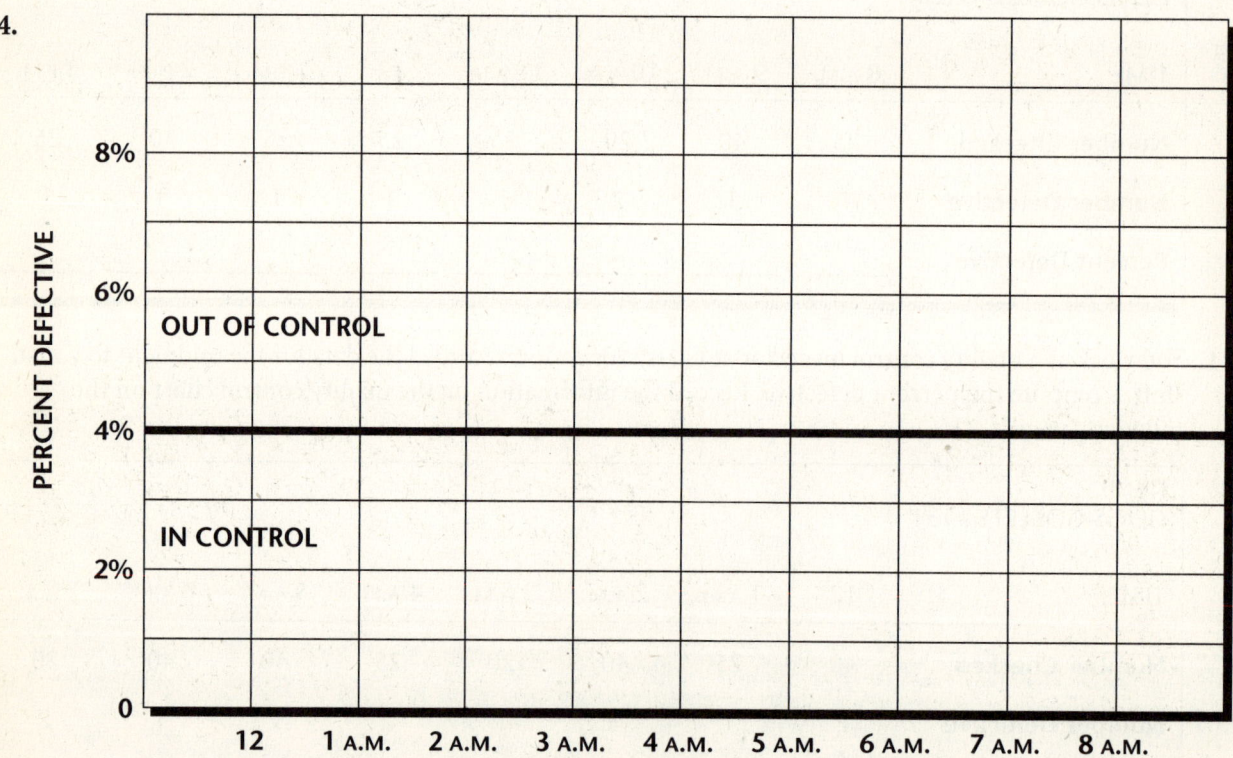

PERCENT DEFECTIVE

8%

6% OUT OF CONTROL

4%

2% IN CONTROL

0

12 1 A.M. 2 A.M. 3 A.M. 4 A.M. 5 A.M. 6 A.M. 7 A.M. 8 A.M.

Student _____ Date _____

Class _____ Instructor _____

SECTIONS 14-4, 14-5 — Time-Study—Number of Units and Percent of Time

A time-study is used to determine the average time an employee takes to do a job or a variety of related activities. You can use the results of a time-study to plan how much time to allow for certain activities.

Number of Units = $\dfrac{\text{Actual Time Worked}}{\text{Average Time Required per Unit}}$

Percent of Time Spent on Activity = $\dfrac{\text{Time Spent on Activity}}{\text{Total Time}}$

1. Eric Williams prepared a time-study to determine the average time required to process passengers through U.S. Customs at the new international airport.

    a. Calculate the average time required for each task in the table, to the nearest hundredth of a minute.

    b. How many passengers can be inspected by 1 customs officer in 1 hour?

    c. What percent of the inspector's time is spent on completing required documents/forms?

OBSERVATION IN MINUTES

Task	#1	#2	#3	#4	#5	Average Time
Open suitcases	0.6	0.7	0.5	0.6	0.3	_____
Inspect suitcases	3.0	2.9	3.2	3.9	2.8	_____
Close suitcases	1.1	1.0	1.1	1.3	1.2	_____
Complete required documents/forms	2.5	2.1	3.1	3.1	2.5	_____
					Total	_____

2. The Forest Valley Schools prepared a time-study of Rosella Ruiz's job as manager of a computer lab. What is the average time required for each task? What is the average number of hours worked each day? With respect to the average time, what percent of Ruiz's time is spent on each task?

TIME IN HOURS

Task	M	T	W	TH	F	Average Time	Percent of Total
Helping students	4.0	3.9	4.1	4.6	4.0	_____	_____
Helping faculty	0.2	0.5	0.6	0.5	0.6	_____	_____
Group instruction	2.1	2.1	3.2	2.0	1.3	_____	_____
Paperwork	0.7	0.7	0.6	0.3	0.9	_____	_____
Reviewing programs	0.6	1.2	0.9	0.8	2.0	_____	_____
Coffee breaks	0.3	0.1	0.4	0.3	0.6	_____	_____
Totals	_____	_____	_____	_____	_____		

Student _____ Date _____

Class _____ Instructor _____

SECTION 14-6 Packaging

Putting your merchandise in containers for shipment is the last step in the production process. The size of the package depends on the size of the finished product.

Dimensions: Length, Width, Height

1. Barry Thigpen packs books for a local warehouse. A new edition of the Standard Dictionary is ready to be boxed for shipment. Each dictionary measures 11 inches by 8.5 inches by 4 inches. The carton for these dictionaries is ⅛-inch thick. What are the dimensions of the carton if the dictionaries are laid flat, in 2 stacks of 6 dictionaries?

   What are the dimensions of the cartons if the dictionaries are arranged in only 1 stack of 8 dictionaries, also laid flat?

2. Action batteries are packed 36 to a carton. The carton is made of 0.6-centimeter-thick cardboard. There are no spaces. One battery measures 10 centimeters by 25 centimeters by 43 centimeters. What are the dimensions of the cartons if the batteries are arranged in 4 stacks of 9 batteries (stacked 1 by 4)?

   What are the dimensions of the cartons if the batteries are arranged in 2 stacks of 18 batteries?

3. You work for a crystal factory. A client ordered 240 goblets. You have to pack each goblet in individual boxes before placing them in containers for shipment. The measurement of each box is 3 inches by 6 inches by 6 inches. The shipping container is made of cardboard ⅛-inch thick. No spacers are needed since each individual box is filled with foam shock absorbers. What are the dimensions of the containers if the boxes are arranged in 3 stacks of 10 boxes?

   How many containers would you need altogether for this shipment?

4. A popular beverage is sold in bottles with dimensions as shown. The bottles are packed 12 to a case for shipping (2 rows with 6 bottles per row). The case is made of ⅛-inch thick corrugated cardboard with ¹⁄₁₆-inch cardboard dividers. An extra layer of ⅛-inch cardboard is placed on the bottom for a cushion. What are the dimensions of the case?

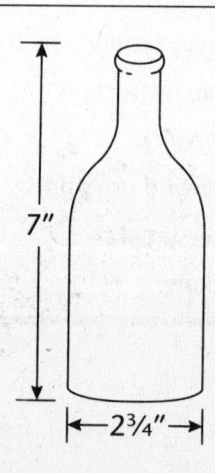

   7″   2¾″

Student _____ Date _____

Class _____ Instructor _____

Spreadsheet Application: Production

DIRECTIONS:

1. Insert your *Student Activity Workbook CD* into your computer and click on Chapter 14 Production. The spreadsheet will appear.
2. Key your name into cell B1. Key the date into cell G1.
3. Key the information below into the appropriate cells. The spreadsheet application will compute the data for you automatically.
4. Save your spreadsheet as Ch14XXX, where XXX are your initials.
5. Print out your spreadsheet.

Input the information below to find the percent defective and whether the process is in or out of control. Then answer the questions that follow.

	Number Tested	Number Defective	Percent Defective	Defective Parts Allowable (%)	Process In or Out of Control
1.	200	6		4%	
2.	300	15		5%	
3.	60	3		4%	
4.	50	2		5%	
5.	200	7		3%	
6.	425	9		2%	
7.	150	9		5%	
8.	250	19		6%	
9.	500	3		1%	
10.	125	4		3%	

11.

Day	Number Tested	Number Defective	Percent Defective	Defective Parts Allowable (%)	Process In or Out of Control
Mon.	180	9		4%	
Tue.	180	7		4%	
Wed.	190	7		4%	
Thur.	180	6		4%	
Fri.	180	8		4%	

12. In #1, what percent of defective parts were found? _____
13. In #1, is the process in or out of control? _____
14. In #2, what percent of defective parts were found? _____
15. In #2, is the process in or out of control? _____

Spreadsheet Application: Production
(CONTINUED)

16. In #3, what percent of defective parts were found? _____

17. In #3, is the process in or out of control? _____

18. What would happen in a situation such as that described in #3?
    _____

19. In #4, what percent of defective parts were found? _____

20. In #4, is the process in or out of control? _____

21. What would happen in a situation such as that described in #4?
    _____

22. In #5, what percent of defective parts were found? _____

23. In #5, is the process in or out of control? _____

24. In #6, is the process in or out of control? _____

25. In #7, is the process in or out of control? _____

26. In #8, is the process in or out of control? _____

27. In #9, is the process in or out of control? _____

28. In #10, is the process in or out of control? _____

29. Describe what happened with respect to being in or out of control in #11.
    _____

30. With respect to being in or out of control, why is what happened in #11 not uncommon?
    _____

Simulation: Manufacturing

You are the production manager of R&J Plastics. The company added 2 new items to the production line 6 months ago. Large sheets of plastic are used to make these items. You have been asked to update the prime cost of manufacturing the new product. Round your answers to the nearest cent.

Item	Cost per Sheet	Pieces per Sheet	Direct Material Cost per Piece	Labor Cost per Hour	Pieces per Hour	Direct Labor Cost per Piece	Prime Cost
Picture Frame	$118.50	150		$10.80	257		
Paper Clip Dispenser	145.96	178		11.60	504		

R&J has decided to raise the selling price. How many units of each product must be made and sold to cover the production expenses at the new price?

	Picture Frame	Paper Clip Dispenser
Total Fixed Costs	$15,467.00	$13,612.00
Variable Cost per Unit	1.41	1.09
New Selling Price per Unit	2.92	2.05
Break-Even Point in Units		

An inspection of 200 units of each item is made every 2 hours. If more than 6 percent of the sample is defective, the process is out of control. Complete the quality control chart for the picture frame.

Time	Number Checked	Number Defective	Percent Defective	In or Out of Control
8:00 A.M.	200	10		
10:00 A.M.	200	13		
12 NOON	200	15		

FINAL THOUGHT

What are the two ways R&J can keep its production costs down?

_____
_____
_____
_____
_____
_____
_____

| Student | | Date | |
| Class | | Instructor | |

Career Path: Cartoonist

Cartoon art appears in many kinds of publications. Cartoons are used in magazines, greeting cards, catalogues, trade journals, and even textbooks. Art, especially art with a punch line, can serve to illustrate a point being made on a page of text, bringing at the same time a laugh and a fresh perspective.

The artists who produce these works are usually freelancers who work from offices or from studios in their homes. The cartoonists who produce the comic strips you read in the daily newspaper work on a strict schedule, or deadline. Their strips are sold and distributed by a syndicate to the newspapers in which they appear. The strip you read in yesterday's paper was probably submitted to the syndicate a few weeks ago.

The typical strip appears in a 3- or 4-panel format 6 times per week, and in a larger format on Sundays. This means the artists and writers must turn out a fixed number of products, each one the same size as the last, every week, every month, every year. That's 313 daily strips and 52 Sundays, all submitted to the syndicate on a deadline. As one professional cartoonist has said, "It's like working in a factory, but it's a factory with really nice chairs."

How does mathematics apply to cartooning? Many of the principles of geometry are used in drawing, with angles and lines and curves all contributing to the creation of perspective and proportion. An artist producing on a deadline must also be able to estimate the time necessary to finish a given number of panels. If you know it takes an average of x hours to produce a single day's strip, and there are 12 dailies to do for the next batch to be submitted to the syndicate, you can calculate the number of work hours needed and distribute them over the number of days between the present and the deadline.

Check Your Understanding

Bud Griese produces the successful comic strip *Order of the Squid*. It appears in 287 newspapers Monday through Saturday and in 161 of them on Sunday. Griese and his syndicate receive $10 per week from each paper for the weekday strip, split 50/50 between him and the syndicate. They receive $20 per week per paper for the Sunday strip.

1. What is Griese's monthly income from the Sunday strips? (Assume 4 Sundays per month.)

2. What does the syndicate earn each year from the *Order of the Squid* daily strips?

3. If each daily strip is 4 panels long and each Sunday strip is 8 panels, how many panels does Greise draw every year? (Assume 52 Sundays per year.) Show your calculations.

4. If *Order of the Squid* did not appear on Sundays, by what percentage would Greise's annual income drop?

5. It takes Greise an average of 3½ hours to draw and ink one daily strip. How many 8-hour workdays per year does he spend producing the dailies?

Student _____ Date _____

Class _____ Instructor _____

SECTIONS 15-1, 15-2 — Trade Discounts and Complement Method

When you buy from a supplier, you usually get a trade discount. This is a markdown from the list price, or catalogue price, and represents a savings for your business. The net price is the amount you actually pay for the item. You can find the net price directly by using the complement of the trade-discount rate.

Trade Discount = Trade − Discount Rate × List Price

Net Price = List Price − Trade Discount

Net Price = Complement of Trade-Discount Rate × List Price

Find the trade discount and net price in the table below. Round answers to the nearest cent.

	List Price	Trade-Discount Rate	Trade Discount	Net Price
1.	$ 810.00	25%		
2.	61.40	40%		
3.	510.00	20%		
4.	310.61	15%		
5.	24.68	3%		
6.	6,318.14	25¼%		

Use the complement method.

7. Craig Milton needs to order paper for his company. In the catalogue a 20 percent trade discount is offered for a price of $481.60. What is the net price? _____

8. The Bennetts own a craft store. They place an order for 100% wool yarn with a supplier who offers them a 17 percent trade-discount rate. The total list price for the yarn is $1,016.14. How much do the Bennetts have to pay? _____

9. Your garage is ordering radial tires for compact cars. National Tire offers you a 15 percent trade-discount rate for 56 tires. The list price for these tires is $61.60 each. Tire Trade has the same tire with a 12.5 percent trade-discount rate. The list price for Tire Trade is $59.90 each. Which supplier is less expensive? _____

How much would you save if you purchased the 56 tires from the less expensive supplier? _____

10. Joe's Hardware receives a 25 percent trade discount from the wholesale hardware supply house. Find the total list price and net price on this invoice.

	Number	Description	Unit Quantity	Unit List Price	Total List Price	Net Price
a.	WH147X	Claw hammer	10	$12.98		
b.	WH271B	Paper towel holder	20	13.95		
c.	WH718XM	Metric bits	15	11.98		
d.	WH791ZE	English bits	25	11.98		
e.	WH918D	Drill	7	36.98		

Student _____ Date _____

Class _____ Instructor _____

SECTION 15-3 Trade-Discount Rate

If you know the list price and the net price of certain items, you can calculate the trade-discount rate.

Trade Discount = List Price − Net Price

$$\text{Trade-Discount Rate} = \frac{\text{Trade Discount}}{\text{List Price}}$$

Complete the table. Round answers to the nearest tenth of a percent.

	List Price	Net Price	Trade Discount	Trade-Discount Rate
1.	$ 210.00	$ 187.95		
2.	21.90	18.62		
3.	18,241.00	14,592.80		
4.	164.00	136.94		
5.	500.00	300.00		
6.	8,143.25	5,252.40		

7. Renee Oswald ordered 10-speed bicycles for her store. The list price was $310 each. She paid $271.25 each. What was the trade-discount rate? _____

8. Michael Riley purchased 12 black walnut tables for his furniture store. The list price for the tables was $2,410 each. Riley paid $2,120.80. What was the trade-discount rate? _____

9. The Valley School ordered new textbooks for the clerical recordkeeping class. The publisher's list price for the total was $1,425. The school paid $1,111.50. How much of a trade-discount rate was offered to the school? _____

10. The Light Company is offering a trade discount to its clients if they purchase 10 or more floor lamps. The manufacturer's list price is $136.98 per lamp. The Light Company is selling them for $104.10 each. How much is the discount? What is the trade-discount rate? _____

11. You are the purchasing agent for a major engineering firm. You have just ordered 30 new computer components. The manufacturer's list price is $791.60 each. You negotiated a net price of $587.76 each. How much of a trade-discount rate did you negotiate? _____

12. If you divide the net price by the list price and take the complement of your answer, you will have the trade-discount rate. Try this by completing the table below.

	List	Net	Net ÷ List	Trade-Discount Rate
a.	$ 90.00	$ 62.55		
b.	164.80	137.61		
c.	294.12	229.42		

108 Mathematics with Business Applications ♦ Section 15-3   Copyright © Glencoe/McGraw-Hill

Student _____ Date _____

Class _____ Instructor _____

SECTIONS 15-4, 15-5 Chain Discounts and Complement Method

Chain discounts are offered to encourage you to place a larger order. A chain discount is a series of individual discounts. Complements may be used to find the net price directly or the single equivalent discount (SED).

Net-Price Rate = Product of Complements of Chain Discount Rates

Net Price = Net-Price Rate × List Price

SED = Complement of Net-Price Rate

Discount = SED × List Price

Fill in the table below. Round answers to the nearest cent.

	List Price	Chain Discount	First Discount	First Net Price	Second Discount	Second Net Price
1.	$1,200.42	16% less 5%				
2.	116.81	30% less 5%				
3.	8,492.80	20% less 7%				
4.	312.90	12% less 8%				

5. Furniture Center offers trade discounts and additional discounts to encourage large orders. What is the net price per item if each invoice total is high enough to get the additional discount?

	Item	List	Quantity	Trade Discount	Additional Discount	Net Price
a.	Oak table	$365.74	15	15%	8%	
b.	Brass bed	749.80	7	22%	4%	
c.	Sofa	514.60	10	18%	5%	

6. Find the net price and SED (nearest tenth percent) for each of these auto parts.

	Part Number	Suggested List Price	Chain Discounts	Net Price	SED
a.	XL461	$ 68.40	30% less 10% less 25%		
b.	ZW912	116.80	30% less 15% less 10%		
c.	RL912	391.96	20% less 20% less 5%		
d.	TK618	8.41	25% less 35% less 10%		

Student _____ Date _____

Class _____ Instructor _____

SECTIONS 15-6, 15-7   Cash Discounts—Ordinary Dating and EOM Dating

If you pay your invoice within a specified number of days, the supplier may offer you a cash discount based on the net price. You then pay the cash price. In ordinary dating, the discount term is from the date of the invoice. In EOM dating, the discount term is from the end of the month.

Cash Discount = Net Price × Cash-Discount Rate

Cash Price = Net Price − Cash Discount

1. The net price of goods from Tree Store to the Smith-Jones law office was $325.09 for indoor plants. The invoice was paid in 7 days. The terms on the invoice were 2/10, net/30. What was the cash discount? What was the cash price?

2. Green Farms sells fresh produce to local markets. It offers a 4/5, n/10 discount to all its clients. Georgie's Market just placed an order for assorted vegetables. The net price was $816.12. How much can Green Farms expect to receive if Georgie's Market paid one day after the date on the invoice?

3. An invoice from Overhead Doors to The Lumber Company had a net price of $12,162.04. The terms were 2/10 EOM. The invoice was dated April 20 and was paid May 9. What was the cash price?

4. An invoice from Standard Goods to Wholesale Grocers carried a net price of $9,618.40. The terms were 5/10 EOM. The invoice was dated August 20 and was paid September 12.

   a. What was the cash price?

   b. What did it cost Wholesale Grocers to pay late?

5. Bob's Department Store received this invoice from the Shoe Gallery.

Date 3/20	Invoice # 81624	Account # 84 102	Store # 126	Terms 1/20 EOM	Vendor # 212
Customer Order #	**Quantity**	**Unit Price**		**Amount**	
812	15	$58.98		_____	
916	10	102.00		_____	
981	25	76.40		_____	
			Total	_____	

   a. Fill in the amount column in the table.

   b. What is the last date that Bob's can take the cash discount?

   c. What is the cash price of the invoice if paid by 4/8?

110   Mathematics with Business Applications ♦ Sections 15-6, 15-7   Copyright © Glencoe/McGraw-Hill

Student _____ Date _____

Class _____ Instructor _____

Spreadsheet Application: Purchasing

DIRECTIONS:

1. Insert your *Student Activity Workbook CD* into your computer and click on Chapter 15 Purchasing. The spreadsheet will appear.
2. Key your name into cell B1. Key the date into cell G1.
3. Key the information below into the appropriate cells. The spreadsheet application will compute the data for you automatically.
4. Save your spreadsheet as Ch15XXX, where XXX are your initials.
5. Print out your spreadsheet.

Input the information below to find the net price and the cash price. Look at the date paid and determine if the cash discount percent should be entered. Then answer the questions that follow.

	List Price	Chain Price	Net Price	Term	Date of Invoice	Date Paid	% Off	Cash Price
1.	$ 500	30%, 20%, 10%		2/10, n/30	Jan. 23	Jan. 30		
2.	460	25%, 20%		net 30	Apr. 14	May 11		
3.	3,820	15%		3/15, n/30	Nov. 11	Nov. 25		
4.	987	20%, 10%, 5%		2/10 EOM	Feb. 3	Mar. 9		
5.	987	25%, 10%		2/10, n/30	Feb. 3	Mar. 1		
6.	4,750	30%, 10%		8/20, n/50	June 13	July 1		
7.	4,750	38%		3/10, n/30	Mar. 23	Apr. 7		
8.	500	10%, 20%, 30%		3/15 EOM	May 21	June 3		
9.	8,259	12.5%, 20%, 50%		2/30, n/60	Aug. 23	Sep. 23		
10.	8,259	65%		2/30, n/60	Sep. 23	Oct. 23		

11. What is the net price in #1? _____
12. What is the cash price in #1? _____
13. What is the cash price in #2? _____
14. What is the net price in #3? _____
15. What is the cash price in #3? _____
16. What is the net price in #4? _____
17. What is the net price in #5? _____
18. In #4 and #5, the list price is the same and the sum of the chain discounts is the same. Why isn't the net price the same?

_____

_____

Spreadsheet Application: Purchasing
(CONTINUED)

19. When is the net price due in #7 if the cash discount is not taken? _____

20. What is the net price in #8? _____

21. What is the net price in #9? _____

22. What is the net price in #10? _____

23. What is the cash price in #9? _____

24. What is the cash price in #10? _____

25. Both #9 and #10 have the same cash discount terms and similar dates but different cash prices. Why is this?

_____
_____
_____
_____
_____
_____
_____
_____

Student _____ Date _____

Class _____ Instructor _____

SECTIONS 16-1, 16-2 Markup and Markup Rate

When your business sells an item, it is at a higher price than the original cost of the item. The difference is the markup. This markup can also be expressed as a percent of the selling price.

Markup = Selling Price − Cost

Markup Rate = $\dfrac{\text{Markup}}{\text{Selling Price}}$

Fill in the table below. Round answers to the nearest cent or tenth of a percent.

	Item	Cost	Selling Price	Markup	Markup Rate on Selling Price
1.	Spray paint, 12 oz	$3.16	$ 4.99		
2.	Linseed oil, 1 gal	9.29	12.49		
3.	Trim brush, 1.5 in	1.94	2.49		
4.	Drop cloth, 9 in x 12 in	4.70	5.99		
5.	Paint remover, 1 qt	2.39	4.19		

6. The Cycle Shop buys new bicycles for $289.40. The bikes are sold for $482.00. What is the markup? _____

   What is the markup rate as a percent of the selling price? _____

7. Home Improvement Center buys kerosene heaters for $119.68 each. The retail selling price is $209.99. What is the markup? _____

   What is the rate of markup? _____

8. American Merchandising distributes pharmaceutical products to various retail outlets. It costs each outlet $2.04 for a 4-ounce bottle of cough syrup. Determine the markup and markup rate as a percent of the selling price for each outlet.

Outlet	Selling Price	Markup	Markup Rate
Foodland Pharmacy	$3.86		
Mainline Pharmacy	2.99		
Phil's Pharmacy	2.89		

9. You work at your local supermarket in the dairy department. Compute the cost per item, markup, and markup rate as a percent of the selling price.

Item	Case Cost	Number per Case	Cost per Item	Selling Price	Markup	Markup Rate
Cream cheese	$28.36	36		$1.39		
Colby cheese, 12 oz	36.85	24		3.49		
American cheese, 1 lb	25.70	24		1.94		

Copyright © Glencoe/McGraw-Hill   MATHEMATICS with Business Applications ◆ Sections 16-1, 16-2   113

SECTIONS 16-3, 16-4 Net Profit and Net-Profit Rate

The markup on the products you sell must cover your overhead or operating expenses. When the markup of an item is greater than its overhead expenses, you make a profit on the item.

Net Profit = Markup − Overhead

Net Profit Rate = Net Profit / Selling Price

Complete the table. Round answers to the nearest cent or tenth of a percent.

	Item	Selling Price	Cost	Markup	Overhead	Net Profit	Net-Profit Rate
1.	Batteries	$ 2.99	$ 1.69		$ 0.15		
2.	Stereo	1,090.00	745.50		131.50		
3.	Paper towels	0.89	0.29		0.03		
4.	Dress	189.99	58.60		21.40		

5. PhotoMart purchased some film for $1.29 per roll. The selling price is $4.12 per roll. The operating expenses are estimated to be 25 percent of the selling price. What is the net profit per roll?

   What is the net-profit rate per roll?

6. The Linen Store is selling white cotton sheet sets for $35.96. An estimated 25 percent is included in the selling price to cover overhead. The original cost of the bedspread was $18.40. What is the net profit for each bedspread?

   What is the net-profit rate?

7. The Sneaker Shoe Shop buys basketball shoes at $54.66 per pair. The selling price is $114.70. Approximately 20 percent of the selling price pays for overhead. What is the net profit per pair?

   What is the net-profit rate?

8. You manage a local convenience store. Included in the selling price of every item sold is 15 percent to pay for overhead. What is the net profit for each item listed below? What is the net-profit rate? Round answers to the nearest cent or nearest percent.

Item	Selling Price	Cost	Markup	Overhead	Net Profit	Net-Profit Rate
Rice	$1.49	$0.76				
Carrots	1.19	0.88				
Coffee	4.99	3.89				
Potato chips	2.19	1.49				

SECTION 16-5 Determining Selling Price—Markup Based on Selling Price

You can use the cost of an item and the desired markup rate based on selling price to figure the best selling price of your products.

Selling Price = $\dfrac{\text{Cost}}{\text{Complement of Markup Rate}}$

Complete the table. Round answers to the nearest cent.

	Cost	Markup Rate (selling price base)	Complement of Markup Rate	Selling Price
1.	$ 75.49	42%		
2.	12.00	50%		
3.	172.00	12%		
4.	89.61	30%		
5.	42.99	60%		
6.	18.50	28%		

7. Plush Furniture sells imported rosewood dining tables. The cost of one model is $762.87. Plush Furniture sells the table at a 15 percent markup based on the selling price. What is the selling price?

8. Universal Sounds sells compact discs at a markup that is 42 percent of the selling price. If one CD costs Universal $5.90 to purchase, what is the selling price?

9. Binder's Bookstore purchases paperback novels from Parker Publishing. The markup for each book is 56 percent of its selling price. Binder's pays $2.90 for each book. What is the selling price?

10. Your company designs small silk-screen prints for $35 each. You sell them to a chain department store at a 25 percent markup based on selling price. It sells the screens to the consumers at a 40 percent markup based on selling price. What is the selling price of one screen to the department store?

    What is the selling price of one print to the consumer?

11. It costs your company $8.89 to manufacture a steering component for a car. You sell the component to a distributor for $10.99. The distributor sells the component to auto parts stores at a 21 percent markup based on selling price. Auto parts stores sell the components to consumers at a 60 percent markup based on selling price. What is the selling price to the consumer?

SECTIONS 16-6, 16-7
Markup Rate Based on Cost and Determining Selling Price— Markup Based on Cost

You can figure out the markup rate by comparing the markup to the original cost of the merchandise. You can use the cost of an item and the desired markup rate based on cost to figure the selling price of the item.

Markup Rate = Markup ÷ Cost

Markup = Markup Rate × Cost

Selling Price = Cost + Markup

Fill in the table. Round answers to the nearest cent.

	Item	Cost	Selling Price	Markup	Markup Rate Based on Cost
1.	Spray paint, 14 oz	$ 3.98	$ 6.99		
2.	Linseed oil, 1.5 gal	12.40	21.19		
3.	Trim brush, 1.75 in	1.01	1.59		

4. Jane Freem buys jeans for a department store. She pays $21.26 per pair. The store sells each pair for $42.50. What is the markup rate based on cost to the nearest tenth percent? _____

5. Happy Home Store buys towels from the manufacturer for $38.16 a dozen. The towels are sold at $9.59 per towel. What is the markup rate based on cost for one towel to the nearest tenth percent? _____

   What is the markup for each towel? _____

6. Carmen Diaz is the chairperson of a charity fund-raising activity. A national direct-sales fund-raising company supplied her with this order form for stationery items. She orders the items at the fund-raiser price. The charity sells the items at a markup rate of 80 percent of cost. Overhead is 7 percent of the selling price.

   a. Find the selling price for each item.

   b. Find the net profit for each item.

Order Code	Number of Items	Page	Catalog Price	Quantity Price	Fund-Raiser Price	Total Amount
80	20	36	$1.54 ea.	$1.18 ea.	$0.91 ea.	
81	16	9	3.13 ea.	2.41 ea.	1.85 ea.	
82	50	48	2.47 ea.	1.90 ea.	1.46 ea.	
83	26	31	1.45 ea.	1.12 ea.	0.86 ea.	
84	31	19	2.13 ea.	1.64 ea.	1.26 ea.	

	80	81	82	83	84
a. Total Selling Price	_____	_____	_____	_____	_____
b. Net Profit	_____	_____	_____	_____	_____

SECTION 16-8 Markdown

When you reduce the selling price of an item, the reduction is called a markdown. The markdown rate is expressed as a percent of the regular selling price of the item.

Markdown = Regular Selling Price − Sale Price

Markdown Rate = Markdown / Regular Selling Price

1. A department store carried this ad. What is the percent markdown?

   _____

   Save 5.00
   11.99 Reg. 16.99
   Men's, Boys' & Youths' Nylon Joggers

2. The Lamp Shop has lamps on sale as shown. Determine the markdown and percent markdown for each item.

   _____ _____ _____
   _____ _____ _____

Large selection of lamps		
REG.		SALE
74.99	Bisque table lamp	50.00
69.99	Pharmacy floor lamp	41.99
49.99	Downbridge floor lamp	29.99

3. World Travel Luggage Store put this ad in the paper. Compute the percent markdown for each item.

   _____ _____ _____
   _____ _____ _____

Rugged luggage		
Was 35.00	tote	24.50
Was 75.00	21-in. carry-on	56.25
Was 95.00	24-in. Pullman	71.25
Was 105.00	26-in. Pullman	84.00
Was 140.00	garment bag	119.00

4. The Sunday newspaper carried an advertisement for All Oak Furniture indicating a savings of $65 on a bookcase. The sale price was $314.99. What was the percent markdown? _____

5. Dottie Hanlen works for Delta Grocery Store. She usually works in stock, but because of a shortage of help she has been asked to price some packages of frozen foods. This pricing guide is the only information she has.

   Hanlen has been asked to mark down the regular selling price of each item 25 percent for a storewide promotion. What is the regular selling price and the sale price of each package?

Description	Case Cost	Packages per Case	Markup Rate Based on Selling Price	Regular Selling Price	Sale Price
Butter top dinner rolls	$9.48	12	25%	_____	_____
Crescent dinner rolls	7.44	12	29%	_____	_____
Banana bread	11.76	12	30%	_____	_____
Apricot nut bread	13.41	9	29%	_____	_____
Oatmeal nut bread	10.08	12	28%	_____	_____
Cranberry nut muffins	10.56	8	30%	_____	_____

Student _____   Date _____
Class _____   Instructor _____

Spreadsheet Application: Sales

DIRECTIONS:

1. Insert your *Student Activity Workbook CD* into your computer and click on Chapter 16 Sales. The spreadsheet will appear.
2. Key your name into cell B1. Key the date into cell G1.
3. Key the information below into the appropriate cells. The spreadsheet application will compute the data for you automatically.
4. Save your spreadsheet as Ch16XXX, where XXX are your initials.
5. Print out your spreadsheet.

Input the information below to find the cost (C), markup (MU), selling price (SP), percent markup based on cost (%M/C), percent markup based on selling price (%M/S), markdown (MD), percent markdown (%MD), or sale price (SALE). Then answer the questions that follow.

	Cost	Markup	Selling Price	%M/C	%M/S	%MD	MD	Sale
1.	$ 45.00			70%	20%			
2.	124.50			50%	30%			
3.	35.75			210%	25%			
4.	124.50			100%	50%			
5.			$ 79.49	300%	25%			
6.			145.78	85%			$ 72.89	
7.			12.96		25%		1.30	
8.			4,985.00		12%		997.00	
9.		$ 35.80		200%				$ 42.96
10.		437.76			40%			711.36

11. What is the selling price in #1? _____
12. What is the sale price in #1? _____
13. What is the selling price in #2? _____
14. What is the selling price in #4? _____
15. The cost is the same in #2 and #4, but the markup in #2 is 50 percent of the selling price and in #4 it is 100 percent of the cost; yet the selling price is the same in #2 and #4. Why?

_____

16. How can the markup possibly be more than 100 percent in #3?

_____

17. What is the markdown in #3? _____

Spreadsheet Application: Sales
(CONTINUED)

18. What is the sale price in #3? _____

19. What is the cost in #5? _____

20. What is the percent markup based on selling price in #5? _____

21. In #5, the cost as a percent of the selling price and the percent markdown are the same (25 percent). The sale price equals the cost ($19.87). Will this always happen? Why or why not?

_____

_____

22. What is the markup in #6? _____

23. What is the percent markdown in #6? _____

24. What is the sale price in #6? _____

25. What is the cost in #7? _____

26. What is the sale price in #7? _____

27. Why are there percents over 100 percent for the percent markup based on cost, but none over 100 percent for the percent markup based on selling price?

_____

_____

28. What is the percent markup based on cost in #8? _____

29. What is the selling price in #9? _____

30. What is the cost in #10? _____

31. What is the percent markdown in #10? _____

Student _____ Date _____

Class _____ Instructor _____

Career Path: Teacher

From a student's point of view, a teacher is just a classroom instructor. His or her job is to come to class, deliver a lecture, hand out tests, and give out grades. Forty-five minutes of talking and you're done. Then, when the school year is over, there's a three-month vacation!

Teachers see it a bit differently. One who spends his or her working life in the classroom has a host of other responsibilities. A teacher is also a writer (of tests and classroom materials), a psychologist, a disciplinarian, a referee, a confidant, a counselor, a grader, and maybe even an interior decorator (especially in preschool and the elementary grades). Add to this mix the extra jobs a teacher can take on—drama director, coach, bandleader—and you've got a very busy schedule. As for those three months off, many teachers take another job for the summer just to make ends meet.

It's not just the math teachers who use math skills on the job. Every teacher of every subject uses math, especially when it's grading time. A teacher must calculate the grades on each test—for instance, add up the number of points taken off for wrong answers, subtract it from the number of points possible, and divide the remainder by the number of points possible.

Check Your Understanding

Use the table below to solve the problems. Show your calculations.

Item	His Cost	Markup
Overhead projector	$147.50	40%
Case of construction paper	32.00	25%
Guillotine paper trimmer	67.90	15%

1. School starts in two weeks, and Mrs. Perry is buying the supplies she needs for her fourth-grade classroom. She needs to buy the items listed above, and her principal has authorized her purchase from petty cash. She can save the school some money, because her brother runs an office supply store and will give her the price he pays before markup. What is the ordinary selling price of the overhead projector?

   _____

2. What would the case of construction paper and the paper trimmer cost a customer buying them together at the retail price?

   _____

3. The principal is also ordering copier paper for the copy machine in the office. The selling price is $3.99 per ream. The office orders 500 reams in the first shipment. The markup is one dollar per ream, and the overhead is 20 percent of the selling price. What is the vendor's net profit on the 500 reams of paper?

   _____
   _____
   _____

4. What is the net profit rate for the paper?

   _____
   _____

SECTION 17-1 Opinion Surveys

An opinion survey can help you determine how well a product is received by the buying public.

Rate of Particular Response = $\dfrac{\text{Number of Times Particular Response Occurs}}{\text{Total Number of Responses}}$

1. The registrar's office conducted a survey on the Student Orientation and Registration (SOAR) program. The 380 students surveyed were asked to choose one answer for this question, "If you consult a counselor, why?" The choices and number of responses received for each were:

   95 _____ a. Counselor understands situation. _____

   146 _____ b. Counselor helps me with registration. _____

   82 _____ c. Counselor gives good advice. _____

   57 _____ d. Counselor makes referrals for special situations. _____

   What is the rate of each response?

2. Your company has decided to conduct an opinion survey to find out how well the new Kitten cat food is selling. The responses were as follows:

Response	Under 20	20–30	31–40	Over 40
Definitely	78	44	84	117
Probably	64	40	61	94
Possibly	51	28	74	106
No	28	18	38	75

   (Age Group column headers)

   a. What percentage of consumers in the 20–30 group gave a "No" response, compared to the total number of responses? _____

   b. What percentage of total responses was in the 31-40 age group? _____

   c. What percentage of consumers gave a "Definitely" or "Probably" response? _____

   d. If 70 percent of "Probably" and "Definitely" responses is needed for the new product to succeed, what do you advise Kitten cat food to do?

   _____

   _____

3. Park's Auto Service conducted a mail survey of all its clients. It asked the question, "If you do *not* bring your car back to our garage for service, why?" The responses were as follows:

   _____ 22 Moved away from vicinity   _____ 39 Crowded service area

   _____ 17 Disliked quality of service   _____ 63 Location not convenient

   _____ 34 Service charges too high   _____ 15 Some other reason

   What is the percent of each response?

Student _____ Date _____

Class _____ Instructor _____

SECTIONS 17-2, 17-3 Sales Potential and Market Share

The sales potential of a product is determined by the percent of potential purchasers, the market size, and the individual rate of purchase. The market share is the ratio of the total product sales to the total market sales.

Annual Sales Potential = Estimated Market Size × Individual Rate of Purchase × Percent of Potential Purchasers

Market Share = $\dfrac{\text{Total Product Sales}}{\text{Total Market Sales}}$

Fill in the table. Round answers to the nearest tenth of a percent.

	New Product	Number in Sample	Number of Potential Purchasers	Percent of Potential Purchasers	Estimated Market Size	Individual Rate of Purchase per Year	Annual Sales Potential
1.	Deodorant	2,000	725		20,000,000	12 sticks	
2.	Computer game	5,000	270		12,000,000	2 games	
3.	Fertilizer	16,000	782		62,000,000	4 bags	
4.	Motor oil	8,400	265		120,000	6 quarts	

5. Modern Optical Company is marketing a new style of soft contact lens. Out of a sample of 7,000 users, 342 preferred the new style. There is an estimated total market of 875,000 users of contact lenses in the city. The average consumer purchases one pair per year. What is the sales potential for the new lenses for one year? _____

6. Electronic Air is a new room air freshener. Out of 7,500 people surveyed, 82 said they would buy it. The estimated market size is 4,500,000. The company estimates that each person would buy 4 per year. What is the annual sales potential? _____

7. Enviro, Inc., sells approximately 3,516,000 beetle traps per year. The insect control industry sells approximately 9,000,000 beetle traps per year. What is Enviro's market share? _____

8. Your company sells pen and pencil sets. Last year sales totaled $74.3 million. The total market sales were $3.6 billion. What was your company's market share? _____

Student _____ Date _____

Class _____ Instructor _____

SECTIONS 17-4, 17-5 Sales Projections and the Factor Method

Sales projections give you an estimate of the dollar volume or unit sales that might occur in the future. You can either use a graph or use the factor method to project sales.

Projected Sales = Projected Market Sales × Market-Share Factor

1. Season's Stores sells storm windows. Its sales history shows:

Year	1985	1990	1995	2000
Sales (in millions)	$2.4	$2.1	$3.2	$3.9

   Construct a line graph to project sales for 2005 and 2010.

   2005: _____

   2010: _____

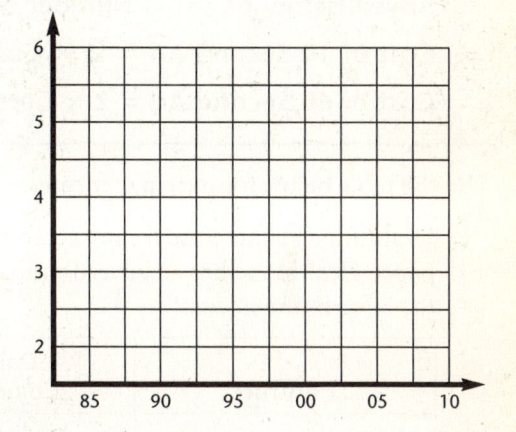

2. At present, Sky Line Foods supplies 46 percent of the meals for ATB flights, earning an income of $6,375,000 per year. The estimated ATB market total for next year is $18,043,533. What is Sky Line Foods' sales projection for next year? Round answer to the nearest dollar. _____

3. You are the Registrar at City College. Your enrollment history for evening courses shows:

Semester	2001–02	2002–03	2003–04	2004–05
Fall	1,350	1,390	1,420	1,450
Spring	1,400	1,420	1,470	1,510

   Construct a line graph to project enrollment for both the fall and spring semesters for 2005-06 and 2006-07.

   2005-06 Fall: _____

   2005-06 Spring: _____

   2006-07 Fall: _____

   2006-07 Spring: _____

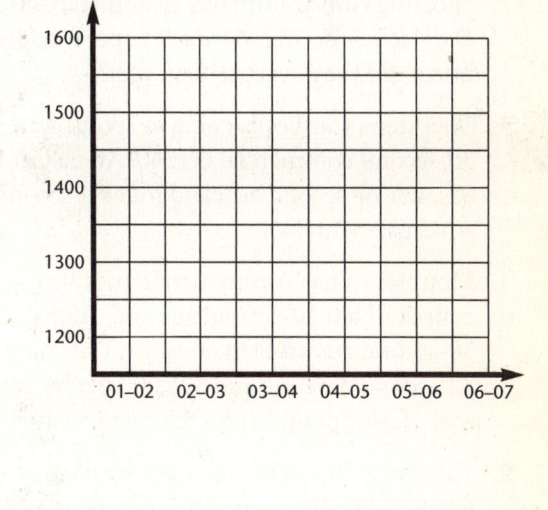

4. Uptown Cleaners has traditionally had 21 percent of the cleaning business in the village of Westerville. The total estimated cleaning business in Westerville for this year is $3,060,000. Next year Westerville anticipates a 10 percent increase in the cleaning business.

   a. What business can Uptown Cleaning estimate for this year? _____

   b. What business can Uptown Cleaning project for next year? _____

SECTIONS 17-6, 17-7 Newspaper and Television Advertising Costs

When you place a newspaper advertisement for your product or service, the cost is determined by the space it occupies and the rate charged per line. When you advertise your product or service on television, the cost depends on the time of day, the program ratings, and the length of the commercial. Television commercials are generally 10, 30, and 60 seconds long.

Advertisement Cost = Number of Column Inches × Rate per Column Inch

Cost of 10-Second Ad = ½ × Cost of 30-Second Ad

Cost of 60 Second Ad = 2 × Cost of 30-Second Ad

Use the table below for newspaper rates.

1. HealthLine has an annual contract for 100 inches of advertising in the Sunday paper. HealthLine has an advertisement equivalent to 16 inches. How much does the advertisement cost?

Contract	Daily per Column Inch	Sunday per Column Inch
No contract	$45.54	$55.28
50 inches	34.90	42.80
100 inches	33.90	41.72

2. Sporting Goods store has an annual contract for 50 inches of advertising in the *Daily Reporter.* In Saturday's paper it had an advertisement of 5 inches. How much did the advertisement cost?

3. The Arena Car Lot is going to sponsor arena sporting events. The rate per 30-second commercial is $540. Arena Car Lot contracts for twenty 30-second ads, ten 10-second ads, and four 60-second ads. What is the total cost for these advertisements?

4. Mountain View Amusement Park's spring television advertising campaign will consist of ten 10-second ads and twenty 30-second ads on daytime TV, and five 30-second ads and ten 60-second ads on prime-time TV. The rates are $6,000 per 30-second daytime and $25,000 per 30-second prime-time ad. What is the total cost of Mountain View's television campaign?

5. You are in charge of publicity for the town fair next month. You are debating whether to have an advertisement equivalent to 31 column inches in the evening paper or a 26-column-inch advertisement in the Sunday paper, or two 30-second TV ads. A 30-second TV ad costs $550. If money is a problem, which one would you select?

   What is the cost of each?

SECTION 17-8 Pricing

The net income of your sales should be high enough to cover all your expenses and still allow you to make a profit.

Possible Net Profit = [Selling Price per Unit − Total Cost per Unit] × Estimated Unit Sales

Round answers to the nearest cent.

1. Complete the table below for Bloomers, a local florist. Which selling price yields the greatest possible profit?

   How many units of the arrangement should be produced to maximum profits?

Selling Price per Unit	Estimated Unit Sales	Total Fixed Costs	Fixed Costs per Unit	Variable Costs per Unit	Total Cost per Unit	Possible Net Profit
$39.99	7,000	$120,000		$5.25		
49.99	5,000	120,000		5.25		
44.99	6,500	120,000		5.25		

2. You are the production manager for Marlin Company. You have assembled these figures about your new Allbright flashlight. Which selling price yields the greatest possible profit?

   How many units of the flashlight should be produced?

Selling Price per Unit	Estimated Unit Sales	Total Fixed Costs	Fixed Costs per Unit	Variable Costs per Unit	Total Cost per Unit	Possible Net Profit
$10.99	15,000	$45,000		$1.35		
9.99	20,000	45,000		1.35		
8.99	25,000	45,000		1.35		

3. CompAdd produces microcircuitry boards. It has a fixed overhead of $240,000. The variable cost to produce each board is $0.15. CompAdd assumes it could sell 1,000,000 boards at $0.55 each; 1,500,000 boards at $0.48 each; and 2,000,000 boards at $0.35 each. What selling price will maximize CompAdd's profits?

Selling Price per Unit	Estimated Unit Sales	Total Fixed Costs	Fixed Costs per Unit	Variable Costs per Unit	Total Cost per Unit	Possible Net Profit
$0.55						
0.48						
0.35						

Student _____ Date _____

Class _____ Instructor _____

Spreadsheet Application: Sales Analysis

DIRECTIONS:

1. Insert your *Student Activity Workbook CD* into your computer and click on Chapter 17 Marketing. The spreadsheet will appear.
2. Key your name into cell B1. Key the date into cell G1.
3. Key the information below into the appropriate cells. The spreadsheet application will compute the data for you automatically.
4. Save your spreadsheet as Ch17XXX, where XXX are your initials.
5. Print out your spreadsheet.

Input the information below to find the fixed costs per unit, total costs per unit, break-even point, gross sales, and possible net profit.

1.

Selling Price per Unit	Estimated Unit Sales	Fixed Costs	Fixed Costs per Unit	Variable Costs per Unit	Total Costs per Unit	Break-Even Point	Gross Sales	Possible Net Profit
$10.95	13,000	$85,000		$3.00				
11.45	12,000	85,000		3.00				
11.95	11,000	85,000		3.00				
12.45	10,000	85,000		3.00				
12.95	9,000	85,000		3.00				
13.45	8,000	85,000		3.00				

2. Electronic Calculator Company developed these figures for its new Model 101 calculator. Compute the fixed costs and variable costs and complete the table below.

Fixed costs:			
Rent	Taxes	Marketing	Manufacturing
$10,200	$62,400	$75,000	$81,500

Variable costs:				
Supplies	Labor	Utilities	Packaging	Shipping
$1.50	$3.75	$0.85	$0.25	$0.25

Selling Price per Unit	Estimated Unit Sales	Fixed Costs	Fixed Costs per Unit	Variable Costs per Unit	Total Costs per Unit	Break-Even Point	Gross Sales	Possible Net Profit
$10.95	900,000							
11.45	800,000							
11.95	750,000							
12.45	400,000							
12.95	200,000							
13.45	150,000							

Student _____   Date _____

Class _____   Instructor _____

Simulation: Major Foods Corporation

Major Foods Corporation is a major breakfast cereal distributor. Before Major Foods markets a new product, thorough research is conducted to determine the product's market potential. As the vice president for marketing, your job is to incorporate all the research data.

Three months ago Major Foods sent 8,000 sample size packages of the new oat cereal CIRCLES to randomly selected customers in the Northeastern region. Enclosed with the sample was a brief questionnaire. Here are the tabulated responses.

Response	Age Group Under 18	18 to 40	40 or Over	Total
Excellent	170	2,480	1,700	4,350
Good	70	377	675	1,122
Fair	25	108	449	582
Dislike	5	45	72	122
Total	270	3,010	2,896	6,176

Round to the nearest tenth of a percent.

Response	Total Number of Responses	Rate of Response	Rate of Response Under 18	18 to 40	40 or Over
Excellent					
Good					
Fair					
Dislike					

Of the 8,000 samples mailed, what percent responded?	
What is the overall rate of "excellent" responses for all age groups?	
Of the three different age groups, which one shows the highest percent of "excellent" responses?	
What percent of this age group rated the cereal as "excellent?"	
How many responses were received from this age group in total?	
This age group is what percent of all the responses received?	

Consumers who rate CIRCLES as "excellent" are most likely to purchase the product. Use the age group with the highest percent of "excellent" responses as a guide to project your estimated annual sales potential.

Total Responses of Age Group	Estimated Number of Purchases	Estimated Percent of Purchasers	Estimated Market	Estimated Individual Rate of Purchase/Year	Estimated Annual Sales Potential
			100,000	20 boxes	

Copyright © Glencoe/McGraw-Hill

Student _____ Date _____

Class _____ Instructor _____

Simulation: Major Foods Corporation
(CONTINUED)

Assume that the estimated percent of purchasers and the individual rate of purchase per year are national trends. Calculate the estimated national sales potential.

Region	Estimated Market Size	Estimated Annual Sales
Northeast	100,000	
South	90,000	
Midwest	110,000	
Pacific Coast	120,000	
Northwest	45,000	
Southwest	80,000	
Alaska	20,000	
Estimated National Annual Sales		

The cost of manufacturing one box of CIRCLES is estimated to be $1.12, which includes direct materials and direct labor. Your overhead is 45 percent of the selling price. Complete the table to calculate the estimated net profit per box.

Estimated Manufacturing Cost/Box	Overhead Rate	Overhead	Markup	Selling Price	Estimated Net Profit/Box
$1.12	45%		$1.87		

Complete the table to project the estimated national net profit and net-profit rate for CIRCLES.

Estimated Net Profit/Box	Estimated National Annual Sales	Estimated National Net Profit	Estimated National Net-Profit Rate

FINAL THOUGHT

Name some media Major Foods can use to promote the new product.

_____
_____
_____
_____
_____
_____

Student _____ Date _____

Class _____ Instructor _____

SECTION 18-1 Storage Space

The area occupied by your products and materials until you are ready to use them is known as the storage space. The size of the storage space depends on the size of the item stored.

Storage Space = Volume per Item × Number of Items

Find the volume and storage space in the table below.

	Item	Carton Dimensions Length	Width	Height	Volume	Number of Items	Storage Space
1.	Cooler	22½ in	16 in	12 in		35	
2.	Jelly jars (12)	10 in	12 in	5¾ in		200	
3.	Office desk	4 ft	2.5 ft	3 ft		30	
4.	Automobile	11 ft	6½ ft	7⅜ ft		12	

5. A popcorn popper is packed in a carton with dimensions of 13½ inches by 13½ inches by 12 inches. How much storage space is required for 40 cartons? _____

6. A CD storage file is packaged in a box measuring 14 inches by 9 inches by 8 inches. Computer Stores received a shipment of 12 files. How much storage space is needed? _____

7. Country Kitchen canning jars are packed 12 to a carton. The carton measures 12½ inches by 9½ inches by 4¼ inches. Walton Food Market has placed an order for 1,440 jars. How much storage space is required? _____

Will a warehouse bin measuring 12 feet by 8 feet by 7 feet hold the jars? _____

8. Teletronics manufactures cellular telephone equipment. Each mobile telephone is packaged in a box that is 20 cm by 15 cm by 12 cm. The boxed telephones are then packed 12 to a carton, arranged as shown. Each carton is made of cardboard that is 0.5 cm thick. There are no spacers in the carton. How many cubic meters of space does Teletronics need to store 120 cellular telephones?

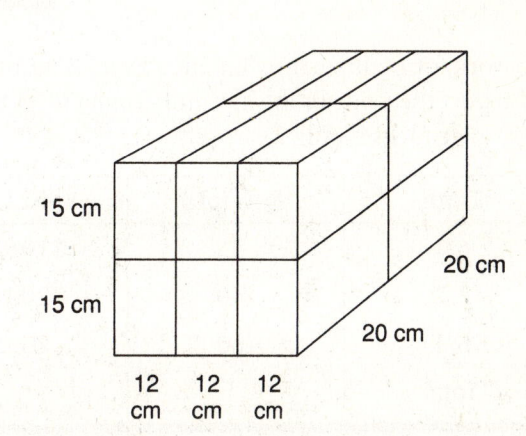

_____

Student _____ Date _____

Class _____ Instructor _____

SECTIONS 18-2, 18-3 Taking an Inventory and Valuing an Inventory

To keep a record of all incoming receipts and outgoing items, you can use an inventory to show what is in stock. You can use the average-cost method to calculate the value of your inventory.

Inventory = Previous Inventory + Receipts − Issues

Inventory Value = Average Cost per Unit × Number on Hand

1. On July 2 Coulder Rugs had 320 rugs measuring 10 feet by 12 feet in its warehouse. By the end of the month it had shipped out 102 rugs and received 35. How many rugs were on hand on August 1? _____

2. Lowland Drugstore had 125 boxes of Axin ointment. It issued 20 boxes through sales and sent 52 to a branch store. It did not receive any shipment that week. How many boxes of the ointment remain in stock? _____

3. Furniture Company orders 50 more model ST-403 end tables. Complete the inventory card below.

Date	Model	Issued	Received	In Stock
9/15	ST-403	6	10	5
9/28	ST-403	—	50	

4. Records for Ingman's Deli show this opening balance and these receipts for Ingman's Mustard from January through July. At the end of July, 52 jars were on hand.

   What is the value of the inventory?

   _____

Date	Receipts	Unit Cost	Total Cost
3/1	60	$1.42	$85.20
4/4	20	1.60	32.00
5/1	40	1.55	62.00
6/2	50	1.45	72.50
7/1	55	1.40	77.00
Total			

5. You work for Maintenance Supplies. Every 3 months you have to update the inventory and report the value of the inventory on hand. What is the value of the inventory for the storage racks if only 15 are left? _____

Date	Receipts	Unit Cost	Total Cost
6/1	35	$196.80	_____
7/1	40	204.90	_____
8/1	60	209.10	_____
Total	_____		_____

Student   Date

Class   Instructor

SECTION 18-4 Carrying an Inventory

The cost of keeping a sufficient inventory of goods includes taxes, insurance, storage fees, and handling charges. The annual cost of carrying an inventory is often expressed as a percent of the inventory value.

Annual Cost of Carrying Inventory = Percent × Inventory Value

1. The Camera Shop maintains a $120,000 inventory. The cost of keeping the merchandise in stock is 22 percent of the value of the inventory. What is the annual cost of carrying the inventory?

2. Pine Furniture maintains a $246,250 inventory. The cost of keeping a sufficient inventory is 32 percent of the value of the inventory. What is the annual cost of carrying the inventory?

3. OPER Laboratories estimates the cost of carrying its inventory of chemicals and apparatus to be 40 percent of the value of the merchandise. How much does it cost OPER annually to carry a $424,000 inventory?

4. Warehouse Food Market estimates the annual cost of carrying its inventory at 25 percent of the value of the inventory as shown. What is the annual cost of each expense if the inventory is valued at $410,000?

Type of Expense	Percent	Annual Cost
Spoilage and physical deterioration	7.0%	
Interest	5.9%	
Handling	3.0%	
Storage facilities	1.8%	
Transportation	1.2%	
Taxes	0.6%	
Insurance	5.5%	
Total		

5. The rate of inventory turnover is the number of times during one year that a business sells its average inventory. Generally, the higher the rate of inventory turnover, the better the business is doing.

Inventory Turnover = Total Cost of Goods Sold / Average Value of Inventory

Calculate the inventory turnover for each business.

	Name	Total Cost of Goods Sold During Year	Average Value of Inventory During Year	Inventory Turnover
a.	Liberty Fabrics	$141,060	$ 31,040	
b.	Loren Industrial	410,295	156,000	
c.	General Stores	930,000	310,000	

Student _____ Date _____

Class _____ Instructor _____

SECTION 18-5 Door-to-Door Transportation Cost

There are a number of ways goods can be shipped, including ship, barge, rail, truck, airplane, or a combination of these. Many shippers transport items door-to-door. The cost of shipping depends on the weight of the item and the speed of the delivery. Next-day delivery costs more than second-day delivery.

Shipping Costs = Weight × Base Rate

Door-to-Door Shipping Cost per 100 Pounds for Selected Routes

City	City	Guaranteed First Arrival	Guaranteed Overnight	Standard Overnight	Guaranteed Second Day	Standard Second Day	BAX Saver
Atlanta	Dallas/Ft. Worth	$196.00	$186.25	$145.30	$127.75	$108.25	$46.00
Boston	Miami	196.00	186.25	145.30	127.75	108.25	46.00
Chicago	Detroit	164.00	155.85	121.62	106.95	90.65	46.00
Denver	Sacramento	196.00	186.25	145.30	127.75	108.25	46.00
Los Angeles	Asheville, N.C.	266.00	252.75	197.10	173.25	146.75	62.00
Tampa	Syracuse	196.00	186.25	145.30	127.75	108.25	46.00

Find the shipping costs for Problems 1–4. Round to the nearest cent.

	From	To	Arrival	Weight in Pounds	Cost/100	Costs
1.	Atlanta	Dallas	Standard Overnight	320		
2.	Boston	Miami	Standard Second Day	8,520		
3.	Denver	Sacramento	Guaranteed Overnight	487		
4.	Tampa	Syracuse	BAX Saver	6,500		

5. A crate of figurines that weighs 240 pounds is shipped from Atlanta to Dallas. The shipment needs to arrive Guaranteed Overnight. What is the total cost of shipping the figurines? _____

6. Auto Plastics is shipping 650 pounds of plastic trim items from Chicago to Detroit. The shipment needs to arrive Guaranteed First Arrival. What is the total cost of shipping the plastic trim items? _____

7. Norberg's Greenhouse in Tampa is shipping strawberries to a customer in Syracuse. The strawberries weigh 400 pounds. The shipment is sent Guaranteed First Arrival. What is the shipping cost? _____

8. A crate of musical instruments that weighs 470 pounds is shipped from Denver to Sacramento. The shipment needs to arrive Guaranteed First Arrival. What is the total shipping cost? _____

9. Jarvis Fullerton is the shipping clerk for Rowley, Inc. He needs to ship 135 pounds of software manuals from the printers in Los Angeles to a trainer in Asheville, North Carolina. Find the difference in shipping cost between the Standard Second Day rate and the Guaranteed First Arrival rate. _____

Student Date

Class Instructor

SECTION 18-6 Transportation by Truck

Your business may use expedited door-to-door direct trucking to ship products. Expedited shipping means that your shipment is given exclusive use of a driver and a truck to move your shipment as quickly as possible. The basic rates differ according to the weight of the goods and the distance that they are being shipped. Most companies charge only for the actual distance the goods are being shipped.

Shipping Cost = Number of Miles × Rate per Mile

Expedited Door-to-Door Motor Freight Rates in Cost per Mile

Weight Group (pounds)	Minimum Charge	1–99 Miles	100–199 Miles	200–299 Miles	300 plus Miles
0–500	$118.00	$1.74	$1.59	$1.52	$1.48
501–3,000	127.00	1.95	1.83	1.75	1.73
3,001–5,000	169.00	2.97	2.73	2.42	2.21
5,001–13,000	225.00	3.32	2.99	2.69	2.39
13,001–45,000	500.00	5.25	4.30	3.64	3.11

Accessorial Charges

Collect-on-Delivery - COD Fee	$ 50.00
Detention Time after 2 Hours - Hourly Rate	50.00
Hand Loading or Unloading - Hourly Rate	35.00
Hazardous Materials	75.00
Lift Gate Required on Truck	125.00
Pickup/Delivery - Holidays	125.00
Second Person - Hourly Rate	50.00
Stop Off - Multiple Drops - Each	50.00

Find the shipping cost and the total cost in the table below.

		Weight	Miles	Basic Rate	Shipping Cost	COD	Lift Gate	Stop Off	Total Cost
1.	Clothing	900	240	$1.75		$50	$125	No	
2.	Detergent	8,000	159	2.99		No	$125	No	
3.	Textbooks	1,563	325	1.73		$50	$125	$50	
4.	Auto Parts	42,632	98	5.25		No	No	No	
5.	Paper	2,654	99	1.95		$50	$125	$150	
6.	GPS Instruments	1,897	560	1.73		$50	No	No	

7. The Radiator Company is shipping 4,400 pounds of radiators via Motor Express. Motor Express will pick up the radiators at the manufacturing plant and deliver them to a truck parts distributor. The total distance is 257 miles. What is the shipping cost? _____

8. A shipment of dairy products is sent by truck from Green Bay, Wisconsin, to St. Louis, Missouri. The distance is 445 miles. The dairy products weigh 5,967 pounds. What is the shipping cost? _____

9. A 44,452-pound shipment of lumber is transported from Marquette, Michigan, to a distribution center in Findlay, Ohio. The distance is 493 miles. What is the shipping charge? _____

10. A shipment of jeep spare parts is sent by truck from Toledo, Ohio, to Green Bay, Wisconsin. The distance is 442 miles. The parts weigh 15,447 pounds. A lift gate is required, and the driver was detained 3.5 hours. What is the total shipping cost? _____

Student _____   Date _____

Class _____   Instructor _____

Spreadsheet Application: Warehousing and Distributing

DIRECTIONS:

1. Insert your *Student Activity Workbook CD* into your computer and click on Chapter 18 Warehousing and Distributing. The spreadsheet will appear.
2. Key your name into cell B1. Key the date into cell G1.
3. Key the information below into the appropriate cells. The spreadsheet application will compute the data for you automatically.
4. Save your spreadsheet as Ch18XXX, where XXX are your initials.
5. Print out your spreadsheet.

Input the information below to find the balance on hand for each date, the total costs, the average cost per unit, and the value of the inventory using the average-cost method. Then answer the questions that follow.

Date	Unit Cost	Receipts (Qty In)	Issues (Qty Out)	Balance on Hand	Total Costs	Average Cost	Inventory Value
01-Oct	$17.45	100					
05-Oct			75				
09-Oct	17.20	80					
12-Oct	17.00	250					
19-Oct			98				
26-Oct			123				
29-Oct	16.50	100					
30-Oct			54				

What is the average cost per unit? _____

What is the inventory value using the average-cost method? _____

1. What is the balance on hand after Oct. 1? _____

2. What is the balance on hand after Oct. 5? _____

3. What is the value of the 80 items received on Oct. 9? _____

4. What is the balance on hand after Oct. 12? _____

5. What is the balance on hand after Oct. 26? _____

6. What is the ending balance on Oct. 30? _____

7. Suppose the unit cost for each receipt (Oct. 1, Oct. 9, Oct. 12, and Oct. 29) equaled $17.00. What would the average cost per unit equal? _____

8. In the situation described in #7, what would be the inventory value using the average-cost method? _____

Spreadsheet Application: Warehousing and Distributing
(CONTINUED)

9. In the given situation, in a declining economy where unit costs are decreasing, would FIFO or LIFO result in the higher valued inventory? Why?

   _____

   _____

   _____

   _____

   _____

10. What is the value of this inventory using FIFO? _____

11. What is the value of this inventory using LIFO? _____

Student _____ Date _____

Class _____ Instructor _____

Career Path: Veterinarian

Every member of the family needs medical attention, and pets are no exception. Animals need treatment for diseases and injuries just as people do. Dogs, cats, rabbits, and ferrets—from time to time they all need examinations, shots, specialized diets, and even prescription drugs. It's the only job in the health care industry in which your patient is likely to lick your hand.

The aspiring veterinarian follows a course of study similar to the one followed by a doctor of human medicine. In the United States, two to four years of college are followed by enrollment in a school of veterinary medicine, for a total of six to eight years of higher education. There are 27 veterinary schools in the country, and admission is competitive. Completion of veterinary school results in the awarding of a Doctor of Veterinary Medicine (DMV) degree.

Many veterinarians work as general practitioners in private practice, either alone or with a small group of veterinarians. Some specialize, limiting their practice to veterinary dermatology, ophthalmology, or radiology. Some work in regulation and food inspection. Others might work for large cattle or poultry companies. Large-animal veterinarians make house calls to take care of farm animals, such as cows, bulls, and horses. Some veterinarians have zoo animals as their patients.

Veterinarians use mathematics in their day-to-day work. For instance, an animal doctor must be able to calculate the dosage of medicine the patient needs based on its body weight, or the precise amount of food needed to help a sick animal lose or gain weight. Since many veterinarians work in private practice, they also have all the responsibilities of a small business involving hours, payroll, taxes, rent, and so on.

Check Your Understanding

For each of the problems below, show your calculations.

1. Dr. Black's veterinary office just got in a shipment of heartworm and flea treatments. Each case measures 14 inches by 8 inches by 6 inches. How many cubic inches of space does Dr. Black need to store 20 cases?

2. How many cubic feet does that equal?

3. Dr. Black's office started the month with 110 units of rabies vaccination on hand. During the next four weeks he used 15, 28, 17, and 24, respectively, and received a shipment of 80 more the third week. How many units were on hand at the end of the month?

4. Dr. Black estimates the cost of carrying his inventory of supplies to be 9 percent of the value of the merchandise. How much does it cost his office annually to carry a $42,925 inventory?

Student _____ Date _____

Class _____ Instructor _____

SECTION 19-1 Building Rental

Your business may rent or lease space in a building on an annual basis. The rent is based on a certain rate per square foot per year. Your total monthly rental charge depends on the number of square feet that your business occupies.

$$\text{Monthly Rental Charge} = \frac{\text{Annual Rate} \times \text{Number of Square Feet}}{12}$$

Find the number of square feet and monthly rental charge in the table below.

	Type of Building	Dimensions	Number of Square Feet	Annual Rate per Square Foot	Monthly Rental Charge
1.	Pharmacy	25 ft by 40 ft		$10.50	
2.	Dry Cleaners	60 ft by 30 ft		6.75	
3.	Gift Shop	35 ft by 25 ft		8.25	

4. The Bargain Barn is considering the rental of additional space at $5.85 per square foot per year. The space Bargain Barn wants to rent measures 150 feet by 150 feet. What monthly rent will Bargain Barn pay for the additional space? _____

5. Brookmans has rented additional mall space to expand its toy operation. The space measures 20 feet by 40 feet and rents for $15.75 per square foot per year. What monthly rent does Brookmans pay for the additional space? _____

6. Tops Sport Shop is opening a store at the Eastland Mall. The rent is $18.95 per square foot per year plus $5\frac{1}{2}$ percent of the store's gross sales. The area of the store is 2,500 square feet. If Tops has $526,000 in gross sales the first year, what monthly rent will it pay? _____

7. Sutter's Fireplace is opening a branch store. The area of the new store is 4,100 square feet. The annual rental charge is $9.65 per square foot per year, plus $4\frac{1}{2}$ percent of Sutter's gross sales for the first year. If Sutter's has $510,000 gross sales the first year, what monthly rent will it pay? _____

8. Your company is looking for a new warehouse to store the incoming inventory. At the Hurt Building, you can rent a space measuring 2,500 square feet for $9.75 per square foot per year. At the Maine Plaza Warehouse, you can rent a space measuring 3,000 square feet for $9.25 per square foot per year. How much is the monthly rental charge at the Hurt Building? _____

How much is the monthly rental charge at the Maine Plaza Warehouse? _____

Which location has a lower rental charge? _____

SECTION 19-2 Maintenance and Improvement

The total cost of keeping your building clean and maintained generally includes a labor charge and a materials charge. The labor charge is usually calculated on an hourly basis for each service person involved.

Total Charge = Labor Charge + Materials Charge

1. Liverpool Real Estate is moving to another location in the city. It takes 4 people 7 hours to complete the move. The hourly rate per person is $9.25 in addition to a packing charge of $54.50. What is the total moving charge?

2. Piazza Pizza Shop hired 3 carpenters to remodel its store. The carpenters each earn $27.90 per hour. Each carpenter worked 16½ hours. The materials charge was $3,160.40. What was the total charge?

3. Long Haul Moving Company needs to reseal its asphalt driveway. It will take 2 workers 6 hours to complete the job using 50 gallons of tar sealer. The charge for the tar sealer is $10.59 per 5-gallon can. The labor cost is $11.25 per person per hour. What is the total cost?

4. The management of Lake View Condominiums hired 2 people to repaint the main lobby. It took the painters 7 hours to finish the job. They used 4 gallons of paint at $17.99 per gallon. The painters charged $14.50 per hour per person for labor. How much did the management pay to repaint the lobby?

5. Your company had minor flood damage. You received these estimates for repair from Faber Repair.

	Hourly Rate	Time Required	Materials Charge
Electrician	$24.10	5 hr	$112.90
Carpenter	21.60	8½ hr	268.40
Plumber	19.25	10 hr	54.60

You must decide if you should hire these 3 people or have your own employees do the job. Materials would cost you $450.10. It would take 4 of your employees 8 hours each to complete the job. Three of your employees earn $8.95 per hour, and one earns $10.95 per hour. If price is the only consideration, which would be less expensive?

6. Shelby Cleaning Service is retained to clean the Harris Law Clinic daily from Monday through Saturday. Two Shelby Cleaning employees work at the clinic for 2 hours each day. One employee is paid $8.15 per hour while the other employee is paid $9.50 per hour. Both earn double time on Saturday. Shelby Cleaning adds 55 percent of the cost of labor to cover overhead. What does Shelby Cleaning Service charge the Harris Law Clinic per week?

SECTION 19-3 Equipment Rental

The cost of renting equipment or furniture for your business is based on the rental charge and the length of time for which you rent them. In some states, a sales tax is added to the rental cost.

Total Rental Cost = (Rental Charge × Time) + Usage Tax

Find the monthly charge and rental cost in the table below.

	Item	List Price	Monthly Charge	Monthly Charge	Time	Usage Tax	Rental Cost
1.	DVD Player	$1,490	10% of list		12 months	6%	
2.	TV/VCR	1,010	6% of list		9 months	5½%	
3.	Computer	5,940	10% of list		3 months	8%	
4.	Wheelchair	495	12% of list		6 months	6.5%	

5. Wendell Construction plans to rent a 300 horsepower bulldozer for 3 months. The rental charge is $41,872.50 per month, without an operator. The delivery and pickup charge amounts to $290 (no tax on delivery and pickup). If the list price for this bulldozer is $465,250, what percent is the monthly rental charge? _____

   What is the total rental charge at the end of 3 months, if a 6½ percent usage tax is applied? _____

6. The Hunter and Williams law office is renting additional furniture for the next 8 months. The rental charge is 10 percent of the list price of the new furniture per month. There is a 6½ percent state tax. They plan to rent:

Item	List Price
4 leather arm chairs	$ 510 each
1 oak conference table to sit 15 people	9,680 each
1 copy/fax/scanner machine	899 each

   What is the total rental charge? _____

7. Your office needs to rent 3 office trailers for 4 months. You received cost information from 2 rental agencies. If price is the only factor, which company should you contact?

   Dena's Rental
   Per month:
   $500 per trailer
   5% insurance charge
   5.5% usage tax
   no transportation charge

   Newman Supply
   Per month:
   $450 per trailer
   no insurance
   6% usage tax
   $25 delivery charge per office trailer

SECTIONS 19-4, 19-5 Utilities Costs—Telephone and Electricity

Your monthly service charge for your telephone service depends on the total minutes per month, the number of phone lines, the type of equipment, and the type of service that you have. A federal excise tax is added to your telephone charge each month. The monthly cost of electricity depends on the demand charge and the energy charge. The fuel adjustment charge may be added by the electric company to help cover the fluctuating cost of generating electricity.

Total Cost for Month = Monthly Service Charge + Cost of Additional Minutes + Cost of Additional Lines + Federal Excise Tax

Total Electricity Cost for Month = Demand Charge + Energy Charge + Fuel Adjustment Charge

---

Use the chart below to solve Problems 1 and 2.

1. Jared's Pharmacy has the $89.99 plan. Jared's has 4 lines and used 1,230 minutes this past month. There is a 5 percent federal excise tax. What is the total cost for the month?

2. Lopez Realty has the $59.99 plan. The realty company has 2 lines and used 650 minutes this past month. There is a 3 percent federal excise tax. What is the total cost for the month?

Monthly Service Charge	Included Minutes	Additional Lines per Month	Additional Airtime per Minute
$ 59.99	up to 500	$19.99	$0.35
89.99	up to 1,000	14.99	0.30
119.99	up to 2,000	9.99	0.25

Refer to the chart below for Problems 3–5.

3. Kilgan's Grocery used 13,000 kilowatt hours of electricity last month. The peak load for the month was 80 kilowatt hours. What is the total cost of electricity for Kilgan's Grocery?

4. P&J Printing used a total of 25,480 kilowatt hours of electricity for the month. The peak load during the month was 135 kilowatts. What is the total cost of electricity for the month?

5. You own the Sunrise Café. Last month you used 9,700 kilowatt hours of electricity with a peak load of 90 kilowatts. In addition to your monthly electricity bill, you have your telephone bill to pay. You are on the $119.99 plan. You have 3 lines and used 1,800 minutes last month. There is a 5 percent federal excise tax.

   a. Calculate last month's telephone cost to the nearest cent.

   b. What was last month's electricity bill?

NORTHWEST POWER

Demand Charge

First 50 kW $6.54/kW
More than 50 kW 5.91/kW

Energy Charge

First 250 kWh $0.1055/kWh
Next 750 kWh 0.0954/kWh
Next 2,000 kWh 0.0644/kWh
Next 2,000 kWh 0.0578/kWh
Next 5,000 kWh 0.0488/kWh
More than 10,000 kWh 0.0455/kWh

Fuel Adjustment $0.0170/kWh

SECTION 19-6 Professional Services

Your business may seek professional advice on a particular problem. Some consultants charge a flat fee; some charge a percent of the cost of the project; and some charge by the hour.

Total Cost = Sum of Consultants' Fees

Find the total fee in the table below.

	Professional Service	Fee Structure	Project Information	Total Fee
1.	Architect	8% of project cost	$925,000	
2.	Real Estate Developer	5.5% of project cost	$510,000	
3.	Contractor	$19.25 per hour	25 hours worked	
4.	Engineer	$54.00 per hour	25 hours worked	

5. Riverview High School hired an in-service training specialist to conduct workshops for all its science teachers. The specialist charged a flat fee of $300 per day. The workshops lasted 2½ days. What was the total cost of the specialist's services?

6. Conner and Helwig, an insurance firm, plans to issue $58,000,000 in bonds to pay for an extensive expansion. One bond broker will sell the bonds for a fee of 2.25 percent of the $58,000,000 face value of the bonds. What will the broker's services cost the firm?

7. Maxwell's, a discount store, wants to change its store's image. It hired Century Interiors to redecorate its store. Century charges $3,500 plus $16.25 per hour for each of the 3 designers assigned to the project. It takes Century designers 38 hours each to complete the design. How much does this project cost Maxwell's in total?

8. Your company has purchased prime real estate in the financial district. You hired an attorney to handle the legal transactions. You were charged $115 per hour plus a $6,500 fee. The attorney devoted 49 hours to the project. How much did your company pay for these legal services?

9. General Hospital hired an industrial engineering firm to conduct a work sampling of the average nurse's day. I.E., Inc., did the work sampling and charged $86.50 per hour. It took I.E. 36 hours to complete the task. What did the work sampling cost General Hospital?

10. Save Rite has installed laser readers at all its checkout stations in all of its 5 stores. Save Rite hired Sheronda Moore to consult on the equipment and its installation. Moore charged 9.5 percent of the total cost. Save Rite hired Don Engel to instruct its employees on the use of the equipment. Engel conducted a 4-hour session at each store. Engel charges $68 per hour. The cost of the equipment and installation totaled $519,480. What was the total cost for professional services?

Student _____ Date _____

Class _____ Instructor _____

Spreadsheet Application: Services

DIRECTIONS:

1. Insert your *Student Activity Workbook CD* into your computer and click on Chapter 19 Services. The spreadsheet will appear.
2. Key your name into cell B1. Key the date into cell G1.
3. Key the information below into the appropriate cells. The spreadsheet application will compute the data for you automatically.
4. Save your spreadsheet as Ch19XXX, where XXX are your initials.
5. Print out your spreadsheet.

Input the information below to find the total square feet, annual rent, monthly rent based on square feet, monthly share of gross sales, and total monthly rent. Then answer the questions that follow.

	Store	Rental Space Dimensions	Total Square Feet	Annual Rent per Sq. Ft.	Annual Rent	Monthly Rent	Plus % of Gross Sales	Annual Gross Sales	Monthly Share Gross Sales	Total Monthly Rent
1.	Video	45' × 60'		$ 7.50			5%	$124,600		
2.	Clothes	90' × 120'		2.75			4%	215,780		
3.	Food	20' × 30'		10.25			0	—	0	
4.	Arcade	60' × 75'		9.80			0	—	0	
5.	Photo	50' × 50'		6.75			3%	156,860		
6.	Shoe	40' × 65'		8.25			2.5%	453,780		
7.	Lunch	35' × 50'		12.50			0	—	0	
8.	Music	50' × 75'		9.50			4.5%	267,750		
9.	Flower	25' × 30'		17.50			2%	98,574		
10.	Deli	35' × 40'		13.60			0	—	0	

11. In #1, what is the monthly rent based on square footage? _____

12. In #1, what is the monthly share of gross sales? _____

13. In #1, what is the total monthly rent? _____

14. In #2, what is the monthly rent based on square footage? _____

15. In #2, what is the monthly share of gross sales? _____

16. In #2, what is the total monthly rent? _____

17. In #1, the rent per square foot per year is almost $5 more than in #2, yet the total monthly rent is less in #1. State two reasons why this is the case.

_____

_____

18. In #3, what is the total monthly rent? _____

142 Spreadsheet Application: Services   Copyright © Glencoe/McGraw-Hill

Student _____ Date _____

Class _____ Instructor _____

Spreadsheet Application: Services
(CONTINUED)

19. In #4, what is the total monthly rent? _____
20. In #5, what is the monthly rent based on square footage? _____
21. In #5, what is the monthly share of gross sales? _____
22. In #5, what is the total monthly rent? _____
23. In #6, what is the annual rent based on square footage? _____
24. In #6, what is the annual share of gross sales? _____
25. In #6, what is the total annual rent? _____
26. In #7, what is the total monthly rent? _____
27. In #8, what is the monthly rent based on square footage? _____
28. In #8, what is the monthly share of gross sales? _____
29. In #8, what is the total monthly rent? _____
30. In #9, what is the total monthly rent? _____
31. In #10, what is the total annual rent? _____
32. In #3, #4, #7, and #10, why does the monthly rent based on square footage equal the total monthly rent?

_____
_____
_____
_____

Copyright © Glencoe/McGraw-Hill

Simulation: The Plaza Five

You are the manager of The Plaza Five, a group of 5 businesses located in the City Squires Shopping Plaza. Complete the table to find the monthly rental charge for each business.

Business	Number of Dimensions	Annual Rate Square Feet	Monthly per Square Foot	Rental Charge
Glamour Boutique	40 ft by 40 ft		$10.50	
Comfort Stores	50 ft by 40 ft		11.20	
Modern Barbers	50 ft by 55 ft		10.75	
Sure-Cut Jewelers	80 ft by 105 ft		11.40	
Quick Stop Grocery	150 ft by 180 ft		9.85	

You will pay for the maintenance and improvement jobs shown below. Complete the table to find the total charge for each job.

Job	Time Required	Number of Employees	Hourly Rate	Labor Charge	Materials Charge	Total Charge
Painting	40 h	4	$18.75		$1,147.50	
Installing Hair Dryers	8 h	4	14.50		924.80	
Carpeting Shoe Store	4½ h	6	10.50		2,745.00	
Installing Security System	12 h	2	15.00		1,245.00	

Complete the table to find the total monthly cost of telephone service for each business shown below. Round to the nearest cent.

Business	Monthly Service Charge	Additional Minutes	Cost per Additional Minute	Cost of All Additional Calls	3% Federal Excise Tax	Total Cost for Month
Glamour Boutique	$119.99	150	$0.25			
Sure-Cut Jewelers	59.99	200	0.35			
Comfort Stores	59.99	0	0.35			
Modern Barbers	89.99	85	0.30			
Quick Stop Grocery	89.99	0	0.30			

What is the total monthly cost of telephone service for Sure-Cut Jewelers when the federal excise tax rate is 2 percent? _____

What is the total monthly cost of telephone service for Comfort Shoes when the federal excise tax rate is 0 percent? _____

Student _____ Date _____

Class _____ Instructor _____

SECTION 20-1 Payroll Register

A payroll register is a record of the gross income, deductions, and net income of your company's employees.

Complete the tables below. Use the Social Security tax rate of 6.2 percent on the first $84,900 earned and Medicare tax rate of 1.45 percent of all earnings. Use the tax tables on pages 178–181 to find the federal income tax (FIT).

1. Donna's Cookie Factory employs 4 people to make deliveries. Donna's pays an hourly rate of $5.50. The only deductions are federal withholding, Social Security, and Medicare. Complete the payroll register for the week.

Employee	Income Tax Information	Hours Worked	Gross Pay	FIT	Soc. Sec.	Medi-care	Total Ded.	Net Pay
Weinberg, S.	S, 1 allowance	40						
Smythe, P.	M, 2 allowances	36						
Penzo, C.	S, 0 allowance	32						
Tao, N.	S, 1 allowance	34						
	Total							

2. Your job is to complete the payroll register for Sport Shoes. A total of 6 salespeople are employed. They are each paid $7.50 per hour. The only deductions are federal withholding, Social Security, Medicare, and a city income tax (CIT) of 0.7 percent of the gross pay.

Employee	Income Tax Information	Hours Worked	Gross Pay	FIT	Soc. Sec.	Medi-care	CIT	Total Ded.	Net Pay
Clark, R.	S, 0 allow.	32							
Griego, R.	M, 3 allow.	40							
Salidar, K.	M, 1 allow.	36							
Nagata, W.	S, 2 allow.	35							
Bichaict, L.	S, 1 allow.	38							
King, J.	M, 2 allow.	32							
	Total	213							

Student _____ Date _____

Class _____ Instructor _____

SECTION 20-2 Business Expenses

Your business must keep accurate records of all its expenses. This information can be used to calculated profit and income tax or to plan future spending. You may calculate the percent of each expense by comparing it to your total expense.

$$\text{Percentage of Total} = \frac{\text{Particular Expense}}{\text{Total Expenses}}$$

1. Holman's Florist and Garden Shop had the following expenses last quarter. Find the total. Find what percentage each expense is of the total.

Item	Amount	Percentage of Total
Payroll	$126,250	_____
Advertising	25,500	_____
Equipment	18,900	_____
Office/garage rental	6,100	_____
Supplies/flowers	110,250	_____
Insurance	8,800	_____
Utilities	6,300	_____
Total	_____	

2. Your business had the following expenses for the last quarter. Find the total. Find what percentage each expense is of the total.

Item	Amount	Percentage of Total
Payroll	$123,000	_____
Advertising	7,000	_____
Raw materials	40,480	_____
Equipment rentals	9,960	_____
Factory rental	9,850	_____
Office rental	2,100	_____
Warehouse rental	1,040	_____
Office supplies	860	_____
Utilities	4,510	_____
Total	_____	

Student _____ Date _____

Class _____ Instructor _____

SECTION 20-3 Apportioning Expenses

Your business may apportion certain expenses among its departments. Often, the amount that each department is charged depends on the space that it occupies.

$$\text{Amount Paid} = \frac{\text{Square Feet Occupied}}{\text{Total Square Footage}} \times \text{Total Expense}$$

1. The Braden Building Corporation apportions the annual cost of utilities among its departments on the basis of space occupied. The total utilities cost for the year was $564,210. The total area of the building is 680,000 square feet. The accounting department occupies an area that is 50 feet by 65 feet. What amount was the accounting department charged for utilities for the year? _____

2. The cost of heating Lental Plastics totaled $58,460 for the winter. Lentel apportions this expense among its departments. If the company occupies a total of 18,900 square feet, how much did the following departments pay for heating?

    Mailroom, 35 feet by 26 feet _____   Accounting, 60 feet by 40 feet _____

3. Your business apportions cost among the departments on the basis of gross sales. The gross sales for last year totaled $4,650,900. Some of the annual expenses were distributed as follows:

Maintenance	Utilities	Security
$5,600	$16,980	$30,600

    The Furniture Department had $490,500 in gross sales last year. How much did it pay for its share of the annual expenses? _____

    The Home Furnishing Department had $812,000 in gross sales last year. How much did it pay for its share of the annual expenses? _____

4. You are the manager for XCEL Development Company that operates the Seasons Shoppers Mall. XCEL apportions the cost of the various items based on the square footage occupied by each store. The utilities cost $90,550, the ads cost $17,600, and the maintenance cost is $154,000. You are to apportion each expense.

Store	Dimensions (in feet)	Square Footage	Utilities	Advertising	Maintenance
Ice Cream Parlor	15 × 20				
Jem's Jewelers	45 × 65				
Jeans Shoppe	40 × 90				
Shoe Barn	30 × 80				
Alley Gifts	30 × 80				
Toy Town	45 × 65				
Kite Corner	15 × 25				
	Total				

Student _____ Date _____

Class _____ Instructor _____

SECTIONS 20-4, 20-5 — Depreciation—Straight-Line Method and Book Value

For tax purposes, the Internal Revenue Service allows you to recognize the depreciation of many of the items that your business owns. The straight-line method is one way to calculate the annual depreciation of an item. The book value is the approximate value of an item after you have owned it for a while.

Annual Depreciation = $\dfrac{\text{Original Cost } - \text{ Salvage Value}}{\text{Estimated Life}}$

Book Value = Original Cost − Accumulated Depreciation

---

1. Use the straight-line method of depreciation to construct depreciation records for a used taxi cab that cost $9,400, has an estimated life of 3 years, and has an estimated salvage value of $1,000.

End of Year	Calculations for Depreciation	Annual Depreciation	Accumulated Depreciation	Book Value
1				
2				
3				

2. Larry Borgen is a computer programmer. He purchased equipment for his department for $13,990. The salvage value of the equipment is estimated to be $725 after 5 years of use. Use the straight-line method to complete the depreciation record.

End of Year	Calculations for Depreciation	Annual Depreciation	Accumulated Depreciation	Book Value
1				
2				
3				
4				
5				

3. Your business is planning to buy a phone mail system. The cost is $15,600. The salvage value is estimated to be $1,200 after 5 years of use. Use the straight-line method to complete the depreciation record.

End of Year	Calculations for Depreciation	Annual Depreciation	Accumulated Depreciation	Book Value
1				
2				
3				
4				
5				

Student Date

Class Instructor

SECTION 20-6 Modified Accelerated Cost Recovery System (MACRS)

The Modified Accelerated Cost Recovery System (MACRS) is another method of computing depreciation.

Annual Depreciation = Fixed Percent × Original Cost

Book Value = Original Cost − Accumulated Depreciation

1. Use the MACRS method to complete the depreciation record for a $90,460 computer. Computers can be depreciated 20 percent the first year, 32 percent the second year, 19.20 percent the third year, 11.52 percent the fourth year, 11.52 percent the fifth year, and 5.76 percent the sixth year.

End of Year	Calculations for Depreciation	Annual Depreciation	Accumulated Depreciation	Book Value
1				
2				
3				
4				
5				
6				

2. Your business purchased 10 new desktop computers and a networking system for a total cost of $32,000. Use the MACRS method to complete the depreciation record for six years. Use the percents in exercise 1.

End of Year	Calculations for Depreciation	Annual Depreciation	Accumulated Depreciation	Book Value
1				
2				
3				
4				
5				
6				

Student _____ Date _____

Class _____ Instructor _____

Spreadsheet Application: Accounting

DIRECTIONS:

1. Insert your *Student Activity Workbook CD* into your computer and click on Chapter 20 Accounting. The spreadsheet will appear.
2. Key your name into cell B1. Key the date into cell G1.
3. Key the information below into the appropriate cells. The spreadsheet application will compute the data for you automatically.
4. Save your spreadsheet as Ch20XXX, where XXX are your initials.
5. Print out your spreadsheet.

Input the information below to compute depreciation using the straight-line method and the modified accelerated cost recovery system (MACRS) method. Then answer the questions that follow.

	Item	Original Cost	Estimated Life	Salvage Value
1.	Delivery Truck	$70,000	5 years	$10,000
2.	Used Taxi	14,500	5 years	2,500
3.	Office Furniture	53,758	5 years	8,758

4. In #1, using the straight-line method:
   a. What is the first year's depreciation? _____
   b. Is it the same each year? _____
   c. What is the book value after the fifth year? _____
   d. Will it always equal the salvage value after the fifth year? _____

5. In #2, using the straight-line method:
   a. What is the annual depreciation? _____
   b. What is the book value after the fifth year? _____

6. In #3, using the straight-line method:
   a. What is the accumulated depreciation after the third year? _____
   b. What is the book value after the fourth year? _____

7. In #1, using the MACRS method:
   a. What is the first year's depreciation? _____
   b. Is it the same each year? _____
   c. What is the book value after the last year? _____
   d. Will it always equal that amount after the fifth year? _____

8. In #2, using the MACRS method:
   a. What is the fourth year's depreciation? _____
   b. What is the book value after the fifth year? _____

9. In #3, using the MACARS method:
   a. What is the accumulated depreciation after the third year? _____
   b. What is the book value after the fourth year? _____

Simulation: Copyfax Center I

You are the manager of Copyfax Center, a small business that does copying, printing, and word processing. Copyfax Center has 3 employees. Here is a chart of the hours they work each day, Monday through Friday.

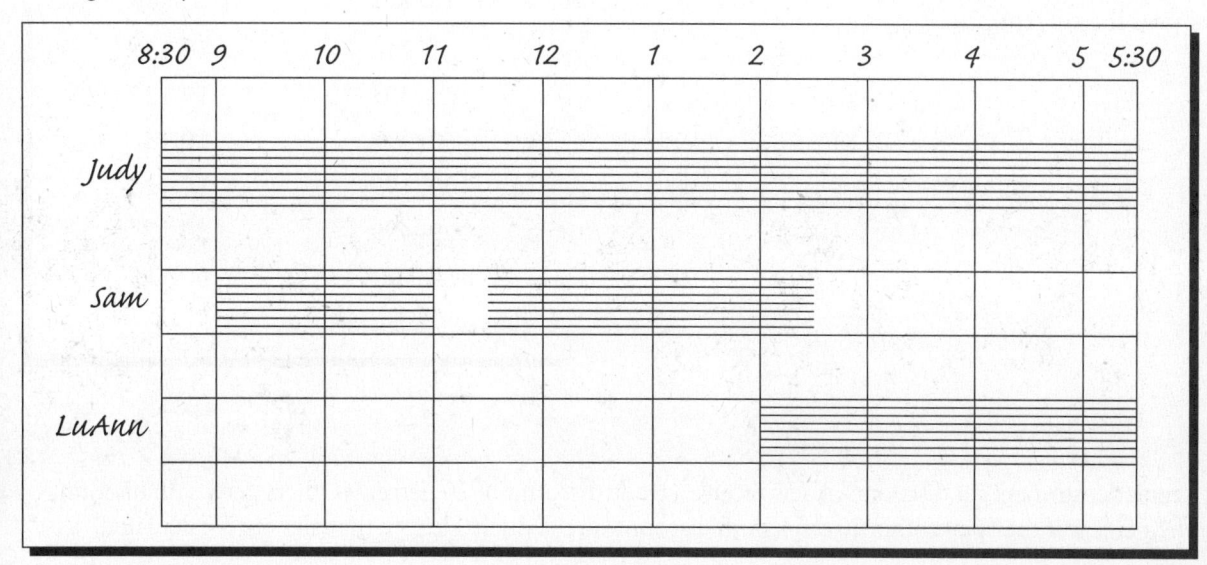

Each week you make up the weekly payroll. Each employee must pay 6.2 percent for Social Security, 1.45 percent for Medicare, and 5 percent for state tax. You pay employees time-and-a-half for overtime.

Use these worksheets to calculate this week's net pay for each employee. Use the tax tables on pages 179–182 to determine the federal income tax (FIT). This week Olson worked 3 hours overtime. Borden and Tate did not work overtime.

	Employee	Hourly Pay	Hours Worked Regular	Hours Worked Overtime	Gross Pay
1.	Judy Olson	$7.60	40.0	3	
2.	Sam Borden	6.50	25.0	0	
3.	LuAnn Tate	7.25	17.5	0	

	Employee	Tax Status	FIT	Soc. Sec.	Medicare	State Tax	Health Ins.	Total Ded.	Net Pay
4.	J. Olson	M, 3 allow.							
5.	S. Borden	S, 2 allow.							
6.	L. Tate	S, 1 allow.							

Simulation: Copyfax Center I
(CONTINUED)

PRICING
The price that Copyfax Center charges for copies depends on the number of copies made. This chart shows the current prices.

Number of Copies	Price per Page*
1–24	$0.15
25–49	$0.135
50–99	$0.13
100–199	$0.125
200–499	$0.12
over 500	$0.115

*plus 6% sales tax

Regular customers get discounts. A few receive a trade discount of 20 percent. Others get a cash discount of 2 percent if they pay within 10 days. Both discounts are deducted before the sales tax is calculated.

Use these invoices to calculate the prices charged to these customers.

7.

COPYFAX CENTER	Invoice no. **2257** Date: *June 15, 20–*
Customer: *Christine's Hardware*	
Number of Copies	800
a. Price per page	
b. Total price	
c. Discount: *20% (trade)*	
d. Net price	
e. Sales tax	
f. Invoice price	

8.

COPYFAX CENTER	Invoice no. **2289** Date: *June 17, 20–*
Customer: *Mike's Travel Service*	
Number of Copies	150
a. Price per page	
b. Total price	
c. Discount: *2% (cash)*	
d. Net price	
e. Sales tax	
f. Invoice price	

9. What is the final price per page (after discount and tax)?

_____

10. What is the price per page (after discount and tax)?

_____

Student _____ Date _____

Class _____ Instructor _____

SECTION 21-1 Assets, Liabilities, and Equity

Assets are the total of your cash, the items that you have purchased, and any money your customers owe you. Liabilities are the total amount of money that you owe creditors. Owner's equity, net worth, or capital is the total value of the assets that you own outright, after you subtract your liabilities.

Owner's Equity = Assets − Liabilities

Find the owner's equity in the table below.

	Assets	Liabilities	Owner's Equity
1.	$ 68,410.04	$10,243.00	
2.	94,014.30	18,480.10	
3.	140,000.00	45,630.40	
4.	76,494.12	21,410.61	
5.	9,140.00	8,721.49	

6. Dot's Dress Shop has these assets and liabilities:

Cash:	$ 2,160.40	Supplies:	$ 270.90	Unpaid merchandise:	$ 5,614.20
Inventory:	10,427.60	Building:	62,000.00	Taxes owed:	912.07
Equipment:	9,160.14	Land:	16,000.00	Real estate loan owed:	16,480.90

What are the total assets? _____

What are the total liabilities? _____

What is the owner's equity? _____

7. First Start Day Care has these assets and liabilities:

Cash:	$ 310.90	Supplies:	$ 416.80	Taxes owed:	$2,160.10
Tuition:	21,000.00	Fixtures:	3,487.95	Wages owed:	3,140.90
Rent owed:	1,600.00	Bank loan owed:	12,910.00		

What are the total assets? _____

What are the total liabilities? _____

What is the owner's equity? _____

8. You are the owner and operator of the Southside Dry Cleaners. You have the following assets and liabilities:

Cash:	$ 2,640.10	Supplies:	$ 3,100.00	Accounts payable:	$ 4,110.90
Inventory:	576.90	Building:	67,800.00	Taxes owed:	2,160.80
Equipment:	26,040.00	Land:	21,000.00	Real estate loan:	59,640.10

What are the total assets? _____

What are the total liabilities? _____

What is the owner's equity? _____

SECTION 21-2 Balance Sheet

A balance sheet shows the financial position of your company on a certain date. You may prepare a balance sheet monthly, quarterly, or annually. The balance sheet shows your total assets, total liabilities, and owner's equity. The sum of the assets must equal the sum of the liabilities and owner's equity.

1. Complete the balance sheet for Morton Auto Parts.

Morton Auto Parts		
Balance Sheet		
November 30, 20—		
Assets		**Liabilities**	
Cash on hand	4 7 1 9 10	Bank loan	2 1 0 9 0 60
Accts. receivable	7 8 4 0 0 90	Accts. payable	1 5 4 9 0 10
Inventory	1 8 1 0 1 40	Taxes owed	1 7 1 0 80
Supplies	4 1 6 80	Wages owed	6 1 2 19
Store fixtures	1 8 1 6 10	Mortgage loan	6 4 9 1 0 00
Building	8 6 4 1 0 00		
Land	2 1 0 0 0 00	Total Liabilities	1 0 3 8 1 3 69
		Owner's Equity	
		Capital	1 0 7 0 5 0 61
		Total Liabilities	
Total Assets		and Owner's Equity	

2. You are the owner of the Seashore Gift Store. You had the following assets and liabilities on July 31. Complete the balance sheet for your gift shop.

Assets
Cash $ 2,160.90
Accounts
  receivable   1,914.06
Inventory   37,519.00
Prepayments   2,160.00
Property   93,575.00
Investments   7,500.00
Other assets   5,617.81

Liabilities
Accounts
  payable $12,070.50
Notes
  payable   65,410.10
Income taxes   2,817.00
Other
  liabilities   5,160.90

Seashore Gift Store
Balance Sheet
July 31, 20—

SECTIONS 21-3, 21-4 — Cost of Goods Sold and Income Statement

An income statement, or profit-and-loss statement, shows in detail your income and operating expenses. If your gross profit is greater than your total operating expenses, your income statement will show a net income, or net profit.

Gross Profit = Net Sales − Cost of Goods Sold

Net Income = Gross Profit − Total Operating Expenses

Cost of Goods Sold = (Beginning Inventory + Receipts) − Ending Inventory

Fill in the table below.

	Total Sales	Returns	Net Sales	Cost of Goods Sold	Gross Profit	Operating Expenses	Net Income
1.	$61,430.00	$9,460.00	$51,970.00	$20,788.00	$31,182.00	$2,618.00	
2.	30,812.90	3,475.00		9,214.00		6,480.90	
3.	646,900.00	6,890.00		81,114.00		28,910.00	

Complete an income statement for each business in Problems 4 and 5.

4. Last month, Ashton Auto Parts had total sales of $16,914.06. Merchandise totaling $312.04 was returned. The auto parts that were sold cost Ashton Auto Parts $8,608.00. Operating expenses for the month were $1,961.02.

Total Sales	Returns	Net Sales	Cost of Goods Sold	Gross Profit	Operating Expenses	Net Income

5. You prepare a quarterly income statement for Duncan Manufacturing Company. For this past quarter, Duncan Manufacturing had a total sales of $212,090, and returns of $6,187. The costs of goods sold amounted to $94,860. Operating expenses for the quarter included: salaries and wages of $55,410, real estate loan payment of $5,440, advertising of $5,000, utilities and supplies of $3,960, bank loan payment of $3,990, and other operating expenses of $4,660.

Income:
    Sales: _____
    Less: Sales returns _____
    Net Sales _____
Cost of goods sold _____
Gross profit on sales _____
Operating Expenses:
    Salaries and wages _____
    Real estate loan payment _____
    Advertising _____
    Utilities and supplies _____
    Bank loan payment _____
    Miscellaneous _____
    Total operating expenses _____
Net income _____

SECTION 21-5 Vertical Analysis

Your business may analyze the dollar amount for the items on its income statement by converting each amount to a percentage of net sales.

Percentage of Net Sales = $\dfrac{\text{Amount for Item}}{\text{Net Sales}}$

1. Duncan Manufacturing had net sales of $205,903. The cost of goods sold by Duncan was $94,860. What is the gross profit as a percentage of net sales? _____

2. Ashton Auto Parts had total sales of $16,914.06. Returns totaled $312.04. The auto parts sold cost Ashton $8,608. What were Ashton's net sales? _____

   What was Ashton's gross profit on sales? _____

   What is the gross profit as a percentage of net sales? _____

3. The income statement for Century Computer Mart for one month showed these figures.

Net sales	$156,910
Cost of goods sold	84,520
Gross profit on sales	

   What is the gross profit on sales? _____

   What is the gross profit as a percentage of net sales? _____

4. You are the proprietor of Hi-Fi Sounds. The income statement for your corporation for the past quarter showed these figures.

Net sales	$84,610
Cost of goods sold	41,010
Gross profit on sales	

Total operating expenses	$16,100
Net Income	

   What is the gross profit on sales? _____

   What is the cost of goods sold as a percentage of net sales? _____

   What is the gross profit on sales as a percentage of net sales? _____

   What are the operating expenses as a percentage of net sales? _____

   What is the net income? _____

   What is the net income as a percentage of net sales? _____

Student   Date

Class   Instructor

SECTION 21-6 Horizontal Analysis

You can compare income statements by computing percentage changes from one income statement to another. When you compute the percentage change, the dollar amount on the earlier statements is the base figure. The amount of change is the difference between the base figure and the figure on the current statement.

$$\text{Percentage Change} = \frac{\text{Amount of Change}}{\text{Base Figure}}$$

Fill in the table below. Round answers to the nearest tenth of a percent.

	Last Year (Base)	This Year	Amount of Change	Percentage Change
1.	$910,400	$847,000		
2.	252,000	296,000		
3.	99,900	93,418		
4.	985,593	798,410		

5. Income statements for Williams, Barnes, and Sampson showed these figures for June and July. Complete the table.

	June	July	Amount of Change	Percentage Change
Net sales	$15,400	$16,800		
Cost of goods sold	9,100	10,010		
Gross profit on sales	6,300	6,790		
Operating expenses	3,610	5,140		
Net income	2,690	1,650		

6. You are the proprietor of Trans-Freight Systems. Your income statements showed the following figures. Complete the table.

	Last Year	This Year	Amount of Change	Percentage Change
Net sales	$216,480	$234,170		
Cost of goods sold	108,240	117,085		
Gross profit on sales	108,240	117,085		
Operating expenses	52,610	54,180		
Net income	55,630	62,905		

Student   Date

Class   Instructor

Simulation: Copyfax Center II

BALANCE SHEET

As the financial manager for Copyfax Center, each month you have to prepare a balance sheet. The balance sheet lists Copyfax Center's assets (what it owns), its liabilities (what it owes), and the owner's equity (assets minus liabilities). Start by listing your assets and liabilities in a running account:

Copyfax Center	December 31, 20—
Cash on hand	$ 3,000
Accounts receivable	$ 3,500
Accounts payable	$ 10,500
Equipment (less accumulated depreciation)	$ 25,798
Inventory (paper, ink, etc.)	$ 2,100
Prepaid insurance	$ 1,800
Office supplies	$ 520
Taxes owed	$ 1,500
Notes payable	$ 9,500

1. Use this form to complete Copyfax Center's balance sheet. Enter the assets and liabilities from your running account.

COPYFAX CENTER
Balance Sheet Dec. 31, 20—

	Assets		Liabilities		
a.					h.
b.					i.
c.					j.
d.					k.
e.			Total Liabilities		l.
f.			Owner's Equity		m.
g.	Total Assets		Total Liabilities and Equity		n.

158 Simulation: CopyFax Center II   Copyright © Glencoe/McGraw-Hill

Simulation: Copyfax Center II
(CONTINUED)

INCOME STATEMENT

Each month you also prepare Copyfax Center's income statement. Here are the sales and expenses you have recorded during the month.

Copyfax Center			December 20—
Wages	$2,510	Insurance	$ 600
Advertising	$ 135	Taxes	$ 500
Delivery	$ 160	Depreciation	$ 660
Postage	$ 300	Supplies	$ 170
Rent	$ 750	Gross sales	$8,002
Utilities	$ 325	Sales discounts	$ 880

2. Use this form to prepare an income statement.

		COPYFAX CENTER		
		Income Statement for Month Ended December 31, 20—		
a.	Income:	Gross sales		
b.		Less sales discounts		
c.		Net sales		
d.	Expenses:			
e.				
f.				
g.				
h.				
i.				
j.				
k.				
l.				
m.				
n.		Total Operating Expenses		
o.		Net Income		

Simulation: Copyfax Center II
(CONTINUED)

ANNUAL REPORT AND COMPARATIVE ANALYSIS

At the end of each year, you prepare an annual income statement. You can then compare Copyfax Center's finances for 2 years, in order to plan for next year.

This chart shows Copyfax Center's income and expenses for last year and this year. Fill in the missing numbers. Then, for each amount, calculate the percent increase from last year to this year. Complete the following statements comparing last year's and this year's figures.

3.

Copyfax Center Annual Income Statement		Last Year	This Year	Percent Increase
Income:	Gross sales	$89,560	$99,480	
	Less sales discounts	9,985	10,750	
	Net sales			
Expenses:	Wages	28,650	30,075	
	Advertising	1,350	1,550	
	Delivery	1,520	1,840	
	Postage	3,260	3,758	
	Rent	8,400	8,800	
	Utilities	3,315	3,900	
	Insurance	4,100	4,200	
	Taxes	4,456	4,826	
	Depreciation	2,100	7,900	
	Supplies	2,136	2,254	
Total Operating Expenses				
Net Income				

4. The expense with the largest percent increase was _____.

5. The next largest was _____.

6. Net sales increased by _____ percent.

7. Total operating expenses increased by _____ percent.

8. Net income changed by _____ percent.

THE BOTTOM LINE

What would you do differently next year to improve Copyfax Center's financial picture?

_____

SECTION 22-1 Corporate Income Taxes

Taxable income is the portion of your company's gross income that remains after normal business expenses are deducted. The structure of federal corporate income taxes is graduated.

Taxable Income = Annual Gross Income − Deductions

Federal Corporate Income Tax

Over −	But not over−	Tax is:	Of the amount over −
$ −	$ 50,000	15%	$ −
50,000	75,000	$ 7,500 + 25%	50,000
75,000	100,000	13,750 + 34%	75,000
100,000	335,000	22,250 + 39%	100,000
335,000	10,000,000	113,900 + 34%	335,000
10,000,000	15,000,000	3,400,000 + 35%	10,000,000
15,000,000	18,333,333	5,150,000 + 38%	15,000,000
18,333,333	−	5,150,000 + 38%	−

Fill in the table below.

	Corporation	Annual Gross Income	Deductions	Taxable Income	Total Tax
1.	Miller, Inc.	$216,750.00	$98,415.00		
2.	Hot Wok	116,418.00	51,420.00		
3.	J. T. Newton	67,800.00	24,950.00		
4.	KMJ	217,400.00	125,350.00		

5. Pappas Manufacturing Company had these business expenses for the year:

Wages	$516,450.00	Property taxes	$74,196.00
Rent	48,000.00	Depreciation	38,750.00
Utilities	113,960.00	Other deductions	14,614.00
Interest	6,247.85		

Pappas had a gross income of $1,826,000 for the year. What is the total of Pappas' business expenses? _____

What is Pappas' taxable income? _____

What is Pappas' federal corporate income tax for the year? _____

6. Dr. Alice McFee formed a medical corporation. The corporation had these business expenses for the year:

Wages	$356,500.00	Property taxes	$4,749.00
Utilities	7,840.00	Depreciation	14,916.50
Interest	6,000.00	Other deductions	6,500.00

The corporation's gross income for the year was $499,620. What is the federal corporate income tax for the year? _____

SECTION 22-2 Issuing Stocks and Bonds

When your company issues stocks and bonds, you must pay certain expenses. The amount that your business actually receives from the sale after paying these expenses is the net proceeds.

Net Proceeds = Value of Issue − Total Selling Expenses

1. Pilgrim Utility Company issued 20,000 shares of stock at $35 per share. Find the net proceeds after these selling expenses are deducted.

Underwriting Expenses		Other Expenses	
Commissions	$42,000	Printing costs	$14,800
Legal fee	6,000	Legal fees	23,000
Advertising	4,700	Accounting fees	15,600
Miscellaneous	2,800	Miscellaneous	5,000

2. Global Corporation sold 400,000 shares of stock at $27.25 per share. The investment banker's commission was 6.3 percent of the value of the stock. The other expenses were 0.6 percent of the value of the stocks. What net proceeds did Global Corporation receive?

3. Riverside Development sold 250,000 shares of stock at $28.75 per share. The underwriting commission was 5.4 percent of the value of the stocks. The other expenses were 0.9 percent of the value of the stocks. What net proceeds did Riverside Development receive?

4. The Tokay Fund is composed of 500 investors who invested $3,000 each. The Fund will be distributed as shown. What are the dollar amounts for each item?

	Percent	Amount
Gross Proceeds	100.00%	_____
Expenses:		
Underwriting commission	12.5%	_____
Acquisition fees	10.0%	_____
Capital reserves	7.5%	_____
Net proceeds		_____

5. You own an engine manufacturing firm. You have plans for a major expansion. To finance the program, you plan to sell 500,000 shares of stock at $40.00 per share.

	Percent	Amount
Gross Proceeds	100.00%	_____
Expenses:		
Underwriting commission	6.3%	_____
Accounting fees	0.4%	_____
Legal fees	0.3%	_____
Printing fees	0.2%	_____
Miscellaneous expenses	0.1%	_____
Net Proceeds		_____

Student _____ Date _____

Class _____ Instructor _____

SECTION 22-3 Borrowing

Your business may take out a commercial loan to buy raw materials, products, or equipment. The maturity value of your loan is the total amount you repay. Commercial loans usually charge ordinary interest at exact time (360 days).

Maturity Value = Principal + Interest Owed

1. Maine National Bank loaned $58,000 to White Mountain Lumber. The term of the loan was 180 days. The interest was 10.5 percent. What was the maturity value of the loan? _____

2. North Industries wanted to purchase the stock of a company that was going out of business. Federal National Finance agreed to loan North $260,000 for 60 days. Federal National charged 9.75 percent interest. What is the maturity value of the loan? _____

3. To take advantage of a special medical supplies sale, College Pharmacy borrowed $17,400 from City Trust Company. City Trust charged 8.4 percent interest on the loan. The term of the loan was 135 days. What was the maturity value of the loan? _____

4. Southwest Bank charges exact interest while Sunshine Trust Company charges ordinary interest. Clark Fox plans to borrow $28,500 for 75 days at 11.8 percent. What is the maturity value if the loan is from:

   a. Southwest Bank _____

   b. Sunshine Trust _____

5. In order to meet its July payroll, Acme Battery Company borrowed $18,500 on July 15 at 9.8 percent ordinary interest at exact time. The due date of the loan is September 25. What is the maturity value of the loan? _____

6. Open Door Company needs to borrow $380,000 for 180 days to help finance the production of a new model door. The business manager arranged for financing from two sources. Each loan charges ordinary interest at exact time. The prime rate is 7.75 percent.

   Georgia Trust Company
   $134,000 for 180 days
   Interest rate: 2% over prime

   Peachtree Investment Company
   $246,000 for 180 days
   Interest rate: 2.5% over prime

   What is the total interest for the two loans? _____

   What is the total maturity value? _____

Student _____ Date _____

Class _____ Instructor _____

SECTIONS 22-4, 22-5   Investments—Treasury Bills and Commercial Paper

Your business may invest surplus cash by purchasing U.S. Treasury bills. These bills are issued on a discount basis. The face value of a Treasury bill is the amount of money you will receive on the maturity date of the bill. Your business can also invest in 30-day to 270-day commercial paper (CP) issued by a company having a high credit rating. Both investments earn ordinary interest at exact time.

Cost of Treasury Bill = (Face Value of Bill − Interest) + Service Fee

Cost of CP = (Face Value of CP − Interest) + Service Fee

Yield = Interest ÷ (Cost × Time)

1. The financial manager of Ortega Manufacturing Company has decided to invest the company's surplus cash in a $100,000 United States Treasury bill for 120 days. The interest rate is 5.00 percent. The bank charges a service fee of $25 to obtain the Treasury bill. What is the cost of the Treasury bill?

2. Determine the yield for the Treasury bill purchased in Problem 1.

3. Software, Inc., has a $500,000 cash surplus. The financial manager used the cash to invest in commercial paper issued by General Motors at 5 percent for 45 days. The bank charges a service fee of $50. What is the cost of the commercial paper?

4. Determine the yield for the commercial paper purchased in Problem 2.

5. The financial manager of Great Lakes Marina made the following investments in commercial paper. The bank charges a service fee of $25. What is the cost of the commercial paper? What is the yield?

   a. Western States Copper Mine $25,000 at 8.4 percent for 40 days.

   _____ _____

   b. Tennessee Lumber $40,000 at 8.75 percent for 90 days.

   _____ _____

6. Your company has just received $400,000 from the sale of a warehouse. As the financial manager, you have to decide the best way to invest the money. You are considering whether to invest in a Treasury bill or in commercial paper. You narrowed it down to these two investments:

U.S. Treasury Bill	Mead/Westvaco, Inc.
91-day bill at 4.5 percent	90-day CP at 4.65 percent
Service fee of $40	Service fee of $40

   a. Determine the net interest and yield for the Treasury bill.

   _____ _____

   b. Determine the net interest and the yield for the CP.

   _____ _____

   c. Where should you invest the money and why?

   _____
   _____

164   Mathematics with Business Applications ♦ Sections 22-4, 22-5   Copyright © Glencoe/McGraw-Hill

Student _____ Date _____

Class _____ Instructor _____

SECTION 22-6 Growth Expenses

You may expand your business in many ways. The cost of expansion may include construction fees, consultation fees, legal fees, and so on.

Total Cost of Expansion = Sum of Individual Costs

1. The Far East Restaurant is expanding its kitchen. It pays $23,500 for construction cost and $2,987 to restock utensils. How much did it pay for this expansion? _____

2. Ashton Real Estate plans to open a new branch office. Ashton purchased property for $32,800. Construction costs for a new building totaled $425,700. In addition, Ashton paid an architect's fee of 13.1 percent of the cost of construction. Legal fees totaled $5,000. New equipment and fixtures cost $12,450. Other expenses came to $4,500. What is the total cost of expansion? _____

3. Your company is expanding by adding a new department. You are converting an area of 1,800 square feet into offices. The costs of expansion are:

Construction permit	$45
Removal of 3 walls	$1,143
New lighting fixtures	$1,575
New office equipment	$6,425
New carpeting	$31.40 per square yard

   What is the total cost of expansion for your company? _____

4. Your computer software firm is planning to expand its business by building a new building. Expenses include:

Land	$ 60,000
Building construction	1,250,000
Architect's fee: 9.5 percent of construction cost	_____
Construction manager:	
5.5 percent of construction cost	_____
Landscaping	8,150
Legal fees	7,500
Equipment and fixtures	84,325
Additional supplies	2,150
Miscellaneous expenses	5,000
Total Growth Expenses	_____

5. Silver Realty plans to open a new branch office in another city. Growth expenses include:

Consultant fees	$ 8,400
Real estate agent: 5 percent of first year rent	
(office space cost is $2,500 per month)	_____
Interior decorator	2,175
New furniture/fixtures	9,498
Legal fees	1,200
Travel expenses	3,650
Total Growth Expenses	_____

Student _____ Date _____

Class _____ Instructor _____

Spreadsheet Application: Financial Management

DIRECTIONS:

1. Insert your *Student Activity Workbook CD* into your computer and click on Chapter 22 Financial Management. The spreadsheet will appear.
2. Key your name into cell B1. Key the date into cell G1.
3. Key the information below into the appropriate cells. The spreadsheet application will compute the data for you automatically.
4. Save your spreadsheet as Ch22XXX, where XXX are your initials.
5. Print out your spreadsheet.

Input the information below to find the value of the issue, the total selling expenses, and the net proceeds. Then answer the questions that follow.

Stock Symbol	Number of Shares	Value per Share	Value of Issue	Percent Commission	Other Expenses	Selling Expenses	Net Proceeds
AMR	500,000	$42.750		4.1%	0.5%		
CSX	250,000	36.000		6.8%	1.0%		
EDO	1,000,000	25.875		5%	2.75%		
GM	300,000	55.625		4.5%	0.5%		
IBM	200,000	87.875		3.75%	0.4%		
K	100,000	35.525		6%	0.36%		
MGM	750,000	15.375		5.5%	1.75%		
ODP	350,000	12.625		6.5%	0.9%		
RSH	600,000	29.250		5.875%	1.66%		
SNA	450,000	32.125		6.25%	0.25%		
URS	750,000	29.625		5.75%	0.35%		
WB	150,000	37.750		6.125%	0.5%		

1. What is the value of the issue for each of these stocks: AMR and URS?

2. What is the selling expense for each of these stocks: CSX and WB?

3. What are the net proceeds for each of these stocks: EDO, GM, MGM, and WB?

4. How many shares of stock must K sell at $37.50 per share to raise $10 million if the underwriter commission is 6 percent and the expenses are 0.36 percent? (Hint: change the number of shares.)

5. How many shares of stock must EDO sell at $25.875 per share to raise $7.5 million if the underwriter commission is 5 percent and other expenses total 1.5 percent of the value of the stock?

6. If ODP could reduce the underwriter commission to 5.5 percent and the other expenses to 0.5 percent, how much more would the net proceeds be?

7. If MGM's stock went up $0.50, how much more would the net proceeds be?

166 Spreadsheet Application: Financial Management Copyright © Glencoe/McGraw-Hill

Simulation: The Stock Market

Your employer has given you a $2,000 bonus. You invest the money in stocks. To help you decide which stocks to buy, you study the past performance of many stocks. You also read financial newspapers and magazines, and talk to people who are well-informed about the stock market.

52 Week High	Low	Stock	Dividend	Yield (%)	PE Ratio	Volume (000)	High	Low	Close	Net Change
26½	23	Cablevsn	—	—	58	265	26½	23½	23	−3½
22⅜	20½	LaZBoy	—	—	67	257	20	20⅞	20	0
59	55⅞	QuakrO	$0.25	6.8%	19	7446	57⅜	55⅛	56⅜	½
8½	5⅜	TCBY	—	—	11	120	7½	6	6⅛	−1½
44⅜	34½	Upjohn	$1.16	7.4%	38	1456	44½	41⅞	42¼	3⅜

1. You purchase 30 shares of LaZBoy stock at today's closing price. What is the cost of the stock? _____

2. Your stockbroker charges a 1.5 percent commission each time you buy or sell stock. What is the commission on this purchase? _____

3. What is the total amount you pay for the stock? _____

4. Of the $2,000 that you want to invest in stock, how much is now available to be invested? _____

5. LaZBoy declares a dividend of $1.25 per share. What is the annual yield? _____

6. What is the total dividend you receive on your 30 shares? _____

7. Including the dividend, how much money is now available to be invested in stocks? _____

Simulation: The Stock Market
(CONTINUED)

BUYING AND SELLING STOCK

During the next year, you continue to study the stock market. Sometimes you buy stocks, starting with the money you have available after buying the LaZBoy stock. Sometimes you sell stock, either because the company is not doing well or because you want the money to buy stocks in a different company. You sell all your stock at the end of the year. While you owned some of the stocks, you received the dividends shown. You add the dividend to the money left to invest. Fill in the table below.

	Name of Stock	Number of Shares	Bought or Sold	Price per Share	Amount Paid	Amount Received	Commission 1.5%	Total Cost	Dividend	Dividend Income	Total Income	Money Left to Invest
	LazBoy	30	B	$20.000	$600.00	—	$9.00	$609.00	$1.25	$37.50	$37.50	$1,428.50
8.	QuakrO	15	B	57.375								
9.	TCBY	25	B	6.125								
10.	Upjohn	8	B	43.000								
11.	QuakrO	10	S	68.500								
12.	TCBY	25	S	7.875								
13.	Upjohn	16	B	40.125								
14.	CityCm	60	B	3.500								
15.	QuakrO	5	S	62.125								
16.	LazBoy	30	S	21.000								
17.	CityCm	80	B	3.875								
18.	Upjohn	24	S	44.875								
19.	CityCm	140	S	3.125								

20. What is the total dividend you received? _____

21. Have you made a net profit or a net loss? How much? _____

22. What is the percent profit or loss on your $2,000 investment? _____

Simulation: The Stock Market
(CONTINUED)

COMPARING MUTUAL FUNDS

You realize at the end of the year that you do not have time to study the stock market. You invest $2,100 in 3 mutual funds. The following table shows the net asset value per share for each fund at the end of each month of the previous year.

23. On graph paper, set up a graph like the one at the bottom of the page. Make a line graph using the values in the table. Use a different color for each fund.

NET ASSET VALUE PER SHARE												
Month	Jan	Feb	Mar	Apr	May	June	July	Aug	Sep	Oct	Nov	Dec
South Bay Fund	$6.42	$6.55	$6.72	$6.89	$6.75	$6.81	$6.97	$7.14	$7.29	$7.50	$7.68	$7.90
Salinas Valley Fund	6.59	6.74	6.89	7.03	6.82	6.85	6.92	7.25	7.41	7.78	7.95	7.83
Central Section Fund	6.54	6.62	6.73	6.84	6.78	6.86	6.95	7.04	7.15	7.24	7.32	7.40

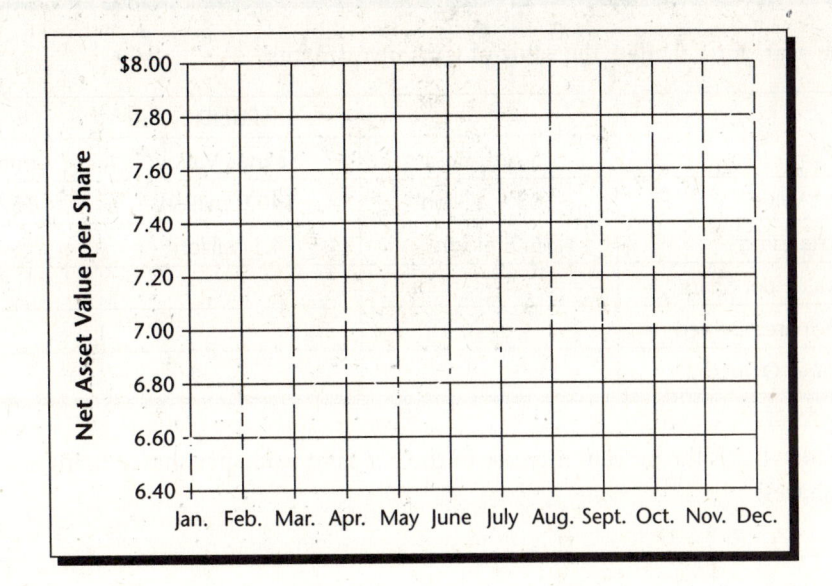

Student _____ Date _____

Class _____ Instructor _____

Simulation: The Stock Market
(CONTINUED)

INVESTING IN MUTUAL FUNDS

You invest $700 in each of the 3 funds. South Bay and Salinas Valley have loading charges. Central Section is a no-load fund.

The table shows the total market value of each fund's portfolio and the number of shares outstanding on the day you make your investments. Calculate the number of shares of each fund you can purchase.

		FUND		
		South Bay	Salinas Valley	Central Section
	Total Market Value	$49.0 million	$30.6 million	$44.1 million
	Shares Outstanding	5.6 million	3.6 million	4.9 million
24.	Net Asset Value per Share			
	Amount Invested	$700	$700	$700
	Loading Rate	10%	8.5%	0
25.	Loading Charge			
26.	Amount Invested Minus Loading Charge			
27.	Number of Shares Purchased			

At the end of the year, you calculate the value of your investments.

		FUND		
		South Bay	Salinas Valley	Central Section
	Total Market Value	$63.4 million	$40.9 million	$52.2 million
	Shares Outstanding	6.0 million	4.1 million	5.2 million
28.	Net Asset Value per Share			
29.	Number of Shares Owned			
30.	Value of Shares Owned			

31. For each fund, what is the percent increase in the net asset value per share during the year you owned the shares?

_____

32. For each fund, what is the percent increase in your $700 investment?

_____

170 Simulation: The Stock Market

SECTION 23-1 Inflation

Inflation is an economic condition during which there are price increases in the cost of goods and services.

The inflation rate is expressed as a percent increase over a specified time period, usually to the nearest one-tenth of one percent.

Inflation Rate = (Current Price − Original Price) / Original Price

The current price can be found by adding the original price to the inflation rate times the original price.

Current Price = Original Price + (Original Price × Inflation Rate)

The original price can be found by dividing the current price by one plus the inflation rate.

Original Price = Current Price ÷ (1 + Inflation Rate)

Fill in the table below.

	Inflation Rate	Current Price	Original Price
1.		$147.79	$ 119.90
2.		27.98	24.99
3.	3.5%		75.49
4.	5.4%		18,500.00
5.	0.8%	14.29	
6.	12.5%	978.65	

7. A new auto that currently sells for $25,000 sold for $24,000 one year ago. Find the inflation rate for autos for that one year.

8. Find the current price of a home that sold for $100,000 2 years ago if the inflation rate for homes over that 2-year period is 10 percent.

9. Find the original price of a lawnmower that currently sells for $595 if the inflation rate for lawnmowers for that period is 5 percent.

10. In 1938, one pound of coffee cost $0.17. Currently, one pound of coffee costs $3.59. What is the inflation rate for coffee from 1938 to present?

11. One year ago bottled water was selling for $1.299 a gallon. The inflation rate for bottled water over the past year is 15 percent. What is the current price for a gallon of bottled water?

12. Find the original price of an outdoor grill that currently sells for $179.98 if the inflation rate for grills for that period is 8.6 percent.

Student _____ Date _____

Class _____ Instructor _____

SECTION 23-2 Gross Domestic Product

The Gross Domestic Product (GDP) is a measure of a nation's economic performance. The GDP is the estimated total value of all domestic goods and services produced within a nation during a year. A nation's GDP can appear to be growing faster than it really is because of inflation. For this reason, the real GDP, or adjusted GDP, is corrected for inflation. The per capita GDP is the GDP distributed over the population.

Real GDP = GDP − (Inflation Rate × GDP)

Per Capita GDP = GDP ÷ Population

Find the real GDP and per capita GDP in the table below.

	GDP	Inflation Rate	Population	Real GDP	Per Capita GDP
1.	$120 billion	5.0%	40 million		$ 3,000.00
2.	96 million	13.4%	480,000		200.00
3.	956,500,000	1.2%	235,000		4,070.21
4.	24.6 billion	0.4%	2.1 million		11,714.29
5.	478.6 million	7.5%	32.4 thousand		14,771.60
6.	13.4 trillion	3.6%	1.2 billion		11,166.67

7. A country has a population of 60,000,000, an inflation rate of 4.0 percent, and a GDP of $300 billion. Find:

   a. the real GDP. _____

   b. the per capita GDP. _____

8. France has a gross domestic product of $1.25 trillion. The population of France is 59,361,000, and the inflation rate of France is 2.2 percent. Find:

   a. the real GDP. _____

   b. the per capita GDP. _____

9. The GDP of Italy is $1.197 trillion, with a population of 56.877 million. The rate of inflation in Italy is 2.8 percent. Find:

   a. the real GDP. _____

   b. the per capita GDP. _____

10. In a recent year, the United States had a GDP of $10.25 trillion and a population of 284.8 million. The rate of inflation for that year was 1.9 percent. Find:

    a. the real GDP. _____

    b. the per capita GDP. _____

SECTION 23-3 Consumer Price Index

The Consumer Price Index (CPI) is a measure of the average change in prices of a certain number of goods and services. The year 1983 is used as the base year and the CPI for 1983 is set at 100. To find the CPI for any given commodity divide, the current cost by the cost in 1983 and multiply by 100 (round to the nearest tenth).

CPI = (Current Cost ÷ Cost In 1983) × 100

If you know the CPI for a given commodity and its cost in 1983, you can find the current cost by multiplying the cost in 1983 by the CPI and then dividing by 100.

Current Cost = (Cost in 1983 × CPI) ÷ 100

If you know the CPI for a given commodity and its current cost, you can find the cost in 1983 by dividing the current cost by the CPI and multiplying by 100.

Cost In 1983 = (Current Cost ÷ CPI) × 100

Complete the table below. Round to the nearest tenth or cent.

		Consumer Price Index (CPI)	Current Cost	Cost in 1983
1.	New home		$148,700.00	$61,068.00
2.	Groceries		80.25	45.70
3.	Dining out	212.8		23.50
4.	New suit	186.3		190.00
5.	New car	180.5	21,840.50	
6.	Bottled water	164.6	1.499	

7. The present cost of a lawn chair is $75.00. The cost in 1983 was $37.50. Find the CPI to the nearest tenth. _____

8. The cost in 1983 of a good pair of gym shoes was $54.75. The CPI for gym shoes is 170. Find the present cost. _____

9. The present cost of a VCR is $97.99. The CPI for VCRs is 78.2. Find the cost in 1983. _____

10. Tickets for a new musical on Broadway are selling for $85.00 each. In 1983, the same tickets would have cost $50.00. What is the CPI for recreational services such as theater tickets? _____

11. In 1983, the Browns paid $50 per month to heat their house. The CPI for heating oil is 504.8. What would it cost the Browns today to heat their house for a month? _____

12. A haircut at the local franchise haircutting salon costs $15.00. The CPI for personal care services such as haircuts is 170. What would a haircut have cost in 1983? _____

SECTION 23-4 Budget

A budget enables a business, governmental agency, or an individual to identify what sources are expected to produce revenue (earn money) and what amounts are allocated to various departments or categories for expenses. Revenue and expenses are assigned as a percent of the total amount. The actual amount spent must be compared with the budget amount.

Budget Allocation = Percent × Total Income

Difference = Actual Amount − Budget Allocation

Find the budget amount and the difference in the table below.

	Total	Percent	Actual	Budget	Difference
1.	$ 60,000	20.0%	$ 11,000		
2.	150,000	30.0%	42,500		
3.	825,000	40.0%	295,000		
4.	4,650,000	17.5%	825,000		
5.	8,548,750	21.8%	1,645,960		
6.	37,986,900	5.4%	1,978,425		

7. Turnkey Limited has a $600,000 budget. For each category determine the amount budgeted and the difference.

	Percent	Actual	Budget	Difference
Salaries	78.8%	$465,780		
Supplies	7.5%	46,500		
Equipment	6.5%	39,000		
Maintenance	5.0%	27,860		
Miscellaneous	2.2%	20,860		
Total				

8. Allocate $2,450,000 in revenue as shown.

   Sales.... 75% _____   Service.... 18% _____   Investments.... 7% _____

9. Mulholland Manufacturing is budgeting total revenues next year of $12,575,000. Out of the total, 90 percent is expected to come from sales, 5 percent from service contracts, 3 percent from investments, and 2 percent from miscellaneous sources. How many dollars has Mulholland budgeted in expected revenues in each category?

10. Mulholland Manufacturing in Problem 9 had actual revenues of $11,450,000 from sales, $598,600 from service contracts, $407,800 from investments, and $232,500 from miscellaneous sources. Did Mulholland reach its revenue goals?

Student _____ Date _____

Class _____ Instructor _____

Spreadsheet Application: Corporate Planning

DIRECTIONS:

1. Insert your *Student Activity Workbook CD* into your computer and click on Chapter 23 Corporate Planning. The spreadsheet will appear.
2. Key your name into cell B1. Key the date into cell G1.
3. Key the information below into the appropriate cells. The spreadsheet application will compute the data for you automatically.
4. Save your spreadsheet as Ch23XXX, where XXX are your initials.
5. Print out your spreadsheet.

Input the information below to find the original price, current price, inflation rate, real GDP, and CPI. Then answer the questions that follow. To work with the CPI, assume the original price occurred in 1983.

	Original Price	Current Price	Inflation Rate	Gross Domestic Product (GDP)	Real GDP	Consumer Price Index (CPI)
a.	$ 18.75	$ 21.45		$45,800,000,000		
b.	219.97	299.99		235.7 billion		
c.	47.79		6.2%	562,000,000		
d.	8,750.00		10.4%	73.9 million		
e.		4.75	7.2%	7,650,000,000		
f.		847.50	1.6%	1,750.6 million		
g.	649.98			2,625.8 billion		215.6
h.	98.98			95,750,000		168.4
i.		75.75		1.4 billion		345.2
j.		549.99		97,748,251,000		116.4

1. What is the inflation rate in part a? _____
2. What is the real GDP in part a? _____
3. What is the CPI in part a? _____
4. What is the current price in part c? _____
5. What is the real GDP in part c? _____
6. What is the CPI in part c? _____
7. What is the original price in part e? _____
8. What is the real GDP in part e? _____
9. What is the CPI in part e? _____
10. What is the current price in part g? _____

Spreadsheet Application: Corporate Planning
(CONTINUED)

11. What is the inflation rate in part g? _____

12. What is the real GDP in part g? _____

13. What is the original price in part i? _____

14. What is the inflation rate in part i? _____

15. What is the real GDP in part i? _____

16. If the current price is less than the original price:

    a. What will be true about the inflation rate?
    _____

    b. What will be true about the CPI?
    _____

    c. Can the CPI ever be negative? Why or why not?
    _____

17. If the current price is equal to the original price:

    a. What is the inflation rate? _____

    b. What is the CPI? _____

    c. How is the GDP related to the real GDP? _____

Appendix

Federal Income Tax Tables

SINGLE Persons—WEEKLY Payroll Period
(For Wages Paid)

If the wages are—		And the number of withholding allowances claimed is—										
At least	But less than	0	1	2	3	4	5	6	7	8	9	10
		The amount of income tax to be withheld is—										
$0	$55	$0	$0	$0	$0	$0	$0	$0	$0	$0	$0	$0
55	60	1	0	0	0	0	0	0	0	0	0	0
60	65	1	0	0	0	0	0	0	0	0	0	0
65	70	2	0	0	0	0	0	0	0	0	0	0
70	75	2	0	0	0	0	0	0	0	0	0	0
75	80	3	0	0	0	0	0	0	0	0	0	0
80	85	3	0	0	0	0	0	0	0	0	0	0
85	90	4	0	0	0	0	0	0	0	0	0	0
90	95	4	0	0	0	0	0	0	0	0	0	0
95	100	5	0	0	0	0	0	0	0	0	0	0
100	105	5	0	0	0	0	0	0	0	0	0	0
105	110	6	0	0	0	0	0	0	0	0	0	0
110	115	6	0	0	0	0	0	0	0	0	0	0
115	120	7	1	0	0	0	0	0	0	0	0	0
120	125	7	1	0	0	0	0	0	0	0	0	0
125	130	8	2	0	0	0	0	0	0	0	0	0
130	135	8	2	0	0	0	0	0	0	0	0	0
135	140	9	3	0	0	0	0	0	0	0	0	0
140	145	9	3	0	0	0	0	0	0	0	0	0
145	150	10	4	0	0	0	0	0	0	0	0	0
150	155	10	4	0	0	0	0	0	0	0	0	0
155	160	11	5	0	0	0	0	0	0	0	0	0
160	165	11	5	0	0	0	0	0	0	0	0	0
165	170	12	6	0	0	0	0	0	0	0	0	0
170	175	13	6	1	0	0	0	0	0	0	0	0
175	180	13	7	1	0	0	0	0	0	0	0	0
180	185	14	7	2	0	0	0	0	0	0	0	0
185	190	15	8	2	0	0	0	0	0	0	0	0
190	195	16	8	3	0	0	0	0	0	0	0	0
195	200	16	9	3	0	0	0	0	0	0	0	0
200	210	17	10	4	0	0	0	0	0	0	0	0
210	220	19	11	5	0	0	0	0	0	0	0	0
220	230	20	12	6	0	0	0	0	0	0	0	0
230	240	22	13	7	1	0	0	0	0	0	0	0
240	250	23	15	8	2	0	0	0	0	0	0	0
250	260	25	16	9	3	0	0	0	0	0	0	0
260	270	26	18	10	4	0	0	0	0	0	0	0
270	280	28	19	11	5	0	0	0	0	0	0	0
280	290	29	21	12	6	0	0	0	0	0	0	0
290	300	31	22	14	7	1	0	0	0	0	0	0
300	310	32	24	15	8	2	0	0	0	0	0	0
310	320	34	25	17	9	3	0	0	0	0	0	0
320	330	35	27	18	10	4	0	0	0	0	0	0
330	340	37	28	20	11	5	0	0	0	0	0	0
340	350	38	30	21	12	6	1	0	0	0	0	0
350	360	40	31	23	14	7	2	0	0	0	0	0
360	370	41	33	24	15	8	3	0	0	0	0	0
370	380	43	34	26	17	9	4	0	0	0	0	0
380	390	44	36	27	18	10	5	0	0	0	0	0
390	400	46	37	29	20	11	6	0	0	0	0	0
400	410	47	39	30	21	13	7	1	0	0	0	0
410	420	49	40	32	23	14	8	2	0	0	0	0
420	430	50	42	33	24	16	9	3	0	0	0	0
430	440	52	43	35	26	17	10	4	0	0	0	0
440	450	53	45	36	27	19	11	5	0	0	0	0
450	460	55	46	38	29	20	12	6	0	0	0	0
460	470	56	48	39	30	22	13	7	1	0	0	0
470	480	58	49	41	32	23	15	8	2	0	0	0
480	490	59	51	42	33	25	16	9	3	0	0	0
490	500	61	52	44	35	26	18	10	4	0	0	0
500	510	62	54	45	36	28	19	11	5	0	0	0
510	520	64	55	47	38	29	21	12	6	0	0	0
520	530	65	57	48	39	31	22	14	7	1	0	0
530	540	67	58	50	41	32	24	15	8	2	0	0
540	550	68	60	51	42	34	25	17	9	3	0	0
550	560	70	61	53	44	35	27	18	10	4	0	0
560	570	71	63	54	45	37	28	20	11	5	0	0
570	580	74	64	56	47	38	30	21	12	6	0	0
580	590	76	66	57	48	40	31	23	14	7	1	0
590	600	79	67	59	50	41	33	24	15	8	2	0

SINGLE Persons—WEEKLY Payroll Period
(For Wages Paid)

If the wages are—		And the number of withholding allowances claimed is—										
At least	But less than	0	1	2	3	4	5	6	7	8	9	10
			The amount of income tax to be withheld is—										
$600	$610	$82	$69	$60	$51	$43	$34	$26	$17	$9	$3	$0
610	620	84	70	62	53	44	36	27	18	10	4	0
620	630	87	72	63	54	46	37	29	20	11	5	0
630	640	90	74	65	56	47	39	30	21	13	6	1
640	650	92	77	66	57	49	40	32	23	14	7	2
650	660	95	80	68	59	50	42	33	24	16	8	3
660	670	98	82	69	60	52	43	35	26	17	9	4
670	680	101	85	71	62	53	45	36	27	19	10	5
680	690	103	88	72	63	55	46	38	29	20	12	6
690	700	106	90	75	65	56	48	39	30	22	13	7
700	710	109	93	77	66	58	49	41	32	23	15	8
710	720	111	96	80	68	59	51	42	33	25	16	9
720	730	114	98	83	69	61	52	44	35	26	18	10
730	740	117	101	86	71	62	54	45	36	28	19	11
740	750	119	104	88	73	64	55	47	38	29	21	12
750	760	122	107	91	75	65	57	48	39	31	22	13
760	770	125	109	94	78	67	58	50	41	32	24	15
770	780	128	112	96	81	68	60	51	42	34	25	16
780	790	130	115	99	83	70	61	53	44	35	27	18
790	800	133	117	102	86	71	63	54	45	37	28	19
800	810	136	120	104	89	73	64	56	47	38	30	21
810	820	138	123	107	92	76	66	57	48	40	31	22
820	830	141	125	110	94	79	67	59	50	41	33	24
830	840	144	128	113	97	81	69	60	51	43	34	25
840	850	146	131	115	100	84	70	62	53	44	36	27
850	860	149	134	118	102	87	72	63	54	46	37	28
860	870	152	136	121	105	90	74	65	56	47	39	30
870	880	155	139	123	108	92	77	66	57	49	40	31
880	890	157	142	126	110	95	79	68	59	50	42	33
890	900	160	144	129	113	98	82	69	60	52	43	34
900	910	163	147	131	116	100	85	71	62	53	45	36
910	920	165	150	134	119	103	87	72	63	55	46	37
920	930	168	152	137	121	106	90	75	65	56	48	39
930	940	171	155	140	124	108	93	77	66	58	49	40
940	950	173	158	142	127	111	96	80	68	59	51	42
950	960	176	161	145	129	114	98	83	69	61	52	43
960	970	179	163	148	132	117	101	85	71	62	54	45
970	980	182	166	150	135	119	104	88	72	64	55	46
980	990	184	169	153	137	122	106	91	75	65	57	48
990	1,000	187	171	156	140	125	109	93	78	67	58	49
1,000	1,010	190	174	158	143	127	112	96	81	68	60	51
1,010	1,020	192	177	161	146	130	114	99	83	70	61	52
1,020	1,030	195	179	164	148	133	117	102	86	71	63	54
1,030	1,040	198	182	167	151	135	120	104	89	73	64	55
1,040	1,050	200	185	169	154	138	123	107	91	76	66	57
1,050	1,060	203	188	172	156	141	125	110	94	78	67	58
1,060	1,070	206	190	175	159	144	128	112	97	81	69	60
1,070	1,080	209	193	177	162	146	131	115	99	84	70	61
1,080	1,090	211	196	180	164	149	133	118	102	87	72	63
1,090	1,100	214	198	183	167	152	136	120	105	89	74	64
1,100	1,110	217	201	185	170	154	139	123	108	92	76	66
1,110	1,120	219	204	188	173	157	141	126	110	95	79	67
1,120	1,130	222	206	191	175	160	144	129	113	97	82	69
1,130	1,140	225	209	194	178	162	147	131	116	100	85	70
1,140	1,150	227	212	196	181	165	150	134	118	103	87	72
1,150	1,160	230	215	199	183	168	152	137	121	105	90	74
1,160	1,170	233	217	202	186	171	155	139	124	108	93	77
1,170	1,180	236	220	204	189	173	158	142	126	111	95	80
1,180	1,190	238	223	207	191	176	160	145	129	114	98	82
1,190	1,200	241	225	210	194	179	163	147	132	116	101	85
1,200	1,210	244	228	212	197	181	166	150	135	119	103	88
1,210	1,220	246	231	215	200	184	168	153	137	122	106	91
1,220	1,230	249	233	218	202	187	171	156	140	124	109	93
1,230	1,240	252	236	221	205	189	174	158	143	127	112	96
1,240	1,250	254	239	223	208	192	177	161	145	130	114	99

MARRIED Persons—WEEKLY Payroll Period
(For Wages Paid)

If the wages are—		And the number of withholding allowances claimed is—										
At least	But less than	0	1	2	3	4	5	6	7	8	9	10
		The amount of income tax to be withheld is—										
$0	$130	$0	$0	$0	$0	$0	$0	$0	$0	$0	$0	$0
130	135	1	0	0	0	0	0	0	0	0	0	0
135	140	1	0	0	0	0	0	0	0	0	0	0
140	145	2	0	0	0	0	0	0	0	0	0	0
145	150	2	0	0	0	0	0	0	0	0	0	0
150	155	3	0	0	0	0	0	0	0	0	0	0
155	160	3	0	0	0	0	0	0	0	0	0	0
160	165	4	0	0	0	0	0	0	0	0	0	0
165	170	4	0	0	0	0	0	0	0	0	0	0
170	175	5	0	0	0	0	0	0	0	0	0	0
175	180	5	0	0	0	0	0	0	0	0	0	0
180	185	6	0	0	0	0	0	0	0	0	0	0
185	190	6	1	0	0	0	0	0	0	0	0	0
190	195	7	1	0	0	0	0	0	0	0	0	0
195	200	7	2	0	0	0	0	0	0	0	0	0
200	210	8	2	0	0	0	0	0	0	0	0	0
210	220	9	3	0	0	0	0	0	0	0	0	0
220	230	10	4	0	0	0	0	0	0	0	0	0
230	240	11	5	0	0	0	0	0	0	0	0	0
240	250	12	6	1	0	0	0	0	0	0	0	0
250	260	13	7	2	0	0	0	0	0	0	0	0
260	270	14	8	3	0	0	0	0	0	0	0	0
270	280	15	9	4	0	0	0	0	0	0	0	0
280	290	16	10	5	0	0	0	0	0	0	0	0
290	300	17	11	6	0	0	0	0	0	0	0	0
300	310	18	12	7	1	0	0	0	0	0	0	0
310	320	19	13	8	2	0	0	0	0	0	0	0
320	330	20	14	9	3	0	0	0	0	0	0	0
330	340	21	15	10	4	0	0	0	0	0	0	0
340	350	22	16	11	5	0	0	0	0	0	0	0
350	360	23	17	12	6	0	0	0	0	0	0	0
360	370	25	18	13	7	1	0	0	0	0	0	0
370	380	26	19	14	8	2	0	0	0	0	0	0
380	390	28	20	15	9	3	0	0	0	0	0	0
390	400	29	21	16	10	4	0	0	0	0	0	0
400	410	31	22	17	11	5	0	0	0	0	0	0
410	420	32	23	18	12	6	0	0	0	0	0	0
420	430	34	25	19	13	7	1	0	0	0	0	0
430	440	35	26	20	14	8	2	0	0	0	0	0
440	450	37	28	21	15	9	3	0	0	0	0	0
450	460	38	29	22	16	10	4	0	0	0	0	0
460	470	40	31	23	17	11	5	0	0	0	0	0
470	480	41	32	24	18	12	6	0	0	0	0	0
480	490	43	34	25	19	13	7	1	0	0	0	0
490	500	44	35	27	20	14	8	2	0	0	0	0
500	510	46	37	28	21	15	9	3	0	0	0	0
510	520	47	38	30	22	16	10	4	0	0	0	0
520	530	49	40	31	23	17	11	5	0	0	0	0
530	540	50	41	33	24	18	12	6	1	0	0	0
540	550	52	43	34	26	19	13	7	2	0	0	0
550	560	53	44	36	27	20	14	8	3	0	0	0
560	570	55	46	37	29	21	15	9	4	0	0	0
570	580	56	47	39	30	22	16	10	5	0	0	0
580	590	58	49	40	32	23	17	11	6	0	0	0
590	600	59	50	42	33	24	18	12	7	1	0	0
600	610	61	52	43	35	26	19	13	8	2	0	0
610	620	62	53	45	36	27	20	14	9	3	0	0
620	630	64	55	46	38	29	21	15	10	4	0	0
630	640	65	56	48	39	30	22	16	11	5	0	0
640	650	67	58	49	41	32	23	17	12	6	0	0
650	660	68	59	51	42	33	25	18	13	7	1	0
660	670	70	61	52	44	35	26	19	14	8	2	0
670	680	71	62	54	45	36	28	20	15	9	3	0
680	690	73	64	55	47	38	29	21	16	10	4	0
690	700	74	65	57	48	39	31	22	17	11	5	0
700	710	76	67	58	50	41	32	24	18	12	6	0
710	720	77	68	60	51	42	34	25	19	13	7	1
720	730	79	70	61	53	44	35	27	20	14	8	2
730	740	80	71	63	54	45	37	28	21	15	9	3
740	750	82	73	64	56	47	38	30	22	16	10	4

MARRIED Persons—WEEKLY Payroll Period
(For Wages Paid)

If the wages are—		And the number of withholding allowances claimed is—										
At least	But less than	0	1	2	3	4	5	6	7	8	9	10
		The amount of income tax to be withheld is—										
$750	$760	$83	$74	$66	$57	$48	$40	$31	$23	$17	$11	$5
760	770	85	76	67	59	50	41	33	24	18	12	6
770	780	86	77	69	60	51	43	34	26	19	13	7
780	790	88	79	70	62	53	44	36	27	20	14	8
790	800	89	80	72	63	54	46	37	29	21	15	9
800	810	91	82	73	65	56	47	39	30	22	16	10
810	820	92	83	75	66	57	49	40	32	23	17	11
820	830	94	85	76	68	59	50	42	33	24	18	12
830	840	95	86	78	69	60	52	43	35	26	19	13
840	850	97	88	79	71	62	53	45	36	27	20	14
850	860	98	89	81	72	63	55	46	38	29	21	15
860	870	100	91	82	74	65	56	48	39	30	22	16
870	880	101	92	84	75	66	58	49	41	32	23	17
880	890	103	94	85	77	68	59	51	42	33	25	18
890	900	104	95	87	78	69	61	52	44	35	26	19
900	910	106	97	88	80	71	62	54	45	36	28	20
910	920	107	98	90	81	72	64	55	47	38	29	21
920	930	109	100	91	83	74	65	57	48	39	31	22
930	940	110	101	93	84	75	67	58	50	41	32	24
940	950	112	103	94	86	77	68	60	51	42	34	25
950	960	113	104	96	87	78	70	61	53	44	35	27
960	970	115	106	97	89	80	71	63	54	45	37	28
970	980	116	107	99	90	81	73	64	56	47	38	30
980	990	118	109	100	92	83	74	66	57	48	40	31
990	1,000	120	110	102	93	84	76	67	59	50	41	33
1,000	1,010	122	112	103	95	86	77	69	60	51	43	34
1,010	1,020	125	113	105	96	87	79	70	62	53	44	36
1,020	1,030	128	115	106	98	89	80	72	63	54	46	37
1,030	1,040	130	116	108	99	90	82	73	65	56	47	39
1,040	1,050	133	118	109	101	92	83	75	66	57	49	40
1,050	1,060	136	120	111	102	93	85	76	68	59	50	42
1,060	1,070	138	123	112	104	95	86	78	69	60	52	43
1,070	1,080	141	126	114	105	96	88	79	71	62	53	45
1,080	1,090	144	128	115	107	98	89	81	72	63	55	46
1,090	1,100	147	131	117	108	99	91	82	74	65	56	48
1,100	1,110	149	134	118	110	101	92	84	75	66	58	49
1,110	1,120	152	136	121	111	102	94	85	77	68	59	51
1,120	1,130	155	139	123	113	104	95	87	78	69	61	52
1,130	1,140	157	142	126	114	105	97	88	80	71	62	54
1,140	1,150	160	144	129	116	107	98	90	81	72	64	55
1,150	1,160	163	147	132	117	108	100	91	83	74	65	57
1,160	1,170	165	150	134	119	110	101	93	84	75	67	58
1,170	1,180	168	153	137	121	111	103	94	86	77	68	60
1,180	1,190	171	155	140	124	113	104	96	87	78	70	61
1,190	1,200	174	158	142	127	114	106	97	89	80	71	63
1,200	1,210	176	161	145	130	116	107	99	90	81	73	64
1,210	1,220	179	163	148	132	117	109	100	92	83	74	66
1,220	1,230	182	166	150	135	119	110	102	93	84	76	67
1,230	1,240	184	169	153	138	122	112	103	95	86	77	69
1,240	1,250	187	171	156	140	125	113	105	96	87	79	70
1,250	1,260	190	174	159	143	127	115	106	98	89	80	72
1,260	1,270	192	177	161	146	130	116	108	99	90	82	73
1,270	1,280	195	180	164	148	133	118	109	101	92	83	75
1,280	1,290	198	182	167	151	136	120	111	102	93	85	76
1,290	1,300	201	185	169	154	138	123	112	104	95	86	78
1,300	1,310	203	188	172	157	141	125	114	105	96	88	79
1,310	1,320	206	190	175	159	144	128	115	107	98	89	81
1,320	1,330	209	193	177	162	146	131	117	108	99	91	82
1,330	1,340	211	196	180	165	149	133	118	110	101	92	84
1,340	1,350	214	198	183	167	152	136	121	111	102	94	85
1,350	1,360	217	201	186	170	154	139	123	113	104	95	87
1,360	1,370	219	204	188	173	157	142	126	114	105	97	88
1,370	1,380	222	207	191	175	160	144	129	116	107	98	90
1,380	1,390	225	209	194	178	163	147	131	117	108	100	91
1,390	1,400	228	212	196	181	165	150	134	119	110	101	93

NOTES

NOTES

NOTES

NOTES

NOTES